EDUCATION FOR PEACE

Also by David Hicks

Minorities: A Teacher's Resource Book for the Multi-ethnic Curriculum
(1981)

*Teaching World Studies: An Introduction to Global Perspectives in the
Curriculum* (1982)
with Charles Townley

World Studies 8–13: A Teacher's Handbook (1985)
with Simon Fisher

EDUCATION FOR PEACE

Issues, principles, and practice in the classroom

Edited by DAVID HICKS

ROUTLEDGE
London and New York

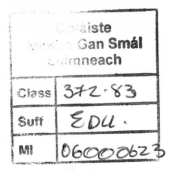

First published in 1988 by
Routledge
11 New Fetter Lane, London EC4P 4EE
29 West 35th Street, New York NY 10001

The collection as a whole
© 1988 Routledge, the individual contributions © 1988 the contributors

Filmset by Mayhew Typesetting, Bristol, England

Printed and bound in Great Britain by
Mackays of Chatham PLC, Chatham, Kent

British Library Cataloguing in Publication Data

Education for peace: issues, principles &
    practice in the classroom. — (Education
    paperback).
    1. Great Britain. Schools. Curriculum
    subjects : Peace studies. Teaching
    I. Hicks, Dave, *1942–* .
    327.1′72′071041
    ISBN 0–415–01329–1

Library of Congress Cataloging-in-Publication Data

Education for peace: issues, principles & practice in the classroom /
    edited by David Hicks.
        p. cm.
    Bibliography: p.
    Includes index.
    ISBN 0-415-01329-1
    1. Peace–Study and teaching. I. Hicks, David, *1942–* .
    UX1904.5.E378 1988
    327.1′72′07–dc 19   88-12205 CIP

A Galactic Viewpoint

Far out in the uncharted backwaters of the unfashionable end of the Western Spiral arm of the Galaxy lies a small unregarded yellow sun.

Orbiting this at a distance of roughly ninety-two million miles is an utterly insignificant little blue green planet whose ape-descended life forms are so amazingly primitive that they still think digital watches are a pretty neat idea.

This planet has – or rather had – a problem, which was this: most of the people living on it were unhappy for pretty much of the time. Many solutions were suggested for this problem, but most of these were largely concerned with the movements of small green pieces of paper, which is odd because on the whole it wasn't the small green pieces of paper that were unhappy.

And so the problem remained; lots of people were mean, and most of them were miserable, even the ones with digital watches.

Many were increasingly of the opinion that they'd all made a big mistake in coming down from the trees in the first place. And some said that even the trees had been a bad move, and that no one should ever have left the oceans.

(Reproduced with permission from *The Hitch Hiker's Guide to the Galaxy* by Douglas Adams, London: Pan, 1979)

To all teachers and educators working for a better world

Contents

Figures

Tables

Notes on contributors

Jen Burnley teaches at the Australian International Independent School in Sydney where she is Head of Geography and International Studies. She has organized and contributed to many conferences on peace education. Her publications include *Peace Education in NSW Schools* (Sydney: Government Printer, 1983) and *From Awareness to Resolution*, two manuals on conflict resolution (Sydney: Miranda Press, 1985). In October 1986 she was given a National Peace Award for her services to peace education and for the establishment of the Peace Education Curriculum Group.

Dave Cooke taught in secondary schools in Zambia and Botswana for nearly ten years. On returning to Britain, while at the Manchester Development Education Project, he worked on materials to help improve teaching about development issues. His recent work as an advisory teacher has involved a two-year secondment to promote the Manchester peace education programme throughout the LEA.

Stefanie Duczek became involved in peace education at the United World College of the Atlantic in South Wales, where she helped to develop the first peace studies course for sixth-formers in 1980–2. She took part in the initial setting up of the Peace Education Network and later became co-ordinator of the York Peace Centre. She was a Research Fellow at the Centre for Global Education, York University, before living for some time at the Findhorn Community in Scotland. She also likes cats.

Gil Fell is Network Development Worker for the Peace Education Network. She provides courses on peace education training skills, disseminating news and views around the network and supporting individual members. She has been involved in the launch of Manchester's guidelines on peace education and has co-edited an introductory manual on peace education. She is involved with the Quaker Facilitators Network and shares her home with two other women, three children, four cats, and a large number of books. She also enjoys knitting and making patchwork quilts.

June Henfrey is Lecturer in Social Studies at the Department of Continuing Education, University of Liverpool. She has special responsibility for education and training for and about socially disadvantaged groups. She was previously Senior Lecturer in Caribbean Studies at Bradford and Ilkley Community College. Her special interests are in the field of race and education. She currently contributes to the design and running of in-service courses for teachers and has also published in this field. She is active in a number of anti-racist initiatives both locally and nationally.

David Hicks is Director of the Centre for Peace Studies at St Martin's College in Lancaster and has been National Co-ordinator for the *World Studies 8–13* curriculum project since 1980. He has written extensively in the fields of peace education, world studies, and multicultural education and has also run workshops in Australia, Italy, and Canada. His books include *Teaching World Studies* (London: Longman, 1982) and *World Studies 8–13: A Teacher's Handbook* (Edinburgh: Oliver & Boyd, 1985). He is also still recovering from a grammar school education.

John Huckle teaches at Bedford College of Higher Education where the majority of his work is with pre-service and in-service courses for geography teachers. He has a particular interest in the ideological nature of current geography and environmental studies curricula in schools and in the methodology of political education. He is editor of *Geographical Education: Reflection and Action* (Oxford: Oxford University Press, 1983), and the author of numerous articles on geographical education. He is presently co-ordinating part of the World Wildlife Fund's Global Environmental Education Programme and is a member of the Labour Party and the Socialist Environment and Resources Association.

Robin Richardson is currently Principal Adviser for the London Borough of Brent. He previously worked as Multicultural Adviser for Berkshire and before that was director of the One World Trust's World Studies Project in London (1973–1980). He has written and lectured extensively in the fields of both world studies and multicultural education, where his thinking has often been of seminal importance.

Richard Slaughter has been an SERC Research Fellow in the Department of Educational Research at the University of Lancaster. He has been a primary teacher and Deputy Head of a special school as well as an occasional lecturer at undergraduate and postgraduate levels. He is a leading expert in the field of futures education and has lectured and written widely in this field. His publications include *Futures Across the Curriculum: A Handbook of Tools and Techniques* (Department of Educational Research, University of Lancaster, 1986). He is now working as a futures consultant in Melbourne.

Toh Swee-Hin is Lecturer in Education, Centre for Social and Cultural Studies in Education, at the University of New England, Armidale, in New South Wales. His specialist interests are peace and development education. He has written extensively on peace and development issues both in terms of research and teacher education. He is a consultant on peace and development in NSW schools and on the National Steering Committee of the Australian

Association for Peace, Justice and Development Education. He has recently been involved in developing a peace education programme for schools in the Philippines.

Tony Weaver was a conscientious objector in the Second World War and is married to a Russian, Alla Perepletnik. He taught in a variety of establishments before becoming a Senior Lecturer in Education at the University of London Goldsmith's College School of Art. He was editor of *New Era*, the journal of the World Education Fellowship 1971–81, and is currently chairman of the board to Housmans bookshop. Tony works with the Peace Education Project of the Peace Pledge Union.

Patrick Whitaker is General Adviser for Primary Education in Derbyshire, before which he spent thirteen years working in primary schools including two headships. He has written books on educational management – *The Primary Head* (London: Heinemann, 1983) and *Managing Primary Schools* (London: Harper & Row, 1985) and he has also written widely on various issues relating to experiential learning, human relations training, and organizational development. In all these activities he is attempting to encourage a more holistic approach to the learning process in schools.

Patricia White is Senior Lecturer in Philosophy of Education and current chairperson of the University of London Institute of Education Philosophy of Education Department. She is author of *Beyond Domination: An Essay in the Political Philosophy of Education* (London: Routledge & Kegan Paul, 1983) and many other papers, particularly on social and political issues within the philosophy of education. She has a longstanding interest in political education, having taught it in schools in the 1960s, and continues to pursue investigations in this area since then. She sees issues of peace and war as having an important place in political education.

Jane Williamson-Fien is Lecturer in History and Social Science at the Kelvin Grove campus of Brisbane College of Advanced Education. She has published widely in the fields of geographical education and historical education and is particularly interested in the insights to be gained from feminist perspectives.

Richard Yarwood worked on a mobile community development education project before travelling in the Far East. He supplemented his income by freelance design work and writing. He is currently on the Peace Education Network Steering Group and is Treasurer of the National Association of Development Education Centres. He is particularly interested in the theory and practice of non-violent direct action and until recently ran the Peace Education Project at the Peace Pledge Union in London.

Preface

Many of the major dilemmas of the late twentieth century relate to issues of peace and conflict, whether increasing levels of violence and the impact of rapid social change or questions of human rights, world development, and the continuing arms race.

These and other issues increasingly impinge on our daily lives and the consciousness of children at school. They cannot be ignored simply because they are controversial, for they are part of, and yet threaten, the very fabric of existence. Indeed future survival may depend on understanding the nature of such problems and taking the action necessary to resolve them peacefully and creatively. Issues of peace and conflict directly affect both our personal lives and the planet as a whole.

The last decade has seen a growing concern that education in schools would take notice of such matters, as witnessed by initiatives in many fields: world studies, multicultural education, political education, development education, and personal and social education. Most recently interest in the field of education for peace has grown rapidly to become a major focus in its own right and this book sets out these concerns in both a clear and practical way.

I would like to express a deep sense of gratitude to all those teachers and educators in the UK, Ireland, Italy, Australia, the USA, and Canada who have inspired me over the years by their commitment and vision. I am also indebted to my contributors, all practitioners in the field, for giving of their experience and expertise. In particular I would like to thank Merrilyn Julian, whose idea it was in the first place; Jane, who encouraged me to go ahead with it; and Dianne Plahuta for her unfailing secretarial support.

David Hicks
December 1987

PART 1

Context

Understanding the field

David Hicks

THE GROWING INTEREST IN PEACE EDUCATION

The last ten years have been marked by an unparalleled interest in the question of what young people should be learning in school, not least in the role schools should be playing in helping them make sense of the world as they approach the twenty-first century. In particular the question of whether, and how, one might teach about issues of peace and conflict in the classroom – from the personal to the global – has been seen as contentious. Interest in this issue has come from young people, parents, politicians, and, of course, teachers themselves. It is also an international concern as well as a national one.

Thus when asked the two questions – Which of the problems facing this country worries you most? Which of the problems facing the whole world worries you most? – a national sample of 10- to 17-year-olds in Britain showed a diverse range of concerns (*Guardian* 1987). In answer to the first question unemployment was most frequently mentioned, followed closely by nuclear weapons and war, then violence and crime. Other problems referred to included nuclear power, drugs, and health. In answer to the second question famine and poverty were most often mentioned, followed again by nuclear weapons and war. Other issues referred to were wars and politics, for example East v. West and South Africa. Given the extent and diversity of their concerns what role, therefore, should schools play in helping students make sense of such issues?

We should, perhaps, be particularly concerned that surveys in several countries, from Australia, Canada, and the USA, to Finland, the USSR, and Britain, indicate a widespread concern amongst young people aɔout the threat of nuclear war. In reviewing this area of research Davies (1984) states:

It often colours their expectations of the future and the choices they feel able to make in the present. Many do not blame 'the enemy' for endangering their future, rather they blame the adult generation as a whole for allowing such a situation to be created. A serious disillusionment is taking place.

More recent work by Davies (1987) indicates that such fears may begin as young as 8 or 9 and affect up to half the school population by 14 to 15 years of age. If this is indeed the case, what are the implications for both parents and teachers?

Public interest in the question of teaching about peace and conflict in school has been largely fuelled by media reports which seem to have been designed more to confuse the debate than to clarify it. Thus on the one hand, headlines such as 'Beware this war for your child's mind' and reports such as that by Cox and Scruton (1984) have been designed to generate alarm rather than to aid in discussion. On the other hand ministers, such as Sir Keith Joseph (1984) when Secretary of State for Education, have acknowledged the need for students to explore issues of peace and war, while researchers such as Galfo (1986) have found no evidence of the indoctrination feared by some, but rather an 'astonishing grasp of the arguments on both sides' amongst older students. What effect, therefore, have these various views had on what actually goes on in schools?

Professional interest amongst teachers in these matters grew gradually during the 1970s and accelerated in the 1980s. The sort of question that many teachers have asked themselves is this: Whatever age children I teach and whatever subject I may teach, are there ways in which I could be helping them to make more sense of a range of issues to do with peace and conflict? In asking such a question teachers have been attempting to respond to problems on at least three interrelated levels. These are first, the state of the planet; second, the state of society; and third, the state of education.

An increasing number of commentators over the last two decades have pointed out that we are facing a series of interrelated global crises. These range from increasing poverty between and within countries, increases in militarism and authoritarian government, denial of human rights and civil liberties, to breakdown of law and order, the rapidly escalating arms race, and often irreversible damage to the biosphere itself. We are inextricably bound up in a web of global interaction, constantly affecting and affected by the choices made by others, whether locally or in more distant parts of the globe. Many people, including teachers, have noted the seriousness of these issues, particularly the threat of nuclear war, and begun to consider how they should respond professionally to young people's interests in, and fears over, such matters.

The conflict and violence that are characteristic of the global stage also affect our own society both directly and indirectly. Acts of terrorism, high unemployment, racist attacks, sexual harassment, issues of law and order, defence and disarmament, all are inescapable features of life in Britain today. We live in a country where the major killer diseases affect the poorest occupational classes more than the rich, where the second most common cause of death among young people is suicide, and where the majority of the population expect a serious nuclear accident before the turn of the century (Jowell, Witherspoon, and Brook 1986). Confronted daily by these issues directly, or indirectly via the media, teachers are concerned about how best to help young people cope with and resolve such dilemmas.

A growing number of teachers are also concerned about the unpeaceful nature of many schools and classrooms, about why so many students feel insulted, bored, or humiliated by their experiences. With both primary and secondary teachers reporting growing numbers of aggressive or disruptive children, a drastic reassessment may be necessary not only of what we teach but also of how we teach. R.D. Laing (1978) put it another way when he wrote:

> A child born today in the United Kingdom stands a ten times greater chance of being admitted to a mental hospital than a university. . . . This can be taken as an indication that we are driving our children mad more effectively then we are genuinely educating them. Perhaps it is our way of educating them that is driving them mad.

Education for peace, then, is an attempt to respond to problems of conflict and violence on scales ranging from the global and national to the local and personal. It is about exploring ways of creating more just and sustainable futures.

THE ORIGINS OF PEACE EDUCATION

Throughout human history there has always been an interest in and a striving for peace. Thus while the contemporary concept of specifically 'educating for peace' may be only a decade or so old its philosophical origins are much older. Accordingly Hutchinson (1986) notes that 'religious and secular notions of peace are probably at least as old as the institution of war' and that those interested in educating for peace today owe 'a considerable debt to cosmopolitan ideas and peace-related ethical concerns of earlier centuries'. During the twentieth century one can discern two traditions that were later to meet in the field of education for peace: the traditions of libertarian education and of personal growth (Roszak 1981). To these one must also add the tradition of education for international understanding which Heater (1984) has examined in his work on the key role of the Council for Education in World Citizenship in promoting this concern from the 1940s up to the present day. Subsequently the work of the One World Trust with its World Studies Project in the 1970s was to provide a firm underpinning for the emergence of education for peace in the 1980s.

5

Figure 1: Defining peace

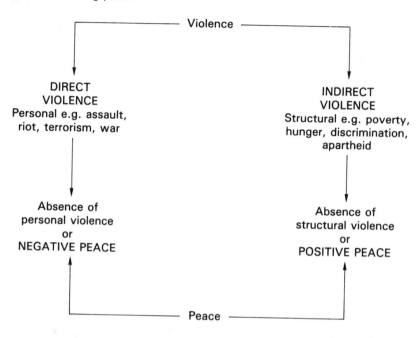

In the 1950s the field of peace research was also emerging in the universities and, while this has had little direct impact on teachers, some of the key concerns identified are extremely relevant to work in schools. The initial emphasis in peace research was on direct (personal) violence, that is violence directed by one person on to another as in the case of assault, torture, terrorism, or war, looking more at conflict than at peace, with the result that peace was defined negatively as merely the absence of war (negative peace). By the late 1960s and early 1970s researchers' attention was shifting from direct to indirect (structural) violence, that is the ways in which people may also suffer as a result of social, political, and economic systems. Such structural violence may equally lead to death and disfigurement or a diminishing of human well-being and potential, as a result of racism and sexism, for example, hunger, denial of human rights, or gross military overspending. This broadening of concern amongst peace researchers to examine issues of freedom and justice also led to broader definitions of peace (see Figure 1). Instead of just being the absence of war, peace was now seen as involving co-operation and non-violent social change, aimed at creating more equitable and just structures in a society (positive peace).

Thus if we are interested in studying issues of peace and conflict, our interests will be broad. One leading peace researcher, Johan Galtung (1976), has suggested that the problems of peace are broadly fivefold, as shown in

Table 1 Studying peace

Problems of peace	Values underlying peace
Violence and war	Non-violence
Inequality	Economic welfare
Injustice	Social justice
Environmental damage	Ecological balance
Alienation	Participation

Table 1. Turned round these five problems give five values which must underpin any definition of peace.

In her comments on peace education Sharp (1984) points out that a variety of approaches exist, not all of which are mutually compatible or mutually exclusive. She thus identifies five broad approaches.

Peace education as peace through strength

This approach is supported by governments and armed forces who see the maintenance of peace being achieved by armed deterrence. The emphasis is on current and recent history and the need to maintain one's military superiority.

Peace education as conflict mediation and resolution

This approach focuses on the analysis of conflict, from the personal to the global, and on ways of resolving such conflicts non-violently. Much can be achieved with this approach, but one needs to recognize the danger of reproducing inequality where an unequal balance of power exists.

Peace education as personal peace

The approach here is primarily interpersonal stressing the need for empathy and co-operation with a focus on the process of education itself and a need to transform hierarchical structures at all levels of society.

Peace education as world order

This approach takes as its starting-point the need for a global perspective and the recognition of structural violence as a major obstacle to peace. This can be utopian unless there is a detailed analysis of the links between personal and global change.

Peace education as the abolition of power relationships

This approach sees people's values as themselves a product of certain structural variables, for example to do with economic, political, and cultural power. The emphasis is therefore on raising awareness of structural violence and identification with the struggles of all oppressed groups.

It will be clear from the above that education for peace may be based on a variety of assumptions and the case studies in this book illustrate some of these differing emphases. In essence (Burns 1983) they are as follows:

1 War and violent conflict are not conducive to human well-being.

2 Neither are they the result of inevitable aspects of human nature.

3 Peace, that is alternative ways of being, behaving, and organizing, can be learnt.

The aims of education for peace are thus to develop the knowledge, attitudes, and skills which are needed in order

1 to explore *concepts of peace* both as a state of being and as an active process;

2 to enquire into the *obstacles of peace* and the causes of peacelessness, both in individuals, institutions, and societies;

3 to *resolve conflicts* in ways that will lead toward a less violent and a more just world;

4 to explore a range of different *alternative futures*, in particular ways of building a more just and sustainable world society.

THE RATIONALE FOR STUDYING PEACE AND CONFLICT

The educational rationale and professional justification for studying peace and conflict has a fourfold basis, relating to first, the aims of education; second, the nature of childhood socialization; third, the need for political education in a democratic society; and fourth, educational ideologies.

In *The Curriculum from 5 to 16* (Department of Education and Science 1985) we are reminded of the broad aims of education, key areas of experience and essential issues which students should be introduced to. Amongst the aims referred to are

1 to help pupils to develop lively, enquiring minds, the ability to question

and argue rationally;

2 to instil respect for religious and moral values, and tolerance of other races, religions, and ways of life;

3 to help pupils to understand the world in which they live, and the interdependence of individuals, groups, and nations.

Amongst the areas of learning and experience to be explored are the human and social, the moral and the spiritual. And amongst the essential issues listed are environmental education, political education, and education in economic understanding. It is to aims and concerns such as these that education for peace is particularly addressed.

Children do not, of course, come to school unaware of the world in which they live. Schools merely intervene in an ongoing educational process, that of childhood socialization, by which children learn the mores expected of their culture, class, and gender. Thus even as young as 5 children are beginning to acquire likes and dislikes about other groups of peoples, and about countries and cultures other than their own. By junior school quite strong prejudices may have been formed, often prior to any factual knowledge. We only need consider how some young children view the Russians, the Irish, or the Germans to exemplify this point.

Children also seem to have fairly well-defined ideas about war and peace by the age of 6 or 7. While they have quite clear images of war it appears that they often have very hazy ideas about the nature of peace. And, as mentioned at the start of this chapter, many children are worried about the threat of nuclear war, whether they actually need to be or not. It is also pertinent to refer to the debate about human aggression, the latter popularly being seen as an innate characteristic of our species. There is much research, however, which indicates that violence and aggression may be culturally learnt (Montagu 1976) and, if this is indeed the case, there may be much more hope for the human condition. Political education is essential in any · democratic society and recognized as such in *The Curriculum from 5 to 16*. It involves learning about political debates in society, the way in which decisions are made and conflicts of interest resolved. This applies, however, not only to matters of central and local government but also to the work-place, school, and family. Some of the key concepts to be explored include rights, justice, power, freedom, participation, and human welfare. Procedural values such as tolerance, fairness, and respect for reason and truth should be actively promoted (Crick and Porter 1978) and, as the Education Act, 1986, states, students need to be 'offered a balanced presentation of opposing views' when looking at any political issue. Teaching about controversial issues is an essential ingredient in any definition of 'good education' and indeed John Slater HMI (1986) has stated clearly that the question is not *whether* we teach about controversial issues, but how and when, that they are neither subject nor phase specific. There has thus also been a renewed

9

interest over the last few years in strategies for teaching about controversial issues in the classroom. Stradling, Noctor, and Baines (1984) have suggested that these fall into three broad categories which they explore in some detail.

First, there is that of giving a *balanced picture* by offering students a range of alternative viewpoints on any issue. Some questions here would be: Does each lesson have to be balanced or is it balance across the whole course that is required? Which is most important: balanced teaching (presuming that students know nothing about an issue) or balanced learning (which will take into account what they may already believe)? Should alternative viewpoints be limited to only broadly agreed ones, for example party political views on, say, defence and disarmament, or should they include the views of pressure groups such as CND and the women at Greenham.

Second, there is the strategy of *teacher neutrality*, which aims to offset the apparent built-in authority of the teacher. Such procedural neutrality is used as a tool to protect divergent viewpoints; it helps avoid the possibility of the teacher using her or his position of authority in order to indoctrinate. The emphasis is on helping students to understand the implications of their own personal viewpoints.

Third, there is the strategy of taking a clearly *committed stance* as there are some issues over which there may be a degree of agreement, for example racial abuse or sexual harassment. Further, it can be argued, that it is important to challenge openly some of the negative values that underpin our society, such as the tacit acceptance of male violence, institutionalized racism, or the stress on ever-continuing consumerism. These strategies are not, of course, mutually exclusive. Different approaches are suited to different occasions and good examples of case studies are available (Wellington 1986). Education for peace is one field which is clearly attempting to grasp this nettle in a creative and imaginative way.

Finally, in clarifying the educational rationale for studying peace and conflict we must look at the role of educational ideologies. Walford (1981), in writing about geography, reminds us that all educational documents, from the school prospectus to the 'official' publication, embody particular assumptions about education and that, broadly, four broad traditions can be identified. In essence these are:

1 The *liberal humanitarian* tradition which is primarily concerned with passing on the basic cultural heritage from one generation to another.

2 The child-centred tradition which values self-development, self-reliance, and social harmony for the individual student.

3 The *utilitarian* tradition which sees the main job of education as equipping students to go well prepared into an already-defined situation.

4 The *reconstructionist* tradition which sees education as a potential instrument for changing society.

Education for peace, by definition, has to be child-centred (valuing the person) and reconstructionist (valuing positive peace), both of which seem particularly appropriate to the turmoil of the late twentieth century. Studying peace and conflict can therefore be justified by reference to the broad agreed aims of education, to work on childhood socialization, to the need for effective political education in a democratic society and to recognized long-standing traditions in education. It offers both a radical critique of much current educational practice but also clear indicators of how to change that practice.

THE NATURE OF PEACE EDUCATION

But what does education for peace actually look like? First, it does need to be made quite clear that we are not talking about a separate subject on the timetable but the creation of a dimension across the curriculum, a concern that may be explored in different ways with any age group and in any subject. A bird's eye view of five classrooms will give some idea of the possibilities.

In the first classroom students are discussing the nature of peace. In particular, in small groups they are identifying and sharing personal experiences of peace: moments of joy, shared endeavour, giving and receiving, creating and celebrating. They then brainstorm some of the main obstacles to peace: fear, prejudice, aggression, indoctrination. Later the students engage in a series of activities aimed at developing their interpersonal skills, especially those to do with listening to, communicating with, and affirming others.

The second classroom is empty. Having learnt how to analyse and resolve some of the everyday conflicts that arise in class, students are turning their attention to conflicts in the local community. They have gone to the public library to look at back copies of the local newspaper. Their specific task is to research a current issue of urban redevelopment so that later they may themselves propose alternative solutions to the planning department.

In the third classroom students are reading comics. In particular they are analysing popular images of war and the different ways in which men and women react to violent conflict. One group feels that women are always the victims, not the perpetrators, of war. They are thus shortly to prepare for a class debate; the motion is that 'It is male society which profits most from war'.

In the fourth classroom students are lying on the floor with their eyes closed. The teacher is leading them through a guided fantasy in which they imagine the world as they would *like* it to be in thirty years' time. Afterwards they record their visions in words and drawings. They then work backwards from the future to the present, listing the steps and changes that

11

had to occur to bring their preferred future about.

In the last classroom students are engaged in a discussion about nuclear issues. They are involved in a role-play which explores six viewpoints on defence and disarmament, and they have short briefing papers on each of the following positions: Conservative, Labour, Alliance, CND, World Disarmament Campaign, and Greenham women. Later they will assess the relative strengths and weaknesses of each case.

What these glimpses all have in common is a shared *process*, that is an attempt to maintain consistency between means and ends: 'There is no way to peace, peace is the way'. The stress in education for peace is thus as much on method as on content. This can best be illustrated by consideration of appropriate curriculum objectives. A visual summary of such objectives is given in Figure 2 and elaborated on in Table 2.

From this list of objectives it can be seen that the substantive subject-matter of education for peace can be grouped under ten broad headings. As stated previously, however, it is rare to find such issues taught as a separate subject on the timetable. If, however, this does occur it can quite correctly be designated as peace studies. More often, however, such issues are taught at different times and different places in the timetable. If this is occurring as a result of conscious curriculum choices, the correct term to use is peace education or, as many would prefer, the more specific education for peace. The local and form of such topics in the curriculum will vary according to the age of students and the subject that is being taught. Good subject-based examples of education for peace are now beginning to appear, as in Fien and Gerber's *Teaching Geography for a Better World* (1988). Education for peace, however, is equally about the development of a range of attitudes and skills as set out in Table 2. The attitudes are a reminder that we must each begin with ourselves, that children need their own peace of mind and self-respect before they can be concerned about others. The strong sense of fairness that many students have can, given appropriate learning experiences, become part of a commitment to justice, to caring for the planet, to becoming involved in political as well as personal change.

But together with the knowledge and attitudes it is the skills that are at the essential core of education for peace. Whatever one is teaching on the timetable these skills can be developed. It is essential in a democratic society that students develop the skill of critical thinking so that they are able to weigh up various arguments in order to make informed choices. It is essential that they are able to recognize propaganda for what it is, whether from a government or a pressure group, and be alert to hidden bias, for example racism, sexism, militarism, both in the media and in teaching materials. Similarly, being able to co-operate and empathize makes conflict resolution more possible and the classroom climate more creative. Being clear about one's needs and able to relate assertively rather than aggressively is also at the heart of good education for peace. Such matters need to be pursued across

Figure 2 A visual summary of objectives

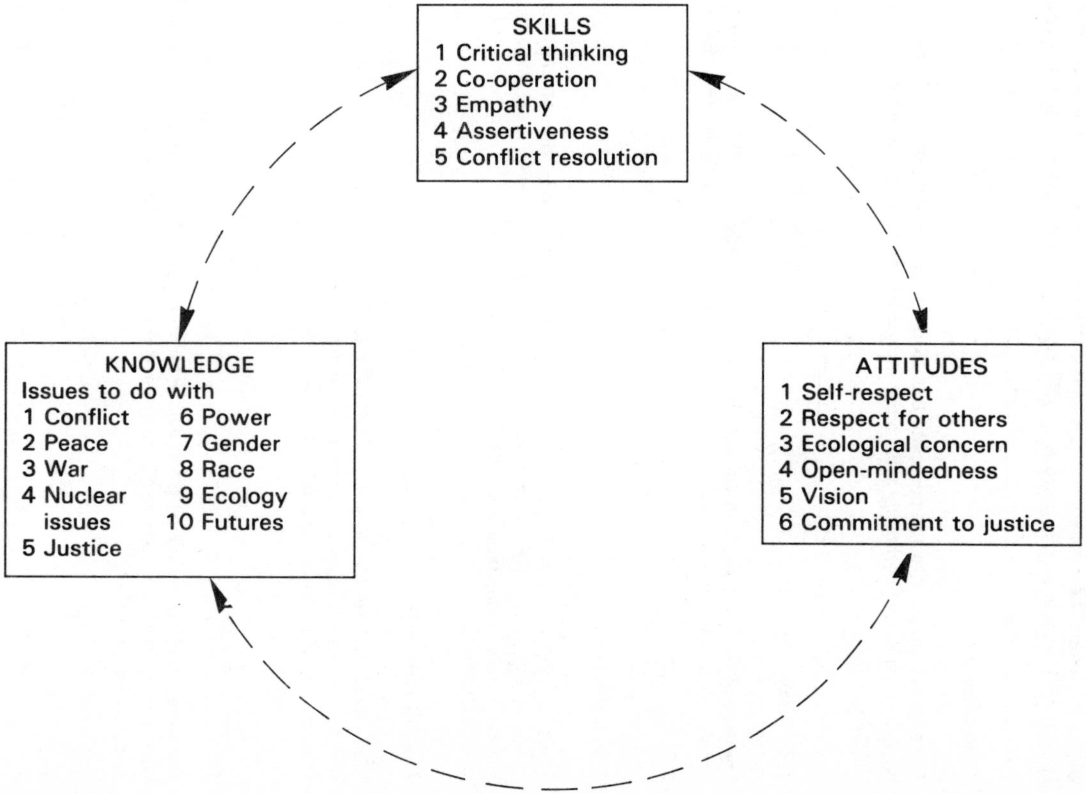

SKILLS

1 Critical thinking
2 Co-operation
3 Empathy
4 Assertiveness
5 Conflict resolution

ATTITUDES

1 Self-respect
2 Respect for others
3 Ecological concern
4 Open-mindedness
5 Vision
6 Commitment to justice

KNOWLEDGE

Issues to do with

1 Conflict   6 Power
2 Peace   7 Gender
3 War   8 Race
4 Nuclear   9 Ecology
  issues   10 Futures
5 Justice

Table 2 Checklist of objectives

SKILLS

1 Critical thinking

Students should be able to approach issues with an open and critical mind and be willing to change their opinions in the face of new evidence and rational argument. They should be able to recognize and challenge bias, indoctrination, and propaganda.

2 Co-operation

Students should be able to appreciate the value of co-operating on shared tasks and be able to work co-operatively with other individuals and groups in order to achieve a common goal.

3 Empathy

Students should be able to imagine sensitively the viewpoints and feelings of other people, particularly those belonging to groups, cultures, and nations other than their own.

4 Assertiveness

Students should be able to communicate clearly and assertively with others, that is not in an aggressive way, which denies the rights of others, or in a non-assertive manner which denies their own rights.

5 Conflict resolution

Students should be able to analyse different conflicts in an objective and systematic way and be able to suggest a range of solutions to them. Where appropriate they should be able to implement solutions themselves.

6 Political literacy

Students should be developing the ability to influence decision-making thoughtfully, both within their own lives and in their local community, and also at national and international levels.

ATTITUDES

1 Self-respect

Students should have a sense of their own worth and pride in their own particular social, cultural, and family background.

Table 2 *contd.*

2 Respect for others

Students should have a sense of the worth of others, particularly of those with social, cultural, and family backgrounds different from their own.

3 Ecological concern

Students should have a sense of respect for the natural environment and our overall place in the web of life. They should also have a sense of responsibility for both the local and global environment.

4 Open-mindedness

Students should be willing to approach different sources of information, people, and events with a critical but open mind.

5 Vision

Students should be open to and value various dreams and visions of what a better world might look like, not only in their own community but also in other communities, and in the world as a whole.

6 Commitment to justice

Students should value genuinely democratic principles and processes and be ready to work for a more just and peaceful world at local, national, and international levels.

KNOWLEDGE

1 Conflict

Students should study a variety of contemporary conflict situations from the personal to the global and attempts being made to resolve them. They should also know about ways of resolving conflicts non-violently in everyday life.

2 Peace

Students should study different concepts of peace, both as a state of being and as an active process, on scales from the personal to the global. They should look at examples of the work of individuals and groups who are actively working for peace.

Table 2 *contd.*

3 War

Students should explore some of the key issues and ethical dilemmas to do with conventional war. They should look at the effects of militarism on both individuals and groups and on scales ranging from the local to the global.

4 Nuclear issues

Students should learn about a wide range of nuclear issues and be aware of the key viewpoints on defence and disarmament. They should understand the effects of nuclear war and appreciate the efforts of individuals, groups, and governments to work towards a nuclear-free world.

5 Justice

Students should study a range of situations illustrating injustice, on scales from the personal to the global. They should look at the work of individuals and groups involved in the struggle for justice today.

6 Power

Students should study issues to do with power in the world today and ways in which its unequal distribution affects people's life chances. They should explore ways in which people and groups have regained power over their own lives.

7 Gender

Students should study issues to do with discrimination based on gender. They should understand the historical background to this and the ways in which sexism operates to the advantage of men and the disadvantage of women.

8 Race

Students should study issues to do with discrimination based on race. They should understand the historical background to this and the ways in which racism operates to the advantage of white people and to the disadvantage of black.

9 Environment

Students should have a concern for the environmental welfare of all the world's people and the natural systems on which they depend. They should be able to make rational judgements concerning environmental issues and participate effectively in environmental politics.

Table 2 *contd.*

---

10 **Futures**

Students should study a range of alternative futures, both probable and preferable. They should understand which scenarios are most likely to lead to a more just and less violent world and what changes are necessary to bring this about.

---

the curriculum by both subject specialists and generalist teachers. They are equally important at both primary and secondary level. They are also, of course, extremely pertinent to issues involving the school as a community and in the community, whether in relation to staff–student relationships, staff–staff relationships, or vandalism, crime, and football violence.

If one is teaching *for* peace and not merely *about* peace, a close relationship needs to exist between ends and means, content and form. If one is concerned about developing self-respect, appreciation of others, concepts of justice and non-violence, they must also be part of the process of learning itself. This puts the teacher in the role of a facilitator rather than in authority, creating a person-centred learning climate which involves much more than just the intellect. Such a climate will encourage participatory and experiential learning, it will involve democracy in action through the development of social and political skills in the classroom. Such approaches to education have been admirably set out by Carl Rogers (1983) and Brian Wren (1986). The most practical exposition for teachers is to be found in Donna Brandes and Paul Ginnis *A Guide to Student-Centred Learning* (1986).

THE UK SCENE

It would be wrong to give the impression that education for peace is a lone innovation of the 1980s, for this is far from the case. Indeed it is only one of a range of initiatives, many of which go back to the early 1970s, all of which aim to help students deal in different ways with ethical dilemmas in a fast-changing world. Other members of this 'family' include: world studies, development education, political education, anti-racist and anti-sexist education, environmental education, and personal and social education. While each may embody a particular set of concerns there is often, in practice, much overlap both in content and methodology. In the final event the terminology used by teachers and schools may well express local or LEA preferences.

The early tone of education for peace in the UK was set by a series of conferences run by the United World College of the Atlantic in the early 1980s. Staff at this international sixth-form college pioneered a peace studies course for the International Baccalaureate and many of the teachers who

17

attended the conferences were later to contribute to developments in this field. One result was the setting up of the Peace Education Network which now employs a full-time worker to advise and support teachers on a national basis. The Centre for Peace Studies was also set up at St Martin's College in Lancaster in 1980 and offers a consultancy service to schools, colleges, and LEAs. As concern about the arms race escalated during the early 1980s so many Teachers for Peace groups sprang up around the country. While their initial concern was often how to teach about nuclear issues members soon came to appreciate the broader concerns of, and legitimation for, education for peace.

Support for concerned teachers came from a variety of organizations, mostly outside the formal sector but often well placed to help. Amongst these were, and are, the Council for Education in World Citizenship, the Peace Education Project of the Peace Pledge Union, the Centre for Global Education, the World Studies Network, and the education staff of bodies such as Pax Christi, the Society of Friends, Oxfam, and Christian Aid. In particular curriculum projects, such as the International and Multicultural Education Project in Scotland and the World Studies 8–13 Project in England, pioneered appropriate and practical classroom approaches with teachers. Good resource books with many classroom ideas are thus now available, including those by Fisher and Hicks (1985) and Pike and Selby (1988).

More formal progress has come where LEAs have adopted their own guidelines and policies on education for peace. Several authorities thus have advisers with responsibility for education for peace or have appointed advisory teachers with this brief. These include Nottinghamshire, Avon, Manchester, Kirklees, Birmingham, and Sheffield, while others may have guidelines such as Wakefield, Lancashire, Barnsley, and Rochdale. Good practice continues to grow in small but, it it is to be hoped, enduring ways. It is also important to remember that similar developments are taking place in Australia, Canada, the USA, Japan, West Germany, Italy, and Sweden too.

This book therefore sets out to provide both a general background to, and specific guidelines on, education for peace. It aims to provide practical activities both for use in the classroom and on in-service courses. It is not just for reading but for using.

REFERENCES

Brandes, D. and Ginnis, P. (1986) *A Guide to Student-Centred Learning*, Oxford: Blackwell.

Burns, R. (1983) *Education and the Arms Race*, Melbourne: Centre for Comparative and International Studies in Education, La Trobe University.

Cox, C. and Scruton, R. (1984) *Peace Studies: A Critical Survey*, London: Institute for Defence and Strategic Studies.

Crick, B. and Porter, A. (1978) *Political Education and Political Literacy*, London: Longman.

Davies, R. (1984) *Children and the Threat of Nuclear War*, Lancaster: Centre for Peace Studies.

—— (1987) *Hopes and Fears: Children's Attitudes to Nuclear War*, Lancaster: Centre for Peace Studies.

Department of Education and Science (1985) *The Curriculum from 5 to 16*, London: HMSO.

Fien, J. and Gerber, R. (eds) (1988) *Teaching Geography for a Better World*, Edinburgh: Oliver & Boyd.

Fisher, S. and Hicks, D. (1985) *World Studies 8–13: A Teacher's Handbook*, Edinburgh: Oliver & Boyd.

Galfo, A.J. (1986) 'Influences of education in the formation of public views of the NATO–Warsaw Pact confrontation: a pilot study conducted in selected schools in the United Kingdom', *Journal of Educational Administration* 18, 2.

Galtung, J. (1976) 'Peace education: problems and conflicts', in M. Haavelsrud (ed.) *Education for Peace: Reflection and Action*, Guildford: IPC Science & Technology Press.

Guardian (1987) 'What are you worried about?' *Young Guardian*, 7 January.

Heater, D. (1984) *Peace Through Education: The Contribution of the Council for Education in World Citizenship*, Brighton: Falmer Press.

Hutchinson, F. (1986) 'Educating for peace: what are its philosophical origins?', in *Educating for Peace: Explorations and Proposals*, Canberra: Curriculum Development Centre.

Joseph, Sir K. (1984) in *Educating People for Peace: Report of a One Day Conference*, London: National Council of Women of Great Britain.

Jowell, R., Witherspoon, S. and Brook, L. (1986) *British Social Attitudes*, Aldershot: Gower.

Laing, R.D. (1978) *The Politics of Experience*, Harmondsworth, Penguin.

Montagu, A. (1976) *The Nature of Human Aggression*, New York: Oxford University Press.

Pike, G. and Selby, D. (1988) *Global Teacher . . . Global Learner*, London: Hodder & Stoughton.

Rogers, C. (1983) *Freedom to Learn for the Eighties*, Columbus, Ohio: Merrill.

Roszak, T. (1981) *Person/Planet: The Creative Disintegration of Industrialised Society*, London: Paladin/Granada.

Sharp, R. (ed.) (1984) *Apocalypse No: An Australian Guide to the Arms Race and the Peace Movement*, Sydney: Pluto.

Slater, J. (1986) 'The teaching of controversial issues in schools: an HMI view', School Curriculum Development Committee seminar, London.

Stradling, R., Noctor, M. and Baines, B. (1984) *Teaching Controversial Issues*, London: Arnold.

Walford, R. (1981) 'Language, ideologies and teaching geography', in R. Walford (ed.) *Signposts in Teaching Geography*, London: Longman.

Wellington, J.J. (1986) *Controversial Issues in the Curriculum*, Oxford: Blackwell.

Wren, B. (1986) *Education for Justice*, London: SCM Press.

2

Curriculum considerations

Patrick Whitaker

One of the characteristics of educational change in recent years has been the recognition that curriculum development can no longer be seen as a sequence of events leading to structural change but should be regarded as a process of continual self-renewal. During the 1980s the curriculum became more closely related to the current realities of social and international life than ever before and schools come under increasing pressure to include in their programmes of work the issues and concerns of the moment, such as vocational training, drug and alcohol education, child abuse, and AIDS. This has created tensions and stresses among and between those partners in the educational enterprise who carry responsibility for the management and organization of schools. Current government policy reflects a need not only to simplify a curriculum which runs the risk of becoming merely responsive to social trends, but also to preserve elements which are regarded as basic and vital to tradition and continuity. The passion of the debate is a symptom of society's confusion in a time of increasingly rapid social, technological, and scientific change. This chapter will explore the nature of the curriculum upheaval we are currently experiencing and in particular consider the implications that education for peace has for this developmental process.

A MODEL OF THE CURRICULUM

Terms and definitions are important. In the *Curriculum from 5 to 16* Her Majesty's Inspectors offer this definition:

> A school's curriculum consists of all those activities designed or encouraged within its organisational framework to promote the intellectual, personal, social and physical development of its pupils. It includes not only the formal programme of lessons, but also the informal programme of so-called extracurricular activities as well as those features which produce the schools ethos, such as the quality of relationships, the concern

for equality of opportunity, the values exemplified in the way that the school sets about its task and the way in which it is organised and managed. (Department of Education and Science 1985)

Such a definition promotes an inclusive view of curriculum design and development and suggests an altogether more holistic approach than we have traditionally been used to. It is a view of the curriculum which must be staunchly defended against the prescriptive and narrowly framed proposals for a national curriculum. The document goes on to present a conceptual framework for curriculum planning which is multidimensional and which attempts to break out of the strait-jacket of subject domination. This is not to suggest that the subject approach is wrong, but rather that it is limited, inhibiting attempts to relate learning in schools to the realities of current social living. The HMI framework is summarized in Figure 3.

Chapter 1 has emphasized the important relationship between content and method in peace education and the attempt to maintain a match between means and ends. These two considerations show a high level of consistency with the curriculum framework summarized above, and suggests that education for peace as defined in this book fits very comfortably within both the structure of the curriculum and the various perspectives that make up its core ingredients.

The model outlined shows that the curriculum as defined is acted upon through four key perspectives: aims, areas of learning, elements of learning, and characteristics. If it is to gain wider respectability, education for peace, like other dimensions of learning, needs to demonstrate consistency with this model. This particular model places considerable emphasis on cross-curriculum issues.

Cross-curriculum issues

In a further attempt to break the stranglehold of separate subjects in curriculum planning and design HMI point to the increasing number of issues which are essentially cross-curricular. Of particular relevance to peace education are

- environmental education
- political education
- education in economic understanding
- careers education
- ethnic minority groups

Such a model of the curriculum is not only clear, precise, and expansive but also essentially pragmatic. It recognizes the crucial importance of linking

Figure 3 A model of the curriculum

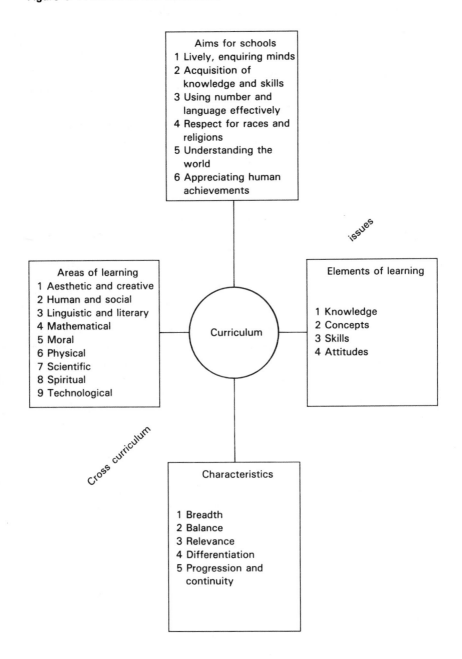

learning with the lives that pupils are currently living and that they might anticipate leading as adults. It provides a framework for planning and development which not only helps to emphasize traditional concerns but also requires attention to current needs and circumstances within a context of rapid social change. Although not listed separately in this list the concerns of peace education are contained both within and between the areas itemized.

The model provides an excellent basis upon which to base curriculum planning in peace education, but before looking at this process in more detail other implications need to be considered.

EDUCATION FOR PEACE AND THE SCHOOLING PROCESS

It is important to see the curriculum implications of peace education within the context of the schooling process with its many contradictions and inconsistencies. In particular it is useful to relate peace education to three considerations:

1 Ambiguity and paradox.
2 Traditional assumptions about learning.
3 A new paradigm for education.

Ambiguity and paradox

It is significant that peace education, which strives for a world free from violence and persecution, should have come in for so much vilification from the present government and its supporters (comment on this is made in Chapter 3). In their concern for respect, understanding, and interdependence the aims for education expressed in the early part of this chapter support the ideas and ideals of peace education. Yet the attempt to organize curriculum approaches designed to satisfy these aims have met with angry opposition. Within schools themselves similar inconsistencies are to be found. School assembly is frequently the forum in which pupils are exhorted to behave with care and consideration to each other, where moral imperatives are expressed, and where Christian virtues are promoted. Yet when the dynamics of a peaceful world are presented within the classroom, this is regarded as deliberate indoctrination. School brochures often present the ethos of the school in terms of 'a caring community' yet only recently has the use of corporal punishment on children been abolished, many years after it was rejected as being unsuitable for adult criminals.

These examples highlight one of the intrinsic difficulties of a nationally administered education service – the reconciling of a rationalist approach with an essentially subjective and personal process. Human behaviour is

23

invariably unpredictable, it defies simple generalization and despite advances in psychology continually resists understanding. It is the failure to grasp this inherent ambiguity that has held back real advances in the quality of education. Successive governments have continued to rely on a belief that attention to either the structure of education or the specific detail of its curriculum holds the clue to success. Neither structural change like the raising of the school leaving age nor comprehensive organization have realized the hopes raised for them; the vast sums of money expended on curriculum and examination reform have not succeeded in creating an education system which is deeply satisfying for its pupils and regarded as successful by society as a whole.

What is missing is the vital 'third way' to educational reform – a concern for the human processes of growth and learning. This third way accepts as fundamental that learning, wherever it takes place, is an intensely personal process more dependent for its success on facts such as self-esteem, motivation, and curiosity than organizational structure and a monolithic curriculum. Peace education, by exposing the paradox of developing peaceful values and attitudes in psychologically violent institutions, has emphasized the importance of this humanistic dimension, recognizing the urgent need to apply to the education system ideas from the fields of organizational theory, humanistic psychology, and adult education.

The current policies of the government illustrate this structural obsession. Reform is seen in terms of schools which have opted for government rather than LEA support, a narrowly defined and imposed national curriculum, and the application of regular objective testing. Totally absent from these proposals are any considerations of how children learn best, how schools can create the safe psychological climate so crucial for successful learning, and how the vital relationship between teacher and taught should be developed.

Not until those who have the responsibility for educational policy can recognize that inconsistencies in human enterprises are to be expected rather than legislated against will the keys to a successful educational future be found. It is surprising that the government has not heeded the experience of successful businesses, which have long recognized that to build an organization only on rationalist and objective principles is to market limitation, inhibition, and conformity. As Peters and Waterman (1986) found in their studies of the USA's best-run businesses, success comes when there is an acceptance of ambiguity and paradox, an organizational climate built on experimentation, risk-taking, and creativity and where individuals are given the freedom to express themselves.

Traditional assumptions about learning

For those teachers who wish to incorporate a peace education approach in their work with pupils it is important to be aware of the assumptions which have traditionally underwritten teaching. Few would argue with the notion that schools are there to prepare children for life. What is in contention is the way that such preparation is handled. Pupils learn very early on in their school career that hard work and good marks are the first indispensable step on the road to success, and if they do not see things that way either they need to be adjusted or they deserve to fail. A.S. Neill (1968) has suggested that schooling is based on the assumption that a child will not grow and develop unless forced to do so, and that those good habits which have not been forced into us in childhood will not develop later on. Carl Rogers (1983) has suggested some other assumptions implicit in our educational system:

1 Pupils cannot be trusted to learn.
2 An ability to pass examinations is the best criterion for selection and judging potential.
3 What a teacher teaches is what a pupil learns.
4 Knowledge is the steady accumulation of facts and information.
5 An academic procedure, e.g. the scientific method, is more important than the idea it is intended to investigate.
6 Pupils are best regarded as manipulative objects, not as persons.

It is certainly true that schools have a preoccupation with the grading and categorizing of pupils. This begins early in infant education with, at times, a paranoid concern for reading ages and quotients. At the age of 16 a pupil can fall into any number of categories of 'pass' or 'fail' or even suffer the final indignity of being 'ungraded'. The normal curve of distribution, while perhaps pandering to the statistician's desire for symmetry, must be one of the most unjust devices yet created to sustain such unpeaceful assumptions. What hope is there for a society in which half the population are by definition 'less able'?

The competitive dynamic in education is one example of structural violence in our schools and it creates and sustains concepts of 'success' and 'failure' to such an extent that some pupils become disaffected with schooling very early on. John Holt has suggested that entry into schooling triggers a decline in the capacity to learn from which few actually ever recover:

Almost every child, on the first day he sets foot in a school building, is smarter, more curious, less afraid of what he does not know, better at finding and figuring things out, more confident, resourceful, persistent and independent, than he will ever again be in his schooling or, unless he is very unusual and lucky, for the rest of his life.

(Holt 1971)

Another factor which also becomes clear early on in school life is that only a part of the pupil is regarded as of any importance – the brain. Most schools make claims in their brochures about being concerned with aesthetic, emotional, and physical development but we know, as indeed the pupils soon learn, that in the end it is their performance in the cognitive domain that will count most. In a few schools, if you are lucky to be not so bright, you might gain rich rewards from a well-planned non-academic curriculum. If you are bright, learning experiences in such areas as art, dance, drama, and home economics will probably be quickly left behind.

It is against this sort of background that attempts are being made to introduce education for peace. The tasks ahead are many and various and need to take account of the whole infrastructure of organized learning. Peace education itself is part of a newly emerging transformative paradigm for education, a paradigm which is attracting both interest and commitment.

A new paradigm for education

The influence of humanistic psychology, particularly through the work of Abraham Maslow (1976) and Carl Rogers (1983), has begun to reach well into the educational system. This can be seen particularly in the growth of pastoral care and counselling in schools and developments in adult education. More recently the identification of personal and social education as a key dimension in the learning process in schools has led to specific programmes such as Active Tutorial Work and the Lifeskills materials. Education for peace and world studies are as much concerned with the process of learning as with their own discrete objectives, and both recognize the importance of personal power in learning – the freedom to take charge of one's own development and growth.

Of key importance in this respect is the work of the libertarian Brazilian educator Paulo Freire (1985). His belief that learning must be tied to the life force of the learner places an individual's personal growth as the central core of the curriculum. If pupils are to become more active and involved in the process of learning in schools they need to be helped out of the 'culture of silence' – that oppressive condition in which people are not aware of the social forces acting upon them. This requires, Freire argues, a process of conscientization. By learning to perceive the social and political contradictions in their lives, people grow in awareness of their social reality and develop a capacity to transform it.

For this transformational process to gain momentum in education it is necessary to work to replace the traditional assumptions of schooling with more enlightened ones and peace education has a critical part to play here. Marylin Ferguson (1982) has suggested that nothing short of a paradigm shift will succeed in freeing the learning that pupils do in schools from the harmful effects already referred to. The new paradigm which she observes emerging points to the nature of learning rather than the content of instruction as the key. She suggests that learning is a journey to be enjoyed rather than a destination to be reached. Among some of the new assumptions she advocates are:

1 In schools the emphasis should be on learning how to learn.

2 Learning is a journey, not a destination.

3 Pupils and teachers should relate to each other as people and not behave towards each other in roles.

4 Priority should be given to the self concept as the key determinant of successful learning.

5 The inner intuitive, emotional, and spiritual experiences of pupils should be regareded as vital contexts for learning.

6 Encouragement should be given to divergent thinking and guesswork as part of the natural process of creative learning.

7 Age-specific learning should give way to variable and flexible age groupings.

8 Greater attention should be given to the design of the learning environment with more attention to colour, comfort, personal space, and privacy.

9 Community education should be seen as an opportunity to break down the traditional association of learning with schools and institutions.

10 Teachers should be regarded as learners too, learning alongside and from the pupils they teach.

Taking account of these ideas and attempting to incorporate them into our work with pupils will assist the transforming of the schooling process. Many of these ideas are central to the concepts of education for peace but there is still much work to be done to convince those bound within their own cultures of silence of their validity and importance.

THE QUESTION OF FIT

Curriculum overload

One of the problems of designing a curriculum in a fast-changing world is that of overload. New ideas, concepts, and frameworks of thinking demand attention and consideration and as what is new fights to replace what is old and outworn, our ways of organizing and disseminating knowledge and information have to reconsidered. The last ten years have seen the emergence of new areas of study in schools. Education for peace along with anti-racist education and anti-sexist education are responses to the movement towards equalization of power in our society. Traditionally oppressed groups – women, minority ethnic groups, the aged, disabled, and sexual minorities –

27

are succeeding as never before in raising the consciousness of their oppressors. Formal recognition of this is contained in legislation designed to outlaw discrimination, but the struggle to affect hearts and minds continues.

More recently we have seen a renewed interest in health education. The government has funded an educational programme aimed to combat the spread of AIDS in society and an increased concern about the various forms of child abuse is creating the need for tighter focus on child safety and care in the teaching programmes of schools. Such developments strain the capacity of a curriculum built on traditional subject areas to cope with change.

The axial tilt of the curriculum

These are but examples of a trend which is likely to continue as social, scientific, economic, and political changes accelerate in our society. Although the national core curriculum might be regarded as an attempt to impede and frustrate these developments, social change is now so fast and so comprehensive that any attempt to impose a narrowly conceived curriculum is likely to be somewhat superficial. These new and varied demands on the curriculum mark the beginning of a fundamental upheaval in the way that learning is organized within our schools, an upheaval that is unlikely to be restrained by the government's attempt to introduce a national core curriculum. As yet we are only witnessing pre-seismic disturbances as we prepare for what can best be described as an axial tilt of the curriculum. This will be a movement so disturbing that few areas of the schooling system will be unaffected by it. This axial tilt is a move from a predominantly vertical and differentiated curriculum to a horizontal and multidimensional one. This curriculum tilting reverberates and responds to developing trends in society and our patterns of living. Issues like the ones referred to above have emerged to test the capacity of the curriculum to adjust creatively and flexibly to new assumptions about living and learning. There is now a tightening tension between a curriculum firmly built on the separation of subjects and one having a more learner-centred perspective, with a concern for human flexibility and all-round capacity. The axial tilt marks the break with a model of learning and teaching that has lasted for the entire history of public education and signals a determination to ground educational theory and practice in experience, with full regard to the changed and constantly changing needs and expectations of learners.

The issue of location

As the curriculum axis tilts and the cross-curriculum dynamic gathers pace there will be an increased pressure on the time/space continuum of curriculum design and planning. We will become increasingly conscious of gaps in our awareness, in our understanding, and in our experience. A key issue relating to education for peace concerns fit and location. Does it belong to the humanities, to personal and social education, or is it a matter for tutorial work or project-based activities. Are we talking about a change in emphasis in our teaching or a whole new focus? It is fashionable to talk about 'dimensions' of the curriculum. Perhaps this is just one more intellectual device to cope with transition, but it demonstrates our preoccupation with identification and labelling, our need for clear definitions, the search for certainty.

The tension between the old and the new in education is increased because new dimensions like education for peace are about the more elusive aspects of learning and growth – attitudes, values, hopes, fears, beliefs, frustrations, and dreams. Our education system has taken upon itself the guardianship and inculcation of attitudes and values. However, our society is now characterized by enormous variations in patterns of attitudes and values. As well as being a pluralist society in terms of culture and race we are a multi-attitude and multi-value society. Increasingly we are becoming a society based on diversity of groups, communities, interests, and concerns. As we can no longer rely on certainty our approach to education for peace must be based on the exploration of attitudes and values, and not merely one of conforming to a predetermined set for all. Within a framework of morality there is considerable scope for such exploration, and peace education has a unique part to play in helping pupils develop a perspectives consciousness and an ability to understand the world with its myriad of value systems and ideologies. Schools will need to take on this task with energy and determination, to devote more time to such explorations than ever before, as pupils struggle to make sense of a world characterized by threat and uncertainty.

What we are experiencing in this axial tilt of the curriculum is the emergence of a set of ideas that are attempting to shift the emphasis in schools from the teaching of a pre-packaged, essentially knowledge-based curriculum to a schooling experience characterized by a recognition of a pupil's innate capacity to grow, learn, and develop fully. One of the important roles of education for peace is to help in the creating of conditions in which this growth and development can flourish. This will require an emphasis on climate, the creating of time and space for pupils to deal with the inner conflicts of their lives, to confront the issues and concerns of the society with which they are striving to identify and to explore personhood with all its awesome possibilities.

It is likely that teachers concerned to develop peace education programmes will be working within one of the following three models.

Subject specific

In this model, areas of learning are defined by specific subjects and

29

consequently peace education is identified as a discrete course or programme. This model has some advantages – it creates a visible space in the timetable which may serve to enhance its status and offer more opportunity for pursuing particular objectives, but it does have the disadvantage of requiring it to compete for timetable space and resource provision.

Inclusion within subjects

Aspects of peace education can occupy appropriate slots in existing subjects. This overcomes the problem of timetable space but can result in token acknowledgement of its importance. Also there may develop uneasy tensions between content and process if knowledge objectives are pursued at the expense of attitudes and skills.

Integration

Within primary schools this involves the inclusion of peace education within topic and thematic approaches. In secondary schools it is provided through broadly based interdisciplinary programmes and courses. This has the distinct advantage of promoting the idea that peace education is best seen as a dimension of the curriculum developing in line with the axial tilt already referred to. This approach enables the considerations of peace education to find a place in all the areas of learning referred to in the HMI curriculum model defined in Figure 3. The disadvantage of this approach is that objectives can become lost during the integrative process and there is a danger that peace education elements will over-focus on 'problems' rather than on the dynamics of positive peace.

Preparing classroom work

The detailed preparation of classroom work also needs to be thorough and systematic. The model shown in Figure 4 suggests there are four key considerations in a systematic approach to planning. The model suggests a dynamic relationship of these four factors in the planning process. While each will demand its own set of considerations and questions, in the end successful learning in the classroom will depend upon how the four elements have been brought together. The following questions are offered as examples to be used in lesson planning and are by no means comprehensive.

Plans

   1 What are the purposes and specific intentions of the lesson?
   2 What specific outcomes are being planned for?
   3 How will the lesson be evaluated?

Figure 4 Preparing classroom work

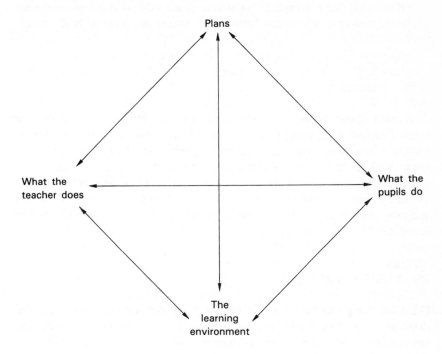

What the teacher does

1 How will the aims and intentions of the lesson be shared so that pupils know
- what they are expected to learn
- how the learning be achieved
- how they will benefit by the learning.

2 How will different teaching methods and techniques be selected?

3 How will relationships be managed
- with individual pupils
- with working groups
- with the class as a whole?

What the pupils do

1 How will pupils perceive the essential relationship between content and process in their peace education learning?

2 How will learning activities reflect the specific and immediate concerns of pupils?

3 How will pupils be encouraged to play an active part in more informal and experiential activities?

The learning environment

1 How will the environment in which peace education programmes are conducted reflect a consistency between the means and ends of peace education?

2 How will materials and resources contribute to the learning?

3 How will a climate of co-operation and shared endeavour be developed in the classroom?

In evaluating the outcomes of lessons it will be important to consider the extent to which means and ends have been compatible and how far teaching has been consistent with the hopes and expectations raised in the planning. Programme design on its own cannot ensure good practice in peace education. The way that the teacher builds relationships with pupils and shares the learning journey with them is far more important than is traditionally realized and peace educators need to be aware of the 'third way' already referred to earlier in this chapter.

AN EVOLVING PEDAGOGY

Education for peace has always emphasized the delicate but crucial relationships between content and process. Although it is important to accept the inevitability of the kinds of ambiguities referred to earlier in the chapter, it is also essential to recognize the dynamic interaction of means and ends in peace education. The point that 'there is no way to peace, peace is the way' has already been made in Chapter 1, but it highlights how important it is for peace education, while pursuing objectives to do with a more just and peaceful world to do it in ways compatible with those intentions. If peace is both the destination and the journey then what we teach and how we teach it must not be separated in our preparations for working with pupils.

Education for peace does not fit easily within a schooling system built on the traditional assumptions referred to earlier. In espousing the new paradigm in education, peace educators need to continue to work actively to help restructure the quality of the relationship between the teacher and the taught and to evolve a pedagogy which places the learner's personal experience, rather than the teacher's subject preoccupation, at the forefront of the educational process in schools.

Key qualities in teachers

Central to the management of this process is the way the teacher relates to the pupils and the extent to which this relationship contributes to and enhances each pupil's capacity to learn effectively. It is important however to work to avoid a developing belief that active, participatory, and experiential learning methods have a place only in the 'soft' areas of the curriculum. Education for peace is as much part of the cognitive domain as it is of the affective. Teachers working exclusively in the cognitive domain need to be helped to realize that person-centred approaches are very 'user friendly' and can bring positive benefits in the form of increased academic performance. In *Freedom to Learn in the Eighties*, Carl Rogers (1983) drew attention to a steadily mounting body of research evidence which supports a person-centred approach to education. In particular he pointed to a study undertaken in the USA and several other countries which set out to determine which particular teacher behaviours were correlated with different kinds of learning outcomes. This research involved the study of 3,700 hours of taped classroom activity from 550 primary and secondary schools. Three particular teacher behaviours turned out to be especially significant:

1 The teacher's ability to understand the meaning that classroom experience is having for each pupil.

2 The respect and positive regard the teacher has for each pupil as a separate person.

3 The ability of the teacher to engage in a genuine person-to-person relationship with each pupil.

It was found that pupils in classes with teachers who demonstrated these qualities to a high degree made significantly greater gains in learning:

1 They became more adept at using higher cognitive skills such as problem-solving.

2 They had a higher self concept.

3 They exercised greater learning initiatives in the classroom.

4 They exhibited fewer discipline problems.

5 They had a lower absence rate.

What is particularly interesting and important is that it was also found that with specific training teachers can begin to change their attitudes and develop the sort of facilitative style described above. The other main characteristics of such teachers were:

1 They had a higher self concept than lower level teachers.

2 They were more open and self-disclosing to pupils.

3 They responded more often and more positively to pupils' feelings.

4 They gave more praise and encouragement.

5 They were more responsive to pupils' own ideas.

6 They engaged in formal didactic teaching less often.

In considering the pedagogic style that would seem to be most consistent with the aims and purposes of education for peace it is essential to give attention to the following skills and qualities:

1 Being emphathetic, a good listener, and sensing pupil experience from the pupil's point of view.

2 Having a warm, caring respect for each pupil as a unique and individual person.

3 Being secure enough to be personally open and honest with pupils.

4 Holding the belief that children are positive and constructive and do want to learn effectively.

Clearly it pays to be human in the classroom. Education for peace offers a unique opportunity to work to develop this third way pedagogy, to honour and celebrate the enormous learning potential that children bring with them into school. It requires the capacity to recognize that the vast resources for healthy learning and living can become minimalized during the process of childhood socialization and that the task of the teacher is to provide the safe psychological climate in the classroom so that this potential for growth and development can become reactivated. Unfortunately schools have tended not to offer this safe and nurturing environment. To reverse this process requires both courage and sensitivity. Above all it demands that we undertake a process of unfolding potential. Theodore Roszak has summarized it well:

> This is what all of us bring into life and school: a wholly unexplored, radically unpredictable identity. To educate is to unfold this identity – to unfold it with the utmost delicacy, recognizing that it is the most precious resource of our species, the true wealth of the human nation.
>
> (Roszak 1979)

Education for peace is a central element in the transformational process in education. It has the capacity to assist further the axial tilt of the curriculum so that the learning programmes we provide more closely relate to the social reality that pupils experience in their lives. It also responds to a yearning in pupils themselves for a schooling process which recognizes and responds to deeply felt fears and aspirations.

REFERENCES

Department of Education and Science (1985) *The Curriculum from 5 to 16*, London: HMSO.

Ferguson, M. (1982) *The Aquarian Conspiracy*, London: Granada.

Freire, P. (1986) *The Politics of Education*, London: Macmillan.

Holt, J. (1971) *The Underachieving School*, Harmondsworth: Penguin.
Maslow, A. (1976) *The Farther Reaches of Human Nature*, Harmondsworth: Penguin.
Neill, A.S. (1968) *Summerhill*, Harmondsworth: Penguin.
Peters, T.J. and Waterman, R.H. (1986) *In Search of Excellence*, New York: Harper & Row.
Rogers, C. (1983) *Freedom to Learn for the Eighties*, Columbus, Ohio: Merrill.
Roszak, T. (1979) *Person/Planet*, London: Granada.

3

Countering the critics

Patricia White

THE VALUE OF CRITICISM

The role of criticism in human life is often vital.[1] Not least when we are chided for not checking which is the earth before wiring the plug or for swallowing the 'aspirins' without reading the label on the bottle. In less dramatic cases criticism can improve things – the cooking, the service. Educational theory and practice is an obvious beneficiary. Without the constructive criticism which has gone on over the years most of us in the teaching profession today would be, I suppose, in the thrall of one ideology or another – child-centredness, Piagetian stage theory, managerialism, sociological relativism – depending upon the sphere of influence we had happened to fall under at some formative stage in our careers. As it is, critics have helped us to stand back from these and many other views and, by raising awkward questions, have deepened our understanding of our practices by indicating some of the limitations of their theoretical underpinnings. So, although in our personal exploits as well as in our professional endeavours *ideally* we would want our friends and colleagues to say, 'Great! That's perfect. Don't do a thing to it!', we know that we do not live in an ideal world. We are fallible and so we are grateful for criticism – or we are when we are being rational.

The critics of peace education enter then to a round of expectant applause. What have they got to say? It seems a good idea to look mainly, though not exclusively, at Cox and Scruton, because all the signs seem to suggest that here we will be getting rigorous criticism of some power. The preface to *Peace Studies: A Critical Survey* (Cox and Scruton 1984: subsequently *PS*) tells us that this paper is one of a stream of 'independent, lucid and authoritative analyses of those political and social factors which impinge on the questions of national and Western security' (*PS*: 5) and John Marks (1984) commends it too as a 'powerfully argued pamphlet'. Let us therefore concentrate on the case presented by Cox and Scruton against peace education in *schools*. Their criticisms extend to the treatment of peace education in institutions of higher education but those will not be dealt with in any detail here.[2]

Certainly Cox and Scruton have a strong conclusion, namely that peace education has no place in schools (with one qualification which we shall come to) or at the very least an optional place. Their case for this conclusion rests on their view of 'the real nature and purpose of a school curriculum' (*PS*: 24). Let us look carefully, therefore, at this attempt to rule out peace education from the school on *educational* grounds.

THE CRITICS' VIEW OF EDUCATION

Cox and Scruton talk in *Peace Studies: A Critical Survey*, seemingly interchangeably, about the purpose of the school curriculum and the purpose of education. Their focus of interest, however, seems to be *school* education, rather than any broader notion of education, and the education provided by the school seems to be identified with the curriculum it offers. They put it like this:

> The purpose of education is to inculcate judgement, to teach the pupil to see the complexity of what confronts him, to hold a question before his mind without begging it.
>
> (*PS*: 25)

This purpose is achieved by 'the old-fashioned curriculum' which is

> built around subjects in each of which there is an accepted body of communicable knowledge. These subjects can be taught to a child at school, and provide the foundation for subsequent learning.
>
> (*PS*: 24)

In *Peace Studies: A Critical Survey* and in other places, Cox and Scruton give examples of subjects – mathematics, history, French – which would be included in such a curriculum.[3] The most complete account is probably that in *Whose Schools? A Radical Manifesto* (Cox *et al.* 1986: subsequently *WS*) where their co-authors are Douglas-Home, Marks, and Norcross. There we are told:

> School education should begin from a sensible and tried curriculum, including reading, writing and mathematics. At the higher level, the curriculum should include, as central disciplines, history, science, mathematics, foreign languages (ancient and modern), the lore and literature of our country, and some of the technical skills which will fit children for participation in a modern society.
>
> (*WS*: 1)

37

We are also told that

> Children need a firm moral and spiritual basis, which will engender the values on which their future happiness depends: honesty, industry, charity, respect for others and for the law.
>
> (WS: 2)

According, again, to the authors of *Whose Schools?*:

> Recreation, sports, music, drama and art are important components of education, and schools should endeavour to provide them.
>
> (WS: 2)

Children also need, it seems, instruction in religious doctrine, in accordance with the wishes and faith of their parents (WS: 2). Other aspects of these views need discussion in their own right. (On what grounds do the authors argue, for instance, that children need instruction in religious doctrine rather than religious education? What are the authors saying in claiming that music, art, sport, and so on, are important but not central aspects of education?) However, in this context comment will have to be restricted to the bearing of these points on the authors' criticisms of peace education.

Cox and Scruton and the other authors of *Whose Schools?* further characterize 'good schools' in the following terms. They are schools concerned with 'real skills and genuine knowledge' and 'based on discipline and order' (WS: 1). The subjects they teach are 'tried and lasting' (WS: 3), 'real and difficult' (WS: 5), 'hard and lastingly useful' (WS: 5), 'proven' (WS: 7). They are concerned with 'serious forms of learning' (WS: 5). Such schools are to be contrasted with those where the 'old educational values' have been replaced by a concern for 'relevance' (WS: 3). In such schools education will be primarily concerned with 'burning issues' and in them 'a child will spend much of his time in the classroom attending to matters which lie beyond his comprehension, and which are in any case the subject of continual dispute and incomprehension even among adults' (PS: 24). Such schools will be 'replacing tried and lasting subjects with spurious "alternatives"' (WS: 3) creating 'new and artificial subjects' like peace studies, '"soft" subjects . . . largely empty of intellectual content,' which merely 'provide a framework into which any nonsense . . . can be fitted', subjects which gradually pollute the whole curriculum (WS: 5).

In a nutshell true education is essentially concerned with the mastering of difficult subjects. Cox and Scruton also say, as we have seen, that children's education needs a moral basis but it is unclear how far they think that *school* education should also provide this. In some places it seems as though they do. They say, for instance, that 'the teaching of the negotiating skills whereby children learn to live peaceably with their kind – has always been and should always be taught' (*PS*: 40). But elsewhere in their paper they seem – it is not clear – to be expressing a different view. They quote, as follows, from the Atlantic College Syllabus:

The student should be able to co-operate in decision-making and action, but where necessary to decide and act alone.

The student should be able to recognise the value and limitation of co-operative and individual action, and to employ means appropriate to the end.

Cox and Scruton comment:

To condense a great amount of sentimental eyewash into a pinch of salt: the student should grow up.

(*PS*: 29)

This seems to suggest that moral education, as such, is not necessary. Perhaps the idea is that students simply develop morally as they grow older; perhaps it is that these things are picked up from the environment without any specific teaching efforts being necessary. Whatever the truth about this particular statement, their general position seems to be that schools must be involved in the teaching of what they call 'good manners'. This, we can take it, includes cultivating the virtues of honesty, industry, charity, respect for others, and respect for the law. Helping pupils to live peaceably with each other also forms a part of this work.

Education, then, in the view of Cox and Scruton and the co-authors of *Whose Schools?* is a matter of mastering difficult subjects and acquiring good manners.

THE CRITICS' OBJECTIONS TO PEACE EDUCATION

Cox and Scruton see peace education as having two aspects – one to do with teaching children to live peaceably with their kind, the good manners aspect, and a more dubious aspect involving the 'contentious and politically charged discussion of peace war and disarmament' (*PS*: 40). Let us look at their objections to both of these.

There seem to be two problems with the good manners aspect. First, it is strictly speaking redundant. Teachers and parents have always been concerned about good manners and therefore there is no need to introduce this aspect into schools as if it were something new. Worse, introducing it as part of a peace education programme is likely to frustrate the achievement of its aims: 'it is never less likely to be taught successfully than when an ideological programme is being advanced by means of it' (*PS*: 32). Second,

39

as this quotation suggests, this aspect of peace education is likely to be used as a cover for the more dubious aspect. Commenting on the report on Peace Education presented to Avon County Council by its Director of Education, Cox and Scruton say:

> Once again, however, the large issue of nuclear disarmament is smuggled into a course which is so vaguely formulated as to suggest little more than an education in manners.
>
> (*PS*: 31–2)

Cox and Scruton have a number of objections to the other aspect of peace education, the 'contentious and politically charged discussion of peace, war and disarmament'. We might as a shorthand call this the Peace Studies aspect.

First, Cox and Scruton consider two linked arguments in favour of the treatment of Peace Studies issues in school, namely that these are major issues of our time and that young people need as citizens to make up their minds about them and should therefore be informed (*PS*: 23). They have a twofold answer to these arguments. The first part is that these and other issues, including sex, socialism, the environment, the market economy, constitutional government, the wisdom and morality of eating animals, of insulting one's parents, of joining the Communist Party, of confessing to religion, and of voting Labour (*PS*: 23–4) cannot be dealt with in school because children have yet to acquire the historical knowledge, articulate expression, and grasp of argument that would enable them to discuss them profitably. The second part is that to attempt to do so would be to forget the 'real nature and purpose of a school curriculum' (*PS*: 24) which is to introduce the pupil to truly educational subjects which force him to understand things which have no immediate bearing on his experience. These are, as we have seen, tried and lasting, real and difficult, proven subjects like mathematics, ancient languages, and history, while Peace Studies is a 'soft' subject, largely empty of intellectual content and not worthy of a place amongst the 'difficult subjects of the traditional curriculum' (*WS*: 5).

Second, Peace Studies is also necessarily indoctrinatory. Not only is it often taught in a biased and irresponsible way, but also it could be taught in no other way (*PS*: 40).

Third, Peace Studies is likely to 'inculcate guilt in the child towards his own inheritance and to encourage him to place blame for conflict in the camp to which he belongs' (*PS*: 30). If some aspects are taken seriously they could even induce nervous breakdowns in pupils (*PS*: 32).

Fourth, even if pupils somehow escape the moral and mental harm of the previous point, Roger Scruton (1986) argues in 'Peace studies: no true subject' in *The Wayward Curriculum* (subsequently *WC*) that they will derive no benefit from this subject.

Nobody comes away from the subject with some useful and decisive piece of information that will enable him to solve some present problem: nobody comes away from it better able to discuss the burning issues of the day, or to take an active and useful part in society.

(*WC*: 111)

Finally, Scruton has a further objection to peace education which straddles the division between good manners and Peace Studies. He claims that some defenders of Peace Studies defend it as a practical subject concerned not to induce theoretical understanding but 'social skills (the skills of peaceful behaviour')' (*WC*: 108). Scruton is sceptical of these claims and writes that if they were true:

We should expect children at schools where peace studies are included in the syllabus to come home from them disposed to conciliate, adapt and compromise and to renounce the ways of war; most of all, we should expect departments of 'peace studies' to be remarkably tranquil and soothing places to which opponents might come and join in the discussion in an atmosphere of calm understanding. However, none of these things seems to be true; indeed it is my experience that a 'peace studies' activist, once questioned in some fundamental tenet of his beliefs, is as disposed as the next man to take the path of confrontation.

(*WC*: 109)

ANSWERING THE CRITICS OF PEACE EDUCATION

Let us accept Cox and Scruton's characterization of peace education as including, broadly speaking, two elements – one concerned with the understanding and explanation of war and the causes of conflict, and another more practical element concerned with learning to control and manage conflict.

Comments on these criticisms of peace education can usefully be divided into two kinds. First, comments on the critics' conception of education and its aims and, second, more heterogeneous comments, not least about indoctrination.

An examination of the educational rationale for the critics' objections

As we saw earlier the critics' objections are launched from the standpoint of a certain view of education, a view labelled in a way designed to make it irresistible. Who could want a silly curriculum which aimed to give students illusory skills and false beliefs and was composed of subjects of ephemeral value? But if we disregard the rhetoric of 'real', 'genuine', 'sensible', 'lastingly useful', 'serious', and so on, what exactly are we being offered? Plainly put, it is an education which gives pupils a grounding in a number of subjects while emphasizing good manners. Now whether or not we buy this content must depend on the reasons backing it. What are these?

The short answer is that the critics give no grounds for their view. This view is simply asserted and, without argument, set up in opposition to a view of school education which would see the creation of citizens as one of its aims. It looks as though Cox, Scruton, *et al.* think that they have removed the need for argument for their position by the use of terms like 'real', 'genuine', and 'truly'. But appeals to such rhetorical devices cannot settle the value questions that confront us when we try to determine what schools should be teaching. The question of what schools should be teaching is to be answered, in large part, in the light of what we think the aims of education should be. What we think the aims of education should be will depend on our conception of human flourishing and of the good society. These are complex value questions, which cannot be answered by educational or any other kind of experts who are able to tell us what means we need to employ to achieve such and such ends. It is precisely the ends which are in question. In any society views on these ends are likely to be many and various (for example, some religiously based, some wholly secular, some emphasizing the well-being of the individual, some emphasizing more communitarian values) and in a liberal democratic society these views will contribute to the public debate on what form education is to take. For the main rationale for such a society is that it is a way of avoiding an unjustifiable authoritarian imposition of values. Since the critics of peace education are implacably opposed to any form of totalitarianism, it is slightly curious that in the papers and manifestos considered here there is no acknowledgement of the view that free and open debate in a democracy is not a matter simply of the assertion of viewpoints but rather the advancing of argued cases for them.[4] If the views of Cox, Scruton, *et al.* on the purpose of school education are to be taken as a serious contribution to that debate they will need to make a case for them which can be examined on its merits. As yet, however, the case for education in a democracy being at least partially concerned with the development of citizens still stands unassailed by the critics.

Cox, Scruton, *et al.* have provided no general argued rationale for their views. The necessity for such a rationale becomes all the more apparent when we look at three of their particular views on peace education which are related to what they assert to be the purpose of education.

First, the claim that Peace Studies is a 'soft' subject can be dismissed fairly briskly. Assuming that it is possible to measure the general hardness and softness of subjects and that on this scale Peace Studies comes out as soft, it is only if our prime criterion for what should be learned in schools is that it should be *hard* that we should remove Peace Studies. If we are concerned about what people need to know as citizens we shall be working within a quite different framework with quite different criteria. Provided that some body of knowledge, hard or soft, is important for future citizens it should be appropriately incorporated in school education. If it is indeed easily mastered, it will occupy little of students' time. It is interesting to speculate how the critics might apply the hardness criterion. Would this not argue for Chinese rather than French, Sanskrit rather than Latin? Their response would probably be that the hardness criterion is to be taken within the framework of our 'tradition of learning' (WS: 7) and the 'precious heritage of our culture' (WS: 3). But on that criterion would we not also have to rule in an initiation into our long democratic tradition? (And, incidentally, in our multicultural society, as part of *our* heritage, Sanskrit and Chinese too? But that is an argument for another occasion.)

Second, Cox and Scruton have another, rather different claim (p. 40): not that Peace Studies is too soft but that it presupposes too many other disciplines and areas of knowledge for it to be able to be taught in school. (On some views of 'hardness' this would perhaps suggest it was hard!) It is thus ruled out on logical grounds. They make the point that there is 'no possibility of introducing [questions concerning peace] into the school curriculum' because to answer these would presuppose a knowledge of many disciplines and fields of study (e.g. philosophy, logic and mathematics, history, theology, military strategy, economics . . .) some at present studied at school level and some at university level. This claim raises a number of questions. On the strictly logical issue, is it the case that if the understanding of one matter presupposes knowledge of another then the temporal order of learning must follow the logical order? It seems clear that the two can be learned at least at the same time. This is in fact how much learning occurs for good psychological reasons. We want to know about x and discover as we delve into x that properly to understand x we need to know y. So we take steps to master y alongside our investigations into x. Furthermore, is it the case that anyone who wishes to have some understanding of nuclear issues must have first thoroughly mastered all the disciplines cited above (and more, see PS: 12)? Cox and Scruton seem to have failed to distinguish between *some* understanding and a complete, global understanding. If however we are concerned with the political education of citizens, this sets some kinds of parameters to the treatment of nuclear issues in school. Future citizens will need to know enough to understand and be able critically to consider the nuclear policies their political leaders are putting before them. This critical understanding will in turn be bolstered by the availability of critical commentary in the press and other media. School education has the function of enabling people to understand and participate in public debate on these issues and where necessary to ask awkward questions and not be fobbed off by bland answers. If one follows the Cox and Scruton line here, it seems to me that one comes close to saying not just that we must rely on nuclear experts to determine questions of peace for us, but that only a kind of nuclear polymath could consider these issues. At which point we might recall Bernard Williams's (1982: 288) comment 'that if a question which affects the lives, the deaths and the future of all of us is one on which only experts can speak, then that fact itself should properly terrify us all'. Cox and Scruton might of course remind us that we are talking about children here who cannot be expected to have the kind of judgement and understanding an adult would, since they are in the process of being educated. If that were to be their response we would be back again to the point that we are concerned with the education of citizens who are actually making political decisions even while they are at school or shortly after.

Third, it is important to make clear that the critics' conception of moral education as good manners (see p. 39) is not something that defenders of peace education could accept as a reasonable account of moral and political education. As suggested earlier, let us take the view expressed in *Whose Schools?* as a gloss on 'good manners':

> Children need a firm moral and spiritual basis, which will engender the values on which their future happiness depends: honesty, industry, charity, respect for others and for the law.
>
> (*WS*: 2)

This list of values suggests a limited and deferential moral education. There is respect for others and respect for the law but where are self-respect, self-esteem, and personal and ethical autonomy? There is charity but not compassion, industry but no hope, something which Mary Warnock (1986) has suggested might be the chief goal of education. Where too is the political education that the citizens of any democracy will need? There is no mention of understanding of the values of justice and freedom, nor as we have seen any mention of the cluster of values associated with autonomy and independent-mindedness. In fact, again surprisingly, in view of the critics' opposition to totalitarianism the list of values given could form the bedrock of education in any totalitarian society. It might be suggested that the values mentioned here are simply examples, but if so why *this* selection of examples? Why no mention of *any* values in the autonomy area?

In sum the *educational* basis of the critics' objections to peace education is little more than a series of unsupported assertions. The activities of peace education are by no means undermined by *assertions* of the real, genuine, true purpose of education or by the suggestion that the kind of moral and political education involved is already covered by an education in deference.

Further comments on the critics' objections

As we have seen (p. 40), one of their major charges against peace education is that it is indoctrinary. In *Peace Studies* Cox and Scruton say:

> We believe that it is now necessary to direct the attention of all concerned
> . . . to the dubious nature of Peace Studies and to persuade them not
> merely that this subject is often taught in a biased and irresponsible way,
> but that it could be taught in no other way.

(PS: 40)

This is a striking claim to say the least. Cox and Scruton are not simply arguing that, as a matter of fact, teachers of peace education sometimes, or even often, indoctrinate their students but that they always *must* do, despite presumably whatever good intentions they may have to introduce their students to the complex issues of peace and war in an open-minded way. Let us elaborate this point to make clear what it is Cox and Scruton are denying.

Let us imagine a school which draws up a programme in moral and political education, or in personal and social education, part of which is devoted to the examination of issues of peace and war, the causes of conflict between groups and individuals and so on. This is drawn up by a staff curriculum development working party, examined further at a staff meeting, and presented to the governing body for their comments before it is finally adopted as a whole school policy document. In the relevant classes teachers use a wide range of sources and encourage their students to examine and compare them. They introduce them to the critics of peace education and in particular to John Marks's report *'Peace Studies' in our Schools: Propaganda for Defencelessness*. Chapter 4, on what is in peace education syllabuses and what is missing from them and, in Marks's view, should be there, is available for students as well as teachers to judge how far their own resources need to be supplemented. One of the dominant aims of the peace education part of the course, as of the whole course, is the development of students' autonomy so that in personal and social matters they are enabled to come to reasoned decisions and to demand, in turn, of public and political bodies that their policies are based on reasoned grounds, which can be open to public scrutiny.

A complementary whole school policy covers the conduct of and decision-making in the school, allowing for as much participation in its running as is compatible with the maturity of its members. This enables students to develop the dispositions and some of the necessary skills of caring and independent-minded members of a moral community.

The approach is through and through reflexive (not for obvious pedagogical reasons to be equated with 'all the time') in that students are encouraged to think how far the aims of their education, and the means used

45

to achieve them, are acceptable. Why, for instance, put such a high value on autonomy and participation?

Faced with this account Cox and Scruton have to show, on their view, that the peace education element of it *must* be indoctrinatory. They do not say much about indoctrination in *Peace Studies* but Scruton, Ellis-Jones, and O'Keefe (1985) identify five characteristics of indoctrination in *Education and Indoctrination* (subsequently *EI*):

1 Conclusions are foregone. (The signs of this are many, principal among them being loaded questions, loaded references, and loaded vocabulary.)

2 The conclusions form part of a constellation, whose meaning is to be found in a 'hidden unity', based in emotional or political attitude.

3 The conclusions are premises to action, and form the fundamental starting-point of a political 'programme'.

4 The conclusions are also part of a closed system of mutually confirming dogma, which serves to consolidate and validate the emotional unity from which it springs.

5 They are typically established not by open discussion, but by closing the mind to alternative viewpoints, and perhaps even by vilifying or denouncing opposition.

(*EI*: 26)

It is necessary to quote this account of indoctrination in full, not because it is possible to discuss it in detail here, but to show that, even on a view of indoctrination endorsed by Scruton, the school I have described would not in its peace education programme be guilty of indoctrinating its students. So it is possible to have peace education without indoctrination.

This response to the critics may seem somewhat laboured and rather tediously obvious to people familiar with peace education. For what I have described as a *possible* way to proceed in peace education so as to avoid indoctrination bears all the features of the practice with which they are familiar. Perhaps the only thing to be said is that any similarity to real teachers and real schools is intentional.

The remaining objections to peace education (see pp. 40–1) in *Objections to Peace Education* can be dealt with quite quickly. We need to raise questions about the critics' assumptions and make requests for the evidence supporting their claims – familiar activities to those working in peace education since they constitute the very stuff of many of their teaching activities.

First, Cox and Scruton suggest that Peace Studies 'is likely to inculcate guilt in the child towards his own inheritance and to encourage him to place blame for conflict in the camp to which he belongs' (*PS*: 30). Are Cox and Scruton here making certain questionable assumptions themselves about how students should view the world? Is it appropriate to see oneself as a member of a camp opposed to others in some other, presumably hostile, camp? In peace education much useful work is done on the role of the notion of the enemy in human life.[5]

Second, Cox and Scruton are worried that if children are to be 'encouraged to be aware of their responsibility for world disarmament' this may lead them to have nervous breakdowns. They ask, 'What mental outlook would enable a child to assume "responsibility" for "world disarmament"?' (*PS*: 32). Cox and Scruton have no reason for anxiety because the suggestion is not that individuals should assume *total* responsibility for world disarmament (a curious misreading of this suggestion?) but that as people with moral concerns living in a political community they should be aware of the part they can play in trying to bring about disarmament. Coming to understand the part one can reasonably play here need not induce despair, or worse: it may give people a proper sense of their own power in this situation and leave them feeling more hopeful and able to carry on (see White 1987). Are Cox and Scruton assuming that it is in some way inappropriate for 'ordinary people' to have such moral and political concerns?

Third, the breathtakingly sweeping claim (see p. 41) that *nobody* derives any benefit at all from Peace Studies' programmes is totally unsupported and yet it needs to be backed by massive empirical research. One is tempted to ask the critics where their 'genuine' knowledge is here.

Fourth, Scruton claims (see p. 41) that peace educators are hopelessly muddled about whether they are attempting to bring about theoretical understanding of the issues or practical skills. It would have been helpful here to have actual examples of such confusion since education is indeed a complex business and it is not uncommon for there to be confusion over the appropriate means to bring about desired ends. In this situation critics often perform a useful service in helping us to get clearer about our ends and how we might best achieve them. One thinks, for instance, of Robert Dearden's (1976) critique of discovery learning. But no such constructive criticism is offered here. Instead a new sort of confusion seems to creep into the picture. Scruton writes

> indeed it is my experience that a peace activist, once questioned in some fundamental tenet of his beliefs, is as disposed as the next man to take the path of confrontation.
>
> (*WC*: 109)

Here Scruton invites us to assume that supporters of peace education are contradicting their own beliefs if they argue strongly for them when questioned. It is however necessary to distinguish between aggressiveness or bullying (of a verbal and non-verbal kind) and defending a position. Scruton gives no evidence of the former and peace educators would certainly see no reason to discourage the latter.

CONCLUSION

Perhaps the most powerful counter to the critics is that in the face of their criticisms the rationale on which the various activities of peace education rest still remains in place. Let us remind ourselves of that rationale.

Briefly the case is this. First, as moral beings we are involved not only with matters to do with immediate personal concerns but also with the social arrangements of our society and even of the world. In other words, our moral concerns do not stop with the personal but extend to the political sphere. The type and strength of these concerns will vary, and it would be foolish to attempt to elaborate on that in detail now: the point is simply that as moral beings we also have obligations as members of a community. Second, it is shortly after, or sometimes during, the secondary stage of education that young people in our society attain the right to vote, and thus to have some influence, as citizens, on political decisions. Third, properly to exercise that right they need to have been morally and politically educated so that at the very least they understand the issues and how their resolution, one way or another, will affect their lives and those of others in their society and beyond it. Given the nature of the necessary elements of that education, indicated below (and more fully developed in White 1983), it is appropriate for it to be the school's responsibility. This is in brief the case for moral and political education in school.

It is into this broad framework that the various aspects of peace education fit. For such a moral/political education in a democracy will involve considerable attention to the knowledge required by future citizens, which it can be argued demands a broad curriculum, as well as space for the discussion of specifically political issues, not least issues of peace and war. It involves attention to certain skills which people will need in a democratic society, not least those to do with assessing the validity of arguments offered by politicians and in the media. Perhaps most importantly it demands the careful nurturing of dispositions about which the critics, with their virtually exclusive attention to intellectual education, have nothing to say. Any worthwhile moral/political education will however pay attention to the fostering of dispositions like, for instance, courage, generous-spiritedness, tolerance, compassion, and a healthy intellectual scepticism. Scruton (1987) claims, it is true, that the acquisition of acceptable habits is an essential part of education but it is not clear from the context whether he has these kinds of wide-ranging dispositions in mind or something more limited. Some of the most interesting work in this area at the moment is precisely the exploration, at the levels of practice *and* reflection, of how these dispositions are to be understood and how they can best be nurtured in the school.[6]

Looking at the contemporary critics of peace education in some detail can generate two thoughts about work in this field. The first is a valuable reminder that peace education activities are *not* peripheral activities for which we have to scratch around for some *ad-hoc* justification. Both the Peace Studies aspect and the more practical moral/political aspects of peace education have a central place in the education of the citizens of a democratic community.

The second and connected thought is that the important work of peace education, in both its aspects, deserves better critics than these.

NOTES

1 I would like to thank David Hicks and John White for helpful comments on this paper and Michael Fielding for bringing the *Pep Talk* treatments of the critics of peace education (see n.2) to my attention.

2 David Aspin (1986: 1987) deals among other things with the attack on Peace Studies in higher education. Cox, Scruton, and Marks's criticisms of peace education are considered from many perspectives, not least to see how far there is common ground between the critics and proponents of peace education, in *Pep Talk* 5 and 6, Summer 1985.

3 See Cox *et al.* (1986) and Scruton (1986).

4 See e.g. Marks (1984), especially ch. 4.

5 Mary Midgley (1983) has an interesting treatment of the philosophical issues here.

6 See e.g. Fielding (1985) and also the burgeoning work in personal and social education at both the theoretical and practical levels. In my own department a couple of us are involved with an ILEA primary school in a project to develop amongst all users of the playground (students, parents, and teachers) a more thoughtful and considerate attitude to the use of this common space.

REFERENCES

Aspin, D. (1986) '"Peace studies" in the curriculum of educational institutions: an argument against indoctrination', in J.J. Wellington (ed.) *Controversial Issues in the Curriculum*, Oxford: Blackwell.

——— (1987) '"Peace studies" and "education": a rejoinder to Scruton', in *Cambridge Journal of Education* 17, 1: 12–19.

Cox, C. and Scruton, R. (1984) *Peace Studies: A Critical Survey*, London: Institute for European Defence and Strategic Studies.

Cox, C., Douglas-Home, J., Marks, J., Norcross, L., and Scruton, R. (1986) *Whose Schools? A Radical Manifesto*, London: Hillgate Group.

Dearden, R. (1976) *Problems in Primary Education*, London: Routledge & Kegan Paul.

Fielding, M. (1985) 'Celebration – valuing what we do', in R. Blatchford (ed.) *Managing the Secondary School*, London: Bell & Hyman.

Marks, J. (1984) *'Peace Studies' in our Schools: Propaganda for Defencelessness*, London: Women and Families for Defence.

Midgley, M. (1983) 'Deterrence, provocation and the Martian temperament', in N. Blake and K. Pole (eds) *Dangers of Deterrence: Philosophers on Nuclear Strategy*, London: Routledge & Kegan Paul.

Scruton, R. (1986) 'Peace studies: no true subject', in D. O'Keeffe (ed.) *The Wayward Curriculum: A Cause for Parents' Concern?*, London: Social Affairs Unit.

—— (1987) 'Expressionist education', *Oxford Review of Education*, 13, 1: 39–44.

Scruton, R., Ellis-Jones, A., and O'Keeffe, D. (1985) *Education and Indoctrination: An Attempt at Definition and a Review of Social and Political Implications*, Harrow: Education Research Centre.

Warnock, M. (1986) 'The education of the emotions', in D.E. Cooper (ed.) *Education, Values and Mind: Essays for R.S. Peters*, London: Routledge & Kegan Paul.

White, P. (1983) *Beyond Domination: An Essay in the Political Philosophy of Education*, London: Routledge & Kegan Paul.

—— (1987) 'Education about nuclear issues: is there any hope?' *Cambridge Journal of Education* 17, 1: 20–5.

Williams, B. (1982) 'How to think sceptically about the bomb', *New Society* 18 November.

PART 2

Case Studies

4

Conflict

Jen Burnley

Students should study a variety of contemporary conflict situations from the personal to the global and attempts to resolve such conflicts. They should also know about ways of resolving conflict non-violently in everyday life.
(Table 2, p. 14)

Introduction

Conflict is a way of communicating and is an inescapable part of our lives. It is inherent in the process of change within individuals and in society, a process which all people can learn to deal with creatively. Education about conflict is an essential part of peace education and should be a concern for all educators in both the formal and informal educational spheres. It has implications for happy and successful schooling, for the development of harmonious community relationships based on tolerance of differences and commitment to social justice, and for the long-term goal of peaceful international relationships where war is no longer considered an acceptable way of solving a dispute.

Education about conflict involves not only knowledge and understanding of conflict itself – types, levels, causes, and courses – but also encompasses learning *for* conflict resolution – experiencing the skills and processes of resolving conflict. Its cognitive aims and objectives must be supported by reliable and informative data, and be enquiry- and problem-centred to encourage the skills of critical thinking, evaluation, and reflection. Above all, imaginative and experiential teaching methods should be employed to bring out the students' communication skills, using situational material related to the concern of their everyday lives and future needs. Language appropriate to the level and interest of the students is a key element of education about conflict, as it is in all aspects of peace education.

This chapter discusses conflict in four ways. The first section places conflict in the school context, emphasizing the students' perceptions of conflict. The second specifically addresses teachers on learning about conflict and conflict resolution. The third section contains ideas for dealing with conflict. Three examplar exercises, for infants, primary, and secondary school levels, comprise the fourth and final section.

CONFLICT IN CONTEXT

Students experience conflict directly in their everyday lives and indirectly through the media, their reading, or through the experiences of others. Its omnipresence may have contributed to its apparent legitimacy in the minds of the students. Schools give it institutional support and conflicts of interest there frequently result in an incremental sense of injustice, and the resultant reactive behaviour further feeds the cycle. Examination of the context of conflict gives insight into the effects of contention on the formation of students' attitudes and values and on the effectiveness of their coping and communication mechanisms.

Students enter the formal educational phase of their lives already well versed in the various types of conflict and its language while little of the process of resolution has generally come their way. Generally their view of conflict is one-sided and negative, and they have a lively appreciation of its accentuated phase, violence. Violence is the life-blood of much media reporting. From such exposure alone children have absorbed 'information' that violence wins, is socially acceptable, and guarantees results. Violence is associated with images of success. It is easy to see why many so readily accept the idea that violence is normal and that people are inherently violent. Children also perceive teachers as powerful beings who will always fight kids' ideas and this is regrettably reinforced by exposure to school structures. Most children are rewarded for passivity, conformity, and blind obedience, for few are the schools which encourage the conscious co-operation of the students in creating their learning structures, or in at least having a voice which will be heard and acted upon. Many students' sole experience has been of structures which teach acceptance of power and authority (as though it is not our democratic right to learn to question) and of teachers who use praise to manipulate or who use physical violence, threats, sarcasm, and other inappropriate means of control. Some students accept all this as 'what teachers do'. For others the tension and conflict-ridden atmosphere leads to rejection of school and all it stands for.

Conflict in the school context incorporates internal, interpersonal, and intergroup conflict. Internal conflicts may arise out of school or home events, from impaired self-esteem or other causes, can seriously affect attitude and behaviour and cause many teachers to say, 'I can't understand her, she used to be *such* a good girl and now look at her.' Interpersonal conflicts involve the relationships between student–student, student–teacher, teacher–teacher,

teacher–parent, parent–student, or any combination of these. Especially significant is the perceived conflict of the union of teacher–parent against student. Some students take a strong dislike to a teacher and vice versa; some become teachers' pets. Individual or group hositility may be based on ethnicity, religion, gender, or just 'I don't like his face.'

Much conflict arises over values. Education for what? Many students see the offered subject matter as profoundly irrelevant to their present and future lives. Many teachers overtly or covertly express doubts about it too. Perceived irrelevancy leads to boredom, boredom to misbehaviour and involvement with, for example, extra-curricular arson, graffiti writing, and vandalism. More causes for conflict. Other values differences occur over systems of control and effective decision-making. Should discipline be imposed? Can it be? What about self-discipline? Conflicts over discipline/authority and homework are legion.

For many students there is a reluctance to face conflicts. Without the skills of conflict resolution, and having absorbed the forms of conditioning and socializing of our society, many see no further than win/lose possibilities. Losing involves loss of face. It may damage the stability of classroom friendships, increase vulnerability, and impair self-esteem. Consequently many either withdraw from, suppress, or avoid conflict, or become entrenched in their attitude, with determination to gain for oneself rather than to solve the problem. Either way conflict remains unresolved, leading to anger, anxiety, tension, and loneliness. The longer a conflict remains unresolved, the less manageable it becomes. Yet students have a lively appreciation of the ramifications attached to the term conflict, together with their acceptance that conflict is part of the maelstrom of their lives.

When first-year secondary students were asked to draw a free word association from the word *conflict* almost all the 11- and 12-year-old students' first association was *war*. Their language associations were not only of the implements of war but also of its corollary – death, maiming, sadness, and grief. Older students, from fourth-year secondary school, recognized war as *one* form of conflict. Very few mentioned the weapons of war. Most found links between intolerance, misunderstandings, and arguments with conflict, and many searched for words to describe forms of resolution (for example compromise, discussion, resolution, organization, settlement, bonding, friendship, security, apology, restoration of relations, love, conciliation, understanding). For many of the older students, their interpretation of conflict was not wholly negative, while for most of the younger students it was. Conflict makes people uncomfortable. For the younger children it was associated with the inability to envisage successful resolution, especially at the interpersonal level, hence their use of distancing mechanisms and concrete non-emotional words.

The perception of conflict need not be negative. Conflict gives a creative opportunity for development and change. The nature of conflict is such that there exists an incompatibility of ideas, values, or goals. Instead of seeing it as a message of destruction or as something to avoid, clarification of the issues can be seen as stimulating, positive, with gains to be made in communication skills, thought processes, and solutions. Instead of the adversarial, inflammatory mode, handling conflict by processes such as conciliation, mediation, or through the use of good offices, requires students to communicate their positions, beliefs, and attitudes regarding the dispute and they actually listen to the perceptions of the opposing parties. Together they will consider a range of solutions, discussing, clarifying, realistically appraising the stakes involved. We *need* conflict. We need to permit disagreement, diversity of opinion, to allow for the constructive part of the discussion process. Conflict is not all disruptive. It is not good or bad. Conflict is a *signal*. It is the actions which arise from unresolved conflict which may lead to undesirable consequences.

LEARNING ABOUT CONFLICT AND CONFLICT RESOLUTION

The study of conflict

There is a place for the study of conflict in all areas of the formal curriculum. The aim of such studies should be to raise awareness of the different levels of conflict – personal, interpersonal, community/group, national, global; to understand the significance of the medium of communication as a factor in conflict; and to encourage critical thinking about actual conflicts, engaging in creative problem-solving and lateral thinking to assist students in understanding the processes of choice and decision-making. An analysis of structures, both school-based and external, which lead to conflict should be included.

It is a common mistake for teachers to ignore, belittle, or resist resolving the very real problems which exist in the students' lives, whether they are at home, in the classroom, or dealing with the wider community. Complex issues and contradictions in society are often glossed over by teachers in the interest of consensus or conformity. Conflicts are assumed easily resolved within accepted boundaries. Students are expected to accept glibly that individuals are governed by commonly agreed rules, that members of families are governed by law and that people's peaceful interaction depends on social controls. Real dialogue with students about conflict and its resolution must involve critical thinking and a process of analysis and inquiry. Teachers will need to look deeply at structural conflict and at the incompatibilities between existing structures, at real injustice and inequalities at all levels.

Students will need to be aware of the distinction between conflict management and conflict resolution. Management often involves establishing social controls through top-down judgements, using status, authority, or power to impose a solution or maintain the status quo. Clearly this may perpetuate an injustice, such as a denial of rights. Conflict resolution, on the other hand, embodies an understanding and skilled application of democratic processes which encourage social responsibility and creative response to change. A good example of the distinction between conflict management and resolution is demonstrated when establishing classroom 'discipline' or classroom 'rules'. Conflict resolution principles are practised by building up mutual trust and respect, by training students in co-operative techniques and by consciously allowing students to participate in establishing, effecting, and maintaining those rules. In other words, classroom management has a focus. It heightens awareness of any social, political, or other factors which are conducive to conflict, and of the subtle manipulation of language by both teachers and students in the process of conflict resolution. It allows the teacher to assess and apply alternative solutions – with the co-operation of students. Such a democratic process may be extremely threatening both to the classroom teachers and to the establishment, not only because of the political overtones but also because of the traditional view of conflict 'resolution' as being only for the weak.

Within schools, whether it is considering conflict as a science or in working for the resolution of a specific dispute, three aspects must be taken into account: the *context* (actual situation) of a conflict, the *attitude* of the parties involved, and their *behaviour*. If one of these three interlinking aspects changes, it will alter the conflict. For example if the actual situation changes, the immediate conflict may be averted. However, if the behaviour or attitudes of the protagonists do not change, the chances of conflict recurring are high.

Allied to both attitude and behaviour are the goals or purposes of the parties which for some reason are incompatible and thus produce conflict. Unless the underlying reason for the conflict can be defined, there is less chance of a successful resolution, for the process of resolution will be determined by the context. In the school context, as at other levels, the behaviour of the protagonists is often exhibited as seeking attention, power, or revenge. Such behaviour tends to accentuate conflict, and will affect the attitudes of those involved. The level of analysis of what is behind the conflict situation and the behaviour will of course vary with the age and maturity of the students.

Using conflict and its resolution

For senior students, conflict studies can be placed in their theoretical context and can be analysed as actual events, drawing examples from in-school situations as well as from the wider world's social, economic, and political spheres. Senior students should be exposed to the various theories of conflict – biological, sociological, and psychological-social as, apart from providing a theoretical framework, they can then assess the values of theory in understanding causality, management, and resolution of conflict. In addition senior students should further extend their skills in the procedures of conflict resolution. Peer support groups – where 'families' of students of about ten, from the most junior to the most senior, are formed for mutual benefit and support – are valuable areas in which to gain skills in non-violent conflict resolution.

For junior secondary students (age 8–13) the emphasis should be on gaining skills and understanding of the various procedures of conflict resolution, once the analysis of context, attitude, and behaviour of the protagonists is understood. Skills may be formally practised through role play in the classroom or used as a method to solve any dispute which arises (either with teacher assistance or, if the process is sufficiently well understood, to reach a solution among themselves). Community and international disputes should be examined from the points of view of cause, course, and resolution, and why these happened. Junior secondary students can practise four types of conflict resolution: avoidance; reconciliation; compromise or negotiation; and arbitration or judicial processes.

Often a conflict is avoided when one of the parties leaves, changes direction, or simply stops provoking conflict. Otherwise a conflict can be resolved only by using specific techniques or procedures. Two processes relevant to the junior secondary level include negotiation and compromise. In negotiation the disputants control their own resolution-seeking process without outside help. They may be able to work through by steps, identifying the conflict and expressing their feelings about it, discussing possible solutions, before deciding on one and then working on how to put it into effect. In compromise, both sides give up something in order to decide on something.

Empathy, one of the basic skills for successful conflict resolution, is difficult for children, and using negotiation or compromise involves active listening, empathy, and the use of appropriate assertiveness – all three attained only after considerable practice and through acquiring sensitivity to a situation.

A major difficulty with both negotiation and compromise is that the stronger, more forceful, more stubborn personality or better communicator may dominate or wear down the other and so the decision, if reached, may set the scene for further conflicts. The potential for power games by a stronger personality is obvious.

The 'judicial' approach requires the involvement of people who are not directly connected with the dispute. In schools, the teacher or Head is often used as the judge. The resolution is imposed and there is generally no possibility of appeal to a 'higher court'. Such settlements may or may not allow the protagonists to state their case. Regrettably we are all too familiar with this scenario. Judicial process involves applying the rules as they stand. The possibility for change or for finding a creative solution is limited.

A variation of the judicial process is forming a panel to decide a course of action. Parents and teachers, or teachers alone, may assess the case of the disputants. While this provides for discussion it still imposes a decision on the disputing parties and such decisions are generally binding. Students may feel resentful that adults have imposed once more, that adults never listen to them anyway. They may accede to the decision only because they cannot see what else they can do.

Both the judicial and arbitration processes favour the win/lose option and, in the school context especially, are top-down solutions. They may perpetuate a sense of injustice and lay the groundwork for further conflict. Neither relies on the willingness of the parties to reduce the conflict, yet without this there is much less chance of achieving a workable solution.

Another method of resolving conflict through a third party is for either a student or a teacher to take the role of a conciliator. Their job is to clarify the claims of the disputants and to be sufficiently respected by them to be seen as presenting no threat or having no bias towards a particular solution. The conciliator needs to make it clear that s/he wants the dispute to be resolved and needs to be able to show this by the use of supportive techniques to provide a structure which the disputants can use.

A mediator acts as a channel of communication between disputing parties. Unlike the conciliator who plays an active part in the discussion, the mediator merely conveys statements about and interpretations of the conflict from one party to the other, with the aim that gradually the parties will reach a solution. A mediator must be absolutely impartial and unconditionally relay from one to the other anything the disputing parties say.

The varying methods suggested allow for differing points of view to be presented so that the protagonists may express their wants, beliefs about or perceptions of the conflict. They provide for additional information to be presented to help clarify the situation. Positions can be re-examined in the light of this clarification and the parties work towards a resolution. Where a solution is jointly arrived at the possibility of retribution or retaliation may well be avoided.

In primary school one should stress the skills of anticipation and participation as part of conflict resolution skills. Anticipation involves sensitivity to the needs of others, empathy, and co-operation. It means critical thinking and being aware of the strengths, purpose, and results of action. Participation involves whole-hearted involvement with others, appropriate assertiveness while remaining open-minded and respecting differences, and above all, a commitment to justice. Anticipation and participation together lead to creative resolution of conflict.

DEALING WITH CONFLICT

It has been said that for general school, classroom, and discipline conflicts there are only difficult solutions or no solutions at all. Many educators assume that years of experience will help, but this is not so if the experience has been with confrontation 'solutions', old tried and true methods which suppress rather than solve conflicts. Experience is not the same as skill. Educators will have to be prepared to learn and become skilled in new approaches, to think laterally, to believe that outside help may be more useful than to try to resolve everything internally, and to challenge school and classroom structures which perpetuate the avoidance/suppression mechanisms of conflict resolution.

Take an average sort of school conflict – Ross and Michael are bored, spend most of the lesson time talking to each other, consciously disrupt Sam, who joins them in fooling around. What can a teacher do? *Tell* them the solution to the conflict they're creating, 'If you don't behave [i.e. conform] I'll send you to the Head.' Or *bribe, placate, appease* – 'look fellows, just get this down and we'll go on to something interesting'. Do you think the students don't see through this one? Maybe you could *discuss* with them possible solutions to the conflicts they accentuate. Do you choose the one to test out or do they? Does this affect your status, power, or authority? Or can you all *agree* on a solution which threatens none of you but which as the 'lowest common denominator' of agreement may solve nothing either?

Three values are the basis of a co-operative classroom atmosphere, in which a sense of community and dynamic conflict resolution overcome aggression. They are integrity, justice, and consistency. These apply to everyone in the school community. They cannot be imposed by force, but are achieved by understanding, patience, and by application of conflict resolution skills. With these as the base-line, teachers can work for mutual affection with acceptance, and higher self-esteem. Security in these areas allows children to open themselves to other experiences. There are many well-tried activities designed to give children greater security, confidence, and self-esteem. Affirmation exercises, either self- or group-based, explore positive qualities and encourage a sense of personal value.

Active listening is a basic skill in successful conflict resolution. Often children are so involved with their sense of grievance that they cannot listen to the other person's side. Mirroring helps here and can illustrate how misunderstandings arise. It is a useful technique for conflict resolution between two children or for a group situation, though many young children feel frightened to 'open up' in larger groups. In a small group of children (three or five) they feel greater security. Mirroring assures all participants that their feelings about the interpretations of the conflict have been understood.

Communication exercises examine the use of tone as a source of conflict or its resolution and also teach the importance of listening to avoid misunderstanding and potential conflict. 'Passing the news' is one technique where a small group reads and interprets a particular item, then verbally imparts the information to another group, who scatter and each tell it to others. At the end of the exercise the final report is written and compared to the original. Or one child (or group) has a picture or diagram which s/he describes to another who tries to draw what is being described. The recipient may ask no questions but may comment upon what s/he is doing, which should indicate to the describer how well s/he is communicating. Role play of a conflict illustrates the significance of communication. Especially when a conflict has resulted in violence re-creating the conflict leads to an understanding of cause – did it arise from things which have just happened, or from earlier events which may have been inadequately dealt with or ignored? It allows an analysis of the conflict, with communication of gradation of feelings from the initial sense of discomfort or grievance, through the precipitating incident or misunderstanding, to tension and flashpoint.

Other communication exercises deal with the expression of feeling and meaning through voice tone and body language. English is an inflected language and, with changing emphasis, the same words take on an entirely different meaning. Students can decide on a message and act it out giving different meanings through emphasis and body language. Similarly, a range of exercises exists (or you can create your own) designed to raise awareness of which parts of the body are used to express different emotions. In what ways does the body language of anger differ from that of pleasantry? Which body language do most people consistently use and why do some choose to use particular ways to express their feelings?

Communication skill exercises will strengthen understanding of instinctive coping mechanisms. At the initial stage of discomfort did you choose to avoid, deny, suppress, distance yourself from, or handle the conflict? All except handling can lead to the problem becoming unmanageable. Co-operative games can also, of course, be incorporated into any course.

Values clarification exercises signal what is important in conflict management to the class and its individuals. What are their preferred 'weapons' of conflict and its resolution? Why? Could they be arranged in order and what justifications are used for that order? Word flow associations can help the students clarify their thoughts on their preferred solutions. One basic values clarification exercise is on school discipline. Should punishment be different because of gender? For an offence would students prefer a detention or writing lines, or to spend time helping a younger child or in giving some form of service to the school community?

'I' statements are part of both values clarification and communication exercises and are basic to success in conflict resolution. Unless we can be clear about our own needs and how to express them, we often cannot hear the needs of others. It is often useful, therefore, to challenge statements

Figure 5 Conflict-resolution processes

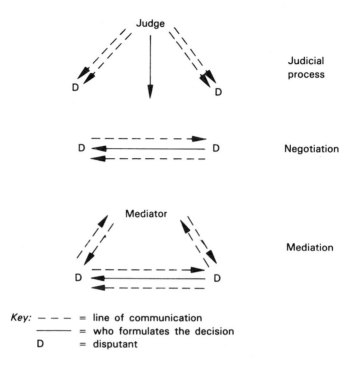

Key: — — — = line of communication
———— = who formulates the decision
D = disputant

beginning 'People feel . . .', 'One should . . .' and ask them to begin '*I* feel
. . .', '*I* should . . .'

HOW CONFLICT RESOLUTION PROCESSES WORK IN THE CLASSROOM

When examining methods of conflict resolution the teacher can effectively
use diagrams such as Figure 5 to illustrate communication flows. In addition
to the processes, teachers should be aware of the different steps which can
be taken to arrive at a successful conclusion to a conflict. Some involve a
few straightforward steps, others are detailed, demanding much time and
patience. A simple structure could involve:

1 Stating one's position on the conflict and listening to others state theirs.
2 Agreeing on common ground.
3 Listing possible solutions.
4 Deciding which to try.

5 Implementing it, and later evaluating its success.

Other structures are more detailed, involving affirmation techniques and considerable introspection. For example disputants working with a conciliator may follow this structure:

1 Conciliator confirms her respect for all the disputants.
2 Disputants express their interpretation of the facts of the dispute together with their feelings about it.
3 Exploration of their feelings before and during the dispute, the depth and reality of these.
4 Conciliator checks the facts of the dispute with each party.
5 Once the facts are agreed upon a solution can be looked for.
6 Range of possible solutions is elicited from the disputants. These are gradually narrowed down to one or two. Use of the 'if' scenario helps here: 'if' we choose this solution then . . . 'if' this changes . . ., 'if' she stops . . .
7 Conciliator draws from the disputants ideas about how feelings would be affected if a particular solution were tried.
8 Disputants discuss feelings freely in association with the solution until they reach agreement.
9 Resolution in effect.

A structure for primary students could be:

1 What is the problem?
2 Who is involved in this problem and how?
3 Who can give information about this problem?
4 What do you feel could be done to help overcome this problem?
5 Which of those ways do you think is worth first try?
6 Why does everyone involved think that this is the way to go?
7 Who takes responsibility for carrying this out?

Great emphasis is placed on affirming, empathy and understanding, tolerance and interdependence within the class. Affirming is doing oneself justice. Empathy helps one understand whether justice has, or has not, been done. Justice is the base on which to build.

SOME WORDS OF ADVICE

When learning about conflict resolution, of overwhelming importance is the commitment to see the process through and to achieve a realistic solution. Conflict begins with a sense of discomfort, whatever the purpose or goal behind the conflict. Recognition of this stage, together with the skills of resolution, will ensure more peaceful learning, teaching and parenting. Therefore:

1 Emphasize the process as well as the result. The result may not work, be achieved, or last. The learning which accompanies the process will.

2 Recognize and reward effort and improvement in conflict-resolution skills. The effort put into it makes a major contribution to the success of the process.

3 Recognize that some things are not negotiable. While as a basic premise conflict resolution procedures and structures should assume equality between adults and students in a school there are some areas where teachers have a responsibility to ensure the safety of their charges.

4 Administer justice without adulteration – there is no difference in justice and there must be no difference in the way it is applied. There should be no difference in justice depending on gender or age for example.

5 Discussion, and good communication, are the basis of conflict resolution. Avoid the 'Devil's Dictionary' definition of discussion as a 'method of confirming others in their errors'.

6 Conflict resolution is a time-consuming process, so enjoy it. It should be beneficial to all involved.

CLASSROOM ACTIVITIES

The two following activities can be adapted for use in a wide range of classroom situations. They each illustrate the kinds of scenarios that can be developed to explore and develop the skills of conflict resolution.

Kathy's Day

Purpose

To illustrate the kinds of conflict which are encountered by younger children in daily life, for example to do with siblings, parents, power struggles between adults and between adults and children.

Preparation

Produce sufficient copies of the scene which you are going to work on. As students get to know the character, Kathy, a more detailed background can be built up. This could take the form of a wall display, using both words and pictures. Also write out and photocopy individual copies of the multiple choice responses for the scene. By offering a series of possible courses of action to take, students have the chance to explore real-life causes of conflict and to discuss their preferred options as solutions.

The scenes offer the opportunity for responses as varied as withdrawal, avoidance, suppression, threat (accentuating the conflict), bargaining, and compromise.

As the character of Kathy becomes familiar to students it may be possible to use the character in role-play or simulation. Kathy can then be used as a foil or the mediator when students want to explore their own real-life conflicts.

Procedure

Students work in groups to devise their own role-plays for the different scenes. A mixture of acting-out and reading of the scenes can be a useful approach.

Scene 1: getting up

A (X)-year-old girl Kathy lives in a high-rise council flat with her parents, young baby sister, and her elder sister. She shares a room with the baby. Her father is unemployed and her mother works nights. Every morning Mum is tired and often cross. Today as she comes home, about 7.00 am, the baby is screaming but Kathy ignores it. Mum comes in and yells at Kathy for not getting the baby her bottle. It is an hour before the time Kathy usually gets up but Mum orders her to get up now. Then she goes into her bedroom and starts shouting at Dad. Kathy

1 hides her head under the pillow and tries to go to sleep again;
2 does as Mum says but feeling cross and resentful;
3 screams back, saying . . .;
4 says it isn't time to get up and can't she get up later?

Scene 2: going to school

Kathy catches a bus to school. After stopping the bus she realizes she does not have her bus pass with her and she has no money. The conductor says she can't get on. Kathy

1 tells him to go to hell and pushes into a crowd of people on the bus who close in behind her to protect her;
2 walks to school;
3 says she's just found her pass and flashes another card at him so quickly the conductor can't see what it is;
4 asks if she can pay tomorrow. The conductor is anxious that the bus keep to time but rules say . . .

Scene 3: in class

Kathy's class is taught by a young male teacher nearly all day. Concerned at the 'groupiness' of various minorities in his class, the teacher has been trying to break up established groups in an effort to lessen the conflict between them. He has just attended a conflict resolution workshop for teachers and is bursting with ideas to try out on his students. Desks and chairs had been in groups of four but now the teacher tells the students to rearrange the room so that tables are in an open U shape. Most of them complain. Kathy is placed next to a girl she has been taunting. She

1 immediately begins to think up further ways to aggravate the girl;
2 sits glumly and does not speak;
3 asks the teacher if she can change seats;

4 accepts that everyone has been changed around and decides to get used to the new pattern.

Scene 4: at the shop

On the way home Kathy has a regular job to do – to collect the bread. She is expected to be home at a specific time. Today there is a crowd in the shop and several more adults come in after Kathy. She is ignored while they are served. One adult inadvertently pushes her. Kathy

1 has had enough of being pushed around and is abusive to the adults;

2 keeps waiting for her turn, while being very worried about being late home;

3 asks the adult in front of her if she would ask the shopkeeper to serve her first;

4 calls out to the shopkeeper that it is her turn.

Heritage Hill: Who stands to gain?

Purpose

To examine the ramifications of a conflict about local redevelopment, using concepts of individual rights versus public responsibility and social justice.

Preparation

First, students and teachers prepare, and add the details to, a base map of the Heritage Hill area. This needs to be large enough for the class to be able to gather around it for general discussion. The map shows

1 The council boundary plus the internal divisions into three wards. One ward contains all the Flats, and the Slope and North Ward are prime residential areas, having views of the river.

2 Route of the main road through the Heritage Hill area.

3 The proposed route of the feeder road to 'cream' heavy traffic from the main road directly to the industrial area of Heritage Flats. This would involve the demolition of some residences, and would bring noisy traffic closer to others.

4 The river adjacent to Heritage Flats.

5 The medium-density housing beside the main road.

6 Middle-class dwellings on Heritage Hill.

7 The location of the Hill Shopping Centre and proposed location of the swimming pool and health care centre.

8 Late-nineteenth-century terrace housing on Heritage Flats.

9 The land for development, on the gentle slope between Heritage Flats and Heritage Hill. This land is currently open land used by the Flats kids as a play area and by the local drunks and down-and-outs.

Second, all students are familiarized with the locational conflicts facing Heritage Hill Council. The Flats have traditionally been areas of working-class homes. They comprise only 20 per cent of the council area and have approximately 30 per cent of the population of the area. Adjacent to the Flats is land zoned as industrial and many of the Flats people work there. The river adjacent to the flat land is suitable

Figure 6 Heritage Hill base map

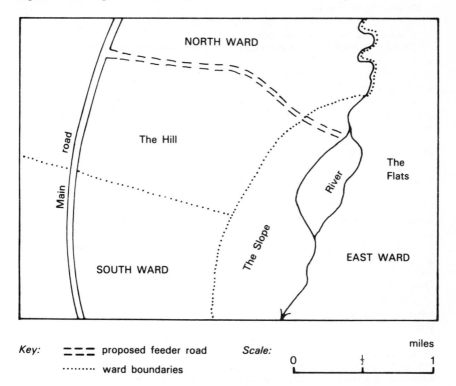

Key: ≡≡≡ proposed feeder road   Scale:

········· ward boundaries

miles

0   ½   1

for transport of goods to and from the industrial sites. It is now proposed that the open space between the Flats and the middle-class area of the Hill, known as the Slope, be re-zoned for light industrial development, thus surrounding the Flats homes with industry. Included in the proposal is the location of a controlled dump for noxious wastes. The Slope land is a gentle slope with good views. The developing firm has promised the council to use profits from the development to build a large indoor swimming pool on the Hill and also to set aside some of the Slope for a playground for children. Funds would also be allocated for a health centre to be located adjacent to the shopping centre of the Hill. The council has control over zoning policy, health care, and leisure facilities.

Many of the Hill people have no transport problems (one- and two-car families), professional and managerial people of 'good taste'. However, on the Flats it is a different matter. Public buses cease at 6.00 pm. Few have cars. Women can shop up the Hill during the day while the buses are running, but they and their children face problems at night. Since the 1970s the corner shop has almost disappeared and shopping is concentrated at the Hill centre.

Third, students choose roles for themselves – 30 per cent are Flats people, 65 per cent are Hill people, some from the apartments, and 5 per cent are developers, architects, and industrial waste experts from outside the local area. Then they should create a dossier about themselves, giving details of place of residence, length of residence, value of home, occupation, number of dependent children, and so on.

Fourth, the issues are

1 Should the Slope be re-zoned?

2 If so, for what kinds of industries and what should be the density of development?

3 If the Slope is re-zoned for light industry, will the noxious dump be allowed and if so, where will it be located and why?

4 If the Slope is re-zoned, is a feeder road necessary? Would it be possible or preferable to use water transport? If a road is built, where should its route lie? Why?

5 Where should the proposed swimming pool and health facility be located, and why choose such sites?

Fifth, the various views are as follows.

People of Heritage Flats

Working class. Mostly both parents working. Acutely aware of the needs of their children – for jobs, leisure facilities, transport, health care. Don't want the new link road – the traffic to and in the existing industrial area is bad enough. Would prefer the Slope to be kept as it is now – open recreational space.

People of Hermitage Hill

1 Middle class, professional, managerial. Relatively affluent. Have private transport. Mostly work and shop outside the area. Keen to preserve and enhance property values. Keen to add to the amenities the Hill offers. Would refuse to support a waste dump unless it was well down the Slope – really on the Flats.

2 Apartment people. Many come from the Flats. Mostly young 18- to 25-year-olds and working outside the area. Rely on public transport. Acutely aware of employment problems, and lack of recreational facilities in the Flats.

Developer

Efficient, large, experienced firm. In it for profit. Ideas of equity not prominent. Links with government over capital support. Believe that any environmental concerns are more than outweighed by the benefits of their proposals to the whole community.

Procedure

Local government elections are due. Candidates present themselves from the three wards; from a class of twenty-five, suggest three per ward, for the two places per ward. Any amount of electioneering is permitted and candidates can decide for themselves the emphasis they will put on the various issues. Posters and leaflets can be prepared and distributed. Public meetings are held in each of the wards.

Once the councillors are elected the classroom becomes the council chamber. The six councillors elect one of their members to be the mayor/ess whose role is to control the agenda of each meeting but who has a vote. Council meetings are open to the public although the public can speak only if representation has been made to the mayor/ess prior to the meeting and s/he has entered it on the agenda. Various pressure groups from the wards do ask for this permission and argue their case before the council.

A series of meetings will be held to reach decisions on the key issues. Council minutes will record salient discussion points and decisions. The public can express their opinions through the local press (letters to the editor being displayed on the class noticeboard).

Points to be considered

1 Who stands for council and why? What part did wealth, power, or prestige, gained from their position in the occupational structure, play? Who stands to gain?

2 What attempts were made towards equity rather than preservation of the relative quality of life of the different social groups?

3 Were decisions made, or were the conflicts of interest too difficult to resolve?

4 Did wealth, power, or knowledge play a part in deciding the location of the salutary/noxious amenities?

5 What processses of conflict resolution were used, with what degree of 'win-win' result? Or was it all 'win-lose'?

6 If either the Hills or Flats people didn't get what they wanted, what options have they got, e.g. move away, use the democratic process, illegitimate means of protest?

7 While the people of the Flats are not disenfranchised, is their voice effectively limited by political or social structures?

8 To what extent was conflict avoided because of the spatial segregation of people of the Flats and Hill?

RECOMMENDED READING

de Bono, E. (1985) *Conflicts: A Better Way to Resolve Them*, London: Harrap. Examines three roads to conflict resolution: fight/litigate; negotiate/bargain; or design a way out. Using the third, he introduces the concept of 'triangular thinking' in which the third party is a creative designer of resolution. An exciting approach, which offers practical proposals for the various levels of conflict, from personal to supranational.

Deutsch, M. (1973) *The Resolution of Conflict: Constructive and Destructive Processes*, New Haven, Conn: Yale University Press. This set of theoretical essays and resource papers is designed to assist the understanding of how to present destructive conflict and initiate co-operation. From the viewpoint of the social psychologist it examines interrelationships between research, theory, and practical application.

Fisher, S. and Hicks, D. (1985) *World Studies 8–13: A Teacher's Handbook*, Edinburgh: Oliver & Boyd. Chapter 5 of this very practical book for teachers is called 'Getting on with others' and contains a variety of classroom activities on themes such as working together, resolving conflicts, and sex-role stereotyping.

Judson, S. (1984) *A Manual on Nonviolence and Children*, Philadelphia, Pa: New Society Publishers. Written for parents or teachers, the exercises in this manual are designed to affirm, to assist in learning to empathize, and to help to establish confidence in solving problems. Such experiential exercises are a vital part of the teacher's repertoire. This book is especially valuable for infants and primary teachers.

Kreidler, W.J. (1984) *Creative Conflict Resolution: More Than 200 Activities for Keeping Peace in the Classroom K-6*, Glenview, Ill: Scott, Foresman. This resource book offers over twenty conflict resolution techniques with examples, fourteen reproducible worksheets, and over 200 class-tested activities and co-operative games. Good on analysing conflicts, helping students settle disputes, ways of dealing with anger, fear, prejudice, and aggression.

Lieberman, M. and Hardie, M. (1981) *Resolving Family and Other Conflicts: Everybody Wins*, Santa Cruz, California: Unity Press. An excellent resource book which sets out very clearly the key issues in relation to self-esteem, expressing feelings, effective communication, active listening, resolving conflicts, and six-step problem-solving.

Nicholas, F.M. (1987) *Coping With Conflict: A Resource Book for the Middle School Years*, Wisbech, Cambs: Learning Development Aids. Deals with issues of conflict and co-operation, violence and peace, both locally and globally. A practical and useful book full of ideas for classroom activities and lessons in art, drama, discussion, research, writing, and maths. Some pages can be photocopied for pupil use.

5

Peace

Gil Fell

Students should study different concepts of peace, both as a state of being and as an active process, on scales from the personal to the global. They should look at examples of the work of individuals and groups who are actively working for peace.

(Table 2, page 14)

DEFINITIONS

In this chapter I will elaborate on how the *processes* of education for peace can be used to explore the concept of peace itself. All too often little time is spent on exploring what we mean by peace, as it is assumed that there is some common understanding. However, this is often not so. Our concepts of peace are many and varied, to quote from Educators for Social Responsibility (1983):

'Give peace a chance', 'Peace with strength', 'Prince of Peace' . . . The rhetoric of peace surrounds us every day as advertisers, politicians, preachers, activists and pop musicians alike appeal for peace. The word appears in all areas of our lives, on all levels. Parents ask their children for 'peace and quiet'. Police officers 'keep the peace' while protesters 'disturb the peace' demanding 'peace now'. We have 'peacekeeping forces' and a nuclear weapon named the 'Peacekeeper'. Many of our consumer products guarantee 'peace of mind' while the people of the Third World cry out for 'peace and justice'. Some of us search for 'inner peace' while others seek 'peace for all peoples'; many seek both. Ronald Reagan is for peace as is Edward Kennedy, yet they might as well be speaking different languages. As we begin to pay attention to the way this seemingly simple word is manipulated, we realise that the nature of peace is complex, its meaning often blurred by rhetoric.

One starting-point for a definition of peace is that given in the resolution of the 18th Session of the General Conference of Unesco (1974) which stated:

> Peace cannot consist solely in the absence of armed conflict but implies principally a process of progress, justice and mutual respect among the peoples designed to secure the building of an international society in which everyone can find his true place and enjoy his share of the world's intellectual and material resources.

At the same time we need to note that such a definition is also culture bound. As Barbara Stanford (1976) points out

> Africans, American Indians and some Asian religious groups have tended to believe that the relationship of human beings with the natural world is also important. Peace with the forces of nature, with other animals, and with the spirits of the ancestors in these cultures is as important as peace with other people.

This chapter attempts to bring into clearer focus the concept of peace as an active, challenging option in the lives of all. One of the central tenets of the chapter is that current, widely held concepts of peace are negative, defining peace in terms of an absence of war or violence rather than as something positive in its own right. Definitions which are couched in the language of their opposite tend to appear passive, as if they have no real meaning except by contrast with their corollary. What is needed are positive concepts, which see peace as the active presence of justice, equality, and so on. Educators and others need a vision of peace as a realistic, hard option worthy of serious consideration, which can offer an alternative to a model of society built on patriarchal concepts. The prevailing model of society is thus one in which war and militarism are glorified and the male values of aggression, competition, and scientific progress are considered to be superior to those values often considered to be innately female, such as co-operation, nurturing, and caring both for others and the planet as a whole.

In the search for a positive concept of peace the negative, 'absence of' definition needs to be turned on its head and the question asked, What must be present for a situation to quality as being peace-ful? One starting-point might be to study our own experiences and think about moments and occasions which have felt peaceful or at peace. The answers may be many and varied. They may be quite concrete, such as working together constructively in a group or sharing a meal with friends, or more abstract such as a concern for justice or human rights; some may be intangible, like feeling good about something that has happened, or tangible as in feeling safe walking along a street alone at night. One task for peace educators is to help those with whom they work to drop some of the bland, passive ideas held about peace and to identify more dynamic and action-centred ideas which can inspire people in their everyday lives.

If we are to be interested in peace, we also have to be interested in violence. Broadly violence within a society falls into two main categories: overt or direct violence, in which people are physically damaged in some way and which is easily recognized, and covert or structural violence. The degree of oppression we experience within a particular society may vary according to our colour, age, sex, class, or sexual orientation. Anything that prevents individuals from being able to realize their full potential or which condemns them to live in poverty or with the denial of basic human rights is inflicting violence just as surely as the direct violence that is the centre of media attention.

Alice Miller (1987) has been searching for the roots of violence in our child-rearing practices. In what she calls 'poisonous pedagogy' she describes how children are taught to obey and respect their parents or teachers, regardless of what is done to them, and also how they are not allowed to express their negative feelings about such treatment openly. Her thesis is that they, in turn, go on to perpetuate their own hurts in the way they themselves deal with the children they encounter. An extension of this is that educational practices dependent on the obedience of the child to the teacher can lead to a loss or devaluing of the child's own sense of self. People with a damaged sense of self, according to Miller, are forever susceptible, to a greater or lesser extent, to being unquestioningly obedient.

This leads to the possibility that one route to building a positive image of peace is through building a positive sense of self. In this light we need to examine and question some of the fundamental assumptions behind our own education system. For example, how much is it designed to mould children into the type of people the educators want them to be, and how much is it designed to fulfil the needs of individual children and allow them to use their potential to the full? And does this vary between, say, primary and secondary schools, as well as between school and school?

Developing a pedagogy that resists the temptation to manipulate and set its own goals implies the development of a system which provides the physical and emotional support children need from adults, it does not imply leaving them to their own devices. Such a pedagogy would, according to Alice Miller, include respect for the children and their rights, a tolerance for their feelings and a willingness to learn from their behaviour.

Being peaceful is often associated with being passive and a state of peace is thought to be one in which there is no conflict. But a moment's thought makes it clear that a world without conflict would be a dull and sterile place. What education for peace recognizes is that conflict is often a springboard for growth; it does not advocate the elimination of conflict, rather it seeks creative and less violent ways of resolving it. The knowledge that there may be better ways of doing things can be a major spur to finding novel solutions and lays a vital role in building a more peaceful environment. No one will suggest that opting for such a path is easy, but it can certainly be dynamic, challenging, and exciting. So, peace is not just a state of being in which individuals become passive acceptors of the status quo, rather it is an active process seeking non-violent and creative ways of being related.

There is also a relationship between peace and justice, particularly social justice for there can be no true peace while major injustice is present within a society or indeed a relationship. Such oppression can take many forms, it may be the oppression of one race or sex by another, it may be the enslavement of one group by another; whatever form the injustice may take, by definition it precludes the possibility of a state of positive peace existing. The question then arises as to whether the use of violence is ever justified in the struggle to achieve social justice. For myself, as a peace educator and pacifist, my answer is that the means used to achieve the end must always be congruent with the end desired, that is non-violence is not merely a tactic in the struggle for social justice but is a way of life which should exert its influence on everything we do.

Surrounded by images of violence in the media and through books, films, and videos, it is hardly surprising that children view war and violence as courageous and exciting. After all the injured hero on television reappears the next week unscathed. Davies (1984) has reviewed the research on children's attitudes to peace and war and writes:

> Perhaps the most important of Alvik's conclusions, from an educational point of view, is that whilst increased intellectual development enables children to make more sophisticated moral judgements about war, there is an alarming inconsistency between the quality of thinking about war, and that about peace. As with the children Cooper studied, peace was often seen in terms of passivity and inactivity. Despite their increasing intellectual maturity, and their ability to make use of more sources of information (e.g. the media, books, other people) their concepts of peace seemed 'stuck' at a relatively immature level.

Even quite young children have positive images for war and conflict while their images of peace are weak and passive. This was borne out by a group of 5- to 9-year-olds I worked with. The images they associated with war and conflict included words such as 'daring', 'adventure', and 'hero' while for peace they include words like 'white', 'dove', and 'silence'. This was despite the fact that, in conversation, they appeared quite clear that fighting often hurts and can lead to killing. It would seem that the way they feel about the words and what they associated with them was different from what they actually knew them to mean.

OBSTACLES TO PEACE

The obstacles to peace are many and varied. One of the central challenges to education for peace is to promote the idea that peace building is an exacting, challenging, and rewarding task. Its vision of a peaceful world is not one in which there is an absence of conflict. Rather, it is a place where conflicts can be resolved in ways that make the outcome as satisfactory as possible for all, and where society is no longer constructed on a model where 'I win' automatically means 'you lose'. Why does the concept of peace as something undesirable and unattainable, the province of dreamers and the unrealistic, hold such sway? One possible answer to this is given by Mary Daly in her book *Gyn/Ecology* (1979) where she says, 'The state of patriarchy is the state of war, in which periods of recuperation from and preparation for battle are euphemistically called 'peace'.' By this she means that we live in a world organized in a competitive and hierarchical way and in which women are required continuously to recreate warriors.

On this issue the Quaker Women's Group (1986) have written

The desire to control and dominate is evident in the crazy way they [men] live out their lives . . . More evidence of the same desire is seen in the rat race, the space race, the conquering of the wilderness, of Everest, the breaking of the four minute mile, the sound barrier and the obsession with breaking record after record. Men spend their lives in isolation from each other, their fear of other men dominating their existence. They turn to women for comfort and support, women whom they see as softer, gentler, weaker and less threatening, and so they lose their ability to reach out to other men. Women are seen as a class apart, not as capable or as powerful as men, serving only as a support for men to make tolerable the intolerable world they have created.

Birgit Brock-Utne (1985) relates this to the impossibility of having a true education *for* peace, as opposed to education *about* peace, without full account being taken of the differing educations given to girls and boys from the cradle onwards. She quotes a group of feminist peace educators meeting in Canada in 1981. Thus 'we could no longer accept the oppression of girls as a non-issue within peace education and peace research'.

When examining the competitive base on which society is founded it is possible to see how methods of non-violent conflict resolution, in which the combatants are encouraged to become 'winners all', strikes at the heart of power structures in society. Such an approach to conflict brings with it an increased personal responsibility for our actions and their consequences, but many have reservations as to whether this can be achieved within an hierarchical education system.

Another obstacle to peace is fear. We all experience it to varying degrees

75

at times, especially in situations of conflict. We may be afraid of our adversary because of the possibility of physical harm that may be inflicted on us, or it may be fear of differences between us that led to conflict arising in the first place. Such differences may be of character, race, or creed and may arise from prejudice because of the stereotypes we receive through the media and other sources. In general we are trained to act initially with suspicion towards those we know to be different from ourselves in some way. One major contribution of education for peace and allied fields such as world studies and multicultural education is to promote celebration of difference as something which contributes to the rich variety of life on this planet.

Popular concepts about human aggression are another major obstacle to peace, for it is commonly believed that we are aggressive by nature and that peace, in part, requires that we restrain and control those impulses. It is vital to recall, however, that there is much debate about the nature of human aggression, indeed there is copious research to indicate that aggression, rather than being part of our biological heritage, is something that we are taught from our first moment on this planet. It is is the case that we *learn* to be aggressive then we can, of course, equally learn to be non-aggressive (Montagu 1976).

Propaganda is often used to fuel prejudice and encourage stereotypes thus enabling the concept of an enemy to be perpetuated. An essential feature of our social organization at present is the concept of an enemy from whom we must, at all times, be ready to defend ourselves. More of our national income is spent annually on defence than on health or education and a large proportion of our scientific research is funded by the military. For such a balance of priorities to be sustained a great deal of effort has to be put into building up the idea of the threat from an outside enemy. In discussing the recent arms reduction talks between the superpowers a radio commentator was heard to say that if there was to be such an agreement, the whole justification for the existence of NATO would be called into question. The notion that it was even possible to contemplate such a thing seemed unthinkable to him and as if it would involve dismantling the very fabric of our society.

STUDYING PEACE

How can positive concepts of peace be worked towards in the classroom and elsewhere? One route is to consider some of the skills and attitudes set out in Chapter 1, in terms of their contribution to the practical implementation of a positive notion of peace at all levels, from the personal to the global. Much of what education for peace proposes is an integral part of the 'good education' practised by many teachers for years. The reason for including these under the umbrella of education for peace is that by so doing those processes become more conscious and clear connections can be drawn between the personal and the political. It can also help to make the philosophical point that underpins much of the practice of education for peace, that the way we live and behave now should be congruent with how we would like things to be; that our means must be compatible with our ends, that is if our vision is for a peaceful non-violent future then the means by which we work to achieve that must also be peaceful and non-violent.

The process of education for peace should not be seen as a 'tool kit' to be brought out in emergencies, but rather as a set of interwoven attitudes and skills which, used consciously, can become an integral part of the ethos of a school. In a sense boundaries between these skills are both artificial and arbitrary, though there are times when one or another may form an appropriate focus for attention.

Affirmation

Affirmation is the open acknowledgement and appreciation of the strengths and potentials within us all. For this potential to develop an environment where our endeavours are encouraged and our doubts reassured is necessary. The purpose of affirmation is to encourage and appreciate qualities that are true about a person so that they can continue to grow in a positive way; it is not to give false praise in order to manipulate and achieve a certain kind of behaviour. Affirmation is a way of showing our faith in people and for this to be effective it needs to pervade the atmosphere of the classroom rather than be used as an occasional activity.

No one grows out of needing or wanting affirmation but they do grow out of expecting to receive it! Children and adults who have their needs for affirmation met are more relaxed and confident and thus are able to learn better. It may sound as if affirming ourselves and others is something that gets done automatically and yet, if we listen carefully, we discover just how often conversation is sprinkled with 'put downs', cutting ourselves and our children down to size. In western culture it seems to be unfashionable to seek out the positive in the behaviour of ourselves and others. As Lois Dorn (1983) has said, 'we find it easier to exchange insulting familiarities than to comfortably express straightforward approval or admiration'.

There seems to be a belief and inbuilt fear that affirmation can lead to arrogance, so there is a tendency to pick up on the negative aspects of a person's personality, keeping their failings and inadequacies to the fore. Maybe this is because a self-confident and assertive person, with a clear, strong sense of self, is less amenable to obeying blindly externally imposed rules and sanctions than one who is unsure of her or his own worth. Negative unconstructive criticism is an essential feature of the structural violence that is built into our education and social system – in our competitive grading system in which only a limited percentage can 'succeed'; within the consumer society which sets standards of perfection against which all but a few can only fail – and is a fact in many classrooms. How often can people be heard saying, 'But I've no ear for music', 'But I can't draw', or 'I've no head for figures'?

To learn a new skill is challenging, but given sufficient lack of positive encouragement it is easier to give up than to struggle to overcome the difficulties. Affirmed individuals, the research shows, are more likely to accept challenges, learn to take control of their own lives, seek active solutions to their problems, and have the confidence to take responsibility for making changes in their own lives.

Affirmation goes beyond praise and criticism. It asserts what is and what might be, helping the individual build on strengths that can be nurtured rather than constantly focusing on weaknesses. However, neither does it shy away from pointing out where changes might be made. To quote an example from Dorn (1983)

> Joe, you have a quick and insightful wit. Sometimes though, people dismiss the important points you make because they think you are just kidding. I think your views deserve to be taken more seriously at times.

The development of healthy self-esteem should become part of the overt and hidden curriculum of the class or school. Individuals with a sense of self-worth are more likely to want to take responsibility for themselves and their learning and will be better placed to react emphatically to the situation of others, whether locally or globally. People who feel positive about themselves are more likely to care about injustice and to have the energy to devote to doing something about it.

Communication

Good communication is one of the key skills to be acquired in education and by education for peace in particular, providing as it does a cornerstone on which, amongst other things, successful conflict resolution can be built. Much of education concerns itself with teaching the arts of written and spoken communication, but in peace education the emphasis is on *listening*, and communication is an active two-way process.

Much teaching is a one-way process – the teacher giving and the pupil receiving – and very little true dialogue occurs. In most interactions there is often a surprising amount of talking but very little listening going on. In conversation or discussion the listener often spends much of the time when the other person is speaking thinking about her reply or formulating the next phase of her argument. Often in conversation the speaker's words get lost as the other person adds her comment before he has finished and in the end the loudest voice triumphs. An ability to listen well and the willingness to do so is an important step in building up understanding and empathy. As Alice Miller (1987) says:

If we are not open to what the other person is telling us, genuine rapport is hardly possible. We need to hear what the child has to say in order to give our understanding, support and love. The child, on the other hand, needs free space if he or she is to find adequate self expression . . . learning is a result of listening, which in turn leads to even better listening and attentiveness to the other person.

It is possible to begin to teach effective listening skills by turning listening into an active process which can be learned and practised. At a most basic level individuals can be given the opportunity of simply being listened to for four or five minutes. During this time the listener's job is to do just that, to listen and pay full attention to what the other person is saying, without asking questions, passing comment, or giving advice. Talking without any prospect of interruption can be daunting but it is also a means of discovering that silence can be acceptable too and, given that extra space which no one feels obliged to fill, often means that the communication takes on greater depth.

Another form of active listening is where the listener reflects back the essence of what the speaker has said, both the gist of the content and the feeling that lies beneath it. For example, if someone has been talking about how unfair it is that he has had to do something, the reflective comment may include, 'You're feeling upset that you've had to . . .' This both shows that the listener has heard what has been said and that she has heard the feeling underlying the statement. It also gives the speaker a chance to clarify what he means, either by acknowledging that the comment correctly reflected what he meant, or by taking the chance to refine his thinking further.

Being listened to attentively helps us take ourselves and what we both say and feel seriously. This then is a way of building self-respect and learning to be aware of the value of what each person has to contribute to life. A useful corallary to practising listening skills is to analyse what helps and what hinders when one is listening or being listened to. The answers to these questions can give useful clues about how to create an environment in which good communication becomes more possible.

Co-operation

Co-operation, in some of its manifestations, such as working together towards a common goal, sharing insights and discoveries, runs counter to much current educational ideology and the hierarchical and competitive structuring of our society. One of the effects of the competitive elements in education is the tendency to guard knowledge, insights, and ideas in case they are appropriated by someone else. This attitude is often fostered by the examination system and with access to higher education dictated by how high up the ladder an individual can climb. The ethic of competition has come to dominate our society and the espousing of co-operation as a valid educational objective is often seen as of doubtful value within many of our pedagogical structures, especially once children have left primary school.

Thus competition is supposed to provide much of the motivation for learning but it is only when the learning is seen as irrelevant by its recipients that such a 'carrot' becomes necessary. How much, too is the fostering of working together in the primary classroom a function of a genuine desire to see true co-operation and how much a device for ensuring satisfactory socialization into compliant behaviour?

One thing is certain. In any competitive situation, from a running race to the arms race, there can be only one winner. The many losers are left to cope with their feelings of failure, disappointment, and frustration which may be expressed by withdrawal or aggressive behaviour. The discovery that more brains are better than one can be an exciting prospect leading to greater depth of thought and the generation of more ideas than is possible when working alone, as any one who has been involved in real team work can testify.

It is difficult to examine the concepts of co-operation and competition in isolation without some reference to the question of power because much of the power in western society rests with those who rise to the top through 'winning' in competitive situations. There is a distinction between 'power-over' and 'power-with'. In the west our predominant world view since Newton has been of a universe consisting of discrete packages of matter – whether these be atoms, human beings, or nation states – which act upon one another much as billiard balls do. Each of these packages is in competition with the other for survival, for space, and resources and, to ensure an adequate supply of these, is also in competition with the others for power over those resources. Modern sub-atomic physics, however, is beginning to challenge the idea that the universe is composed of discrete particles. Instead it is discovering that matter consists of a series of interdependent forces which constantly act on and affect one another. The implication of this web-like interconnectedness is that no individual is in a position to act without that action having repercussions on the whole. Thus the interests of the whole are best served when all the elements are working together and to enable this to take place there must be a shift in emphasis from 'power-over' to 'power-with' or, I win/you win; I lose/we all lose. To quote from Joanna Macy (1983), 'so now we see power in a new light. It is not invulnerability but openness . . . It is important that we do so, because our survival depends on our moving beyond that primitive, competitive, win/lose notions of power.'

In advocating a shift of emphasis from competition towards more co-operation in schools questions are often asked about sport and the sort of co-operation which is embodied in 'team spirit'. My personal qualm is about the purposes for which such a spirit is generated, that is yet again, the defeat of another team or group of people. Competition *per se* is not always negative. For example, competing against oneself can be a spur to greater achievement and one route along the path of seeing oneself as a valuable, valued, and capable individual, not just somebody who is better than X and worse than Y. In schools it should be possible to structure work and play in such a way that all pupils are given positive experiences of working in groups co-operatively and of games where they can be 'winners all'.

Within society those who have gained power often feel a great need to retain it for their own interests. One method of holding on to power unchallenged is by keeping people isolated from one another and setting them in competition against one another. One way in which this is done is by setting up, for example through the media, the idea of the 'social norm' and promoting the idea that anyone who fails to meet that 'norm' is in some way inferior. Groups who are in some way different, perhaps by colour, sexual orientation, or disability, then become 'outsiders'. This notion of 'divide and rule' prevents people coming together, celebrating their differences and discovering the strength inherent in working together for a common cause. When groups do unite they can become powerful and unstoppable forces for change. Think, for example, of Gandhi and the non-violent civil disobedience movement in India, or Martin Luther King and the civil rights movement in the USA.

Conflict resolution

A final powerful strand in our understanding of peace as something creative and positive is gained by consideration of non-violent conflict resolution. Detailed exploration of this area of concern is more fully explored in Chapter 4.

VISIONS AND STRATEGIES

To be creative and positive any concept of peace has to be firmly rooted in a vision of what might be, as an integral part of our thoughts about peace must include hopes and fears about real or imagined futures. For each individual that vision will be unique, though many may have features in common. There is a need to encourage people to dream, to see the value in their visions and those of others, whether they are concerned with something personal, for the school, the local community, or the planet as a whole.

To have a vision is not merely to dream idly. Visioning what might be in a more just and peaceful world is a vital first step towards making that dream a reality. First it is necessary, however, to look critically at where we are now. Pupils should thus develop the ability to examine how we are now with an open mind, and be able to recognize and challenge bias and propaganda, for example, where it occurs. They should also be able to decide what elements of the present they would like to see incorporated into the future.

A group called Educators for Social Responsibility based in the USA have produced a very useful handbook called *Perspectives: A Teaching Guide to Concepts of Peace* (1983), in which they talk about the disillusionment that many young people feel about the world in which they live and the despair which accompanies it. They suggest we need to

> address these feelings of despair from a different perspective: giving young people new, dynamic concepts of peace which include empowerment to act to make a difference in the world; helping them examine the obstacles which often prevent us experiencing progress towards peace in our world; giving them familiarity with specific skills to use to overcome obstacles and resolve conflict; and offering them models of individuals and groups whose peace-making actions have made a difference in the world. All of these are antidotes to the despair students are feeling as they scrutinize the legacy left to them in the present.

Visions and strategies are all very well but without realistic action they remain in the province of daydreams. Imagining how one's school should look in the year 2020 is a mere academic exercise unless the strategies for making the appropriate changes are creatively developed and the action necessary for their implementation made possible. Looking at case studies of how others have acted for change, and a critical analysis of this, are all part of preparing students to work towards a more peaceful future.

However, this does raise the spectre of how we can attempt to build a positive concept of peace within an education system that is hierarchical and full of traps for the unwary, such as awarding a prize for the best essay on co-operation! It is important also to look at the *whole* school and ask how much its ethos and organization seek to promote justice and equality of opportunity. There may well be particular areas where strategies need to be developed and everyone affected by planned changes – administrators, teachers, parents, and pupils – needs to be involved in appropriate dialogue.

There are many examples to illustrate a positive approach to peace building which one can choose from. Possibilities range from the more obvious and easily accessible, such as Gandhi and Martin Luther King, through 300 years of Quaker pacifist witness to contemporary examples of non-violent protest as a critical form of social action today.

CLASSROOM ACTIVITIES

Affirmation tree

Purpose

For students to begin to affirm themselves and begin to feel positive about things they enjoy doing. By so doing they will increase their self-esteem and also get to know more about the others in their group.

Preparation

Either (a) a branch from a tree firmly planted in a tub or (b) a tree drawn and mounted as a wall display. Different shaped pieces of coloured cards are needed, with loops attached for hanging them from the tree; either these can be in bright colours and cut out like gift tags or they can be leaf shaped.

Procedure

Everyone in the class has an opportunity to talk about things s/he enjoys doing or is good at. This can either be a general conversation or something more formal with the children in a sharing circle, taking it in turns to speak. This can sometimes be helped by the presence of a 'magic stone' or shell, the holder of which is the only person allowed to speak at that time. Each person is then encouraged to choose a tag or leaf, write his or her name on it, and draw a picture or write about something s/he likes doing. Everyone then has a turn to tell the others about his or her picture before hanging it on the tree.

Variation

The activity may be varied to fit in with a particular class interest that is being studied, for example friendship or favourite things.

Invisible pictures

Purpose

To explore the differences between one- and two-way communication, to practise listening skills, and to introduce the importance of understanding body-language.

Preparation

Have available for each pair of students two diagrams of your choice, clearly labelled *A* and *B*. These can be geometric or simple line drawings.

Procedure

The class should be divided into pairs, each pair having sufficient space to be able to sit together relatively undisturbed. They should decide who is to be A and who B. A and B then sit back to back. The teacher then gives pencil and paper to A and diagram *B* to B. B has to tell her partner how to draw the diagram she has in front of her which of course A cannot see. No questions are allowed. When they have finished there should be an opportunity for A and B to compare A's diagram with the original and talk about the experience.

Now A and B sit face to face. This time B is given the paper and pencil and A has diagram *A*, with the instruction not to allow B to see it. A has to tell B how to draw the diagram but this time questions are allowed. Again when they have finished allow time to compare the outcomes and to talk about what happened during the activity. Finish with a whole group discussion about the experience, how it felt, what happened, which approach was easiest, and so on. This should provide an opportunity for discussing what we need in order to make listening easier and what tends to make it harder, also how much information we receive from non-verbal cues.

Variation

Instead of diagrams it is possible to do this with photographs.

Washing Line Visions

Purpose

To help students develop particular visions of the future on a common theme.

Preparation

A large roll or large sheets of paper, together with lots of coloured pens, pencils, crayons, or chalks.

Procedure

Students draw out on the paper either a line of washing, or a bed of flowers, or plates for a meal; on each of these will be drawn elements of their vision. Set the scene for students' visions of the future either with a guided fantasy or as the result of a group discussion. The students then have to draw aspects of their vision for the chosen theme on their washing, flowers, or plates. After they have done this give everyone an opportunity to say what s/he has drawn and why. This is perhaps best done in small groups rather than as a whole class. As a result of this it may be possible to link people up with similar areas of concern so they can together plan strategies for making their dream into reality. Creating a group vision in this way can have an immensely unifying effect on a group, giving a strong sense of common purpose, especially if it can be displayed in such a way that it serves as a reminder of future directions which the group wishes to work towards.

Variations

Another approach can be to begin with a line of dustbins in which group members dump all the things they would like to change about an institution or situation – this can provide a useful preliminary to creating the vision!

RECOMMENDED READING

Barnaby, F. (ed.) (1988) *The Gaia Peace Atlas*, London: Gaia Books. This comprehensive resource atlas is both authoritative and visually powerful. Using maps, tables, charts, and illustrations it analyses the roots of peace and conflict, both in the past and the present. It also includes proposals for demilitarization and appropriate peace-building procedures.

Borba, M. and Borba, C. (1982) *Self-Esteem: A Classroom Affair*, San Francisco: Harper & Row (two volumes).These two books are full of useful activities for developing affirmation and building self-esteem. They include copyright-free photocopiable pages and contain many good ideas for working on themes such as friendship.

Educators for Social Responsibility (1983) *Perspectives: A Teaching Guide to Concepts of Peace*, 23 Garden Street, Cambridge, Mass: Educators for Social Responsibility.This remains one of the best resource books for teachers who specifically want to focus on the issue of peace. It looks at concepts of peace, obstacles to peace, peacemaking and conflict resolution peacemakers and imagining the future. It has detailed lesson plans that deal appropriately with all the above concerns at levels from infant to secondary.

McAllister, P. (ed.) (1982) *Reweaving the Web of Life: Feminism and Nonviolence*, Philadelphia, PA: New Society Publishers. This classic work explores in considerable detail the practice and principles of non-violence both as a strategy for social change and as a philosophy of life. It does so via the various critical insights of feminism and thus provides a rich resource on these themes.

Quaker Peace and Service (1986) *Speaking Our Peace: Exploring Nonviolence and Conflict Resolution*, London: Quaker Peace and Service. This manual is based on the experience of the Quaker Peace Action Caravan and its five years on the road. It is a distillation of QPAC's work running workshops on non-violence and conflict resolution with different groups round the country. Its strength is in the graphic detail it gives, both in terms of agendas and individual exercises where both clear instructions and sample scenarios are given.

Wren, B. (1986) *Education for Justice*, London: SCM Press. This important work raises questions both about how we teach and what we teach if we have a concern for justice in the world today. Sets out clearly basic ideas about justice, power, and politics and how this should influence our views of education and learning.

REFERENCES

Brock-Utne, B. (1986) *Education for Peace: A Feminist Perspective*, London: Pergamon.

Daly, M. (1979) *Gyn/Ecology*, London: Women's Press.

Davies, R. (1984) *Children and the Threat of Nuclear War*, St. Martin's College, Lancaster: Centre for Peace Studies.

Dorn, L. (1983) *Peace in the Family*, New York: Pantheon.

Educators for Social Responsibility (1983) *Perspectives: A Teaching Guide to Concepts of Peace*, Cambridge, Mass: Educators for Social Responsibility.

Macy, J. (1983) *Despair and Personal Power in the Nuclear Age*, Philadelphia, PA: New Society Publishers.

Miller, A. (1987) *For Your Own Good*, London: Virago.

Montagu, A. (1976) *The Nature of Human Aggression*, New York: Oxford University Press.

Quaker Women's Group (1986) *Bringing the Invisible into the Light*, Swarthmore Lecture, Quaker Home Service, London.

Stanford, B. (1976) *Peacemaking*, New York: Bantam, in Educators for Social Responsibility (1983) *Perspectives: A Teaching Guide to Concepts of Peace*, Cambridge, Mass: Educators for Social Responsibility.

UNESCO (1974) *Recommendation Concerning Education for International Understanding, Co-operation and Peace*, UNESCO: Paris.

6

War

Richard Yarwood and Tony Weaver

Students should explore some of the key issues and ethical dilemmas to do with conventional war. They should look at the effects of militarism on both individuals and groups and on scales ranging from the local to the global

(Table 2, page 14)

THE PHENOMENON OF WAR

War is defined in the *Oxford English Dictionary* as 'a quarrel usually between nations conducted by force'. Before the twentieth century it was often easier to be clear exactly what 'war' meant – it followed generally accepted rules and the fighting armies were clearly separate from civilians – today there is far less clarity. During the present century, the extent of the area affected by war has increased and the distinction between civilian and military targets has become very blurred. Indeed a whole new vocabulary of terms has been coined to cover new kinds of warfare, for example amongst today's terms are total war, war by proxy, cold war, armed conflict, nuclear war, liberation struggles, and terrorism. The weapons themselves have become more sophisticated, more lethal, and less discriminate and their use reflects a shifting morality. Future wars could involve the use of chemical, biological, or nuclear weapons.

Although there have been hundreds of wars throughout history it is possible to identify four broad reasons which, on their own or in combination, are used as the basis for justifying a declaration of war. These reasons are

1 Self-government: people fighting for the right to rule themselves.

2 Poverty: people fighting for a fairer sharing of wealth and food and a fairer way of running society.

3 Territory and resources: people fighting for more land and resources.

4 Ideology: people fighting for a set of political ideas and/or religious beliefs.

In themselves these four 'reasons' are insufficient to explain why societies resort so readily to war to solve their quarrels. Such a solution reflects attitudes that have been instilled in us for thousands of years. The underlying attitude is that war is a morally acceptable, even inevitable, course of action to be taken when and where necessary to attack by violent means what is perceived to be wrong. Two factors are crucial in the reinforcement of these attitudes: the development of society and particularly the nation state, and the nature/nurture debate on the causes of human behaviour.

It is generally agreed that a turning-point in the evolution of society came between 10,000 and 12,000 years ago with the development of an economy that allowed previously nomadic people to live in villages supported by husbanded food. Agricultural communities are at risk not only from a poor harvest but also from neighbouring marauders who may covet their crops and possessions. The motive which promoted such marauding was the common human desire to secure ease and luxury both in this world and the next, often at the expense of one's neighbours. The growth of city life intensified the division of labour and made possible the privileges of the priesthood and the warrior class, which later became a hierarchy of kings and nobles. Though one of the functions of the ruling class may originally have been held to promote fertility, their time and resources became increasingly devoted to the development of warfare to enforce the dominant position of conquerers over conquered, and also for group defence. Increasingly it became only states, backed by the military-industrial interest groups, that had the resources to wage war. Thus 'war is the health of the state' has been inculcated by militaristic values and validated by the passage of time.

To go to war for what you believe to be right has gradually assumed the status of a moral injunction. Indeed Moltke, the Prussian field marshal, later to be repeated by Fascist followers of Mussolini, stated that 'perpetual peace is a dream . . . war is one of the elements of order in the world established by God. The noblest virtues of men are developed therein. Without war the world would degenerate . . .' (Angell 1911) Thus some take the view that the structures and attitudes of present society make war inevitable and desirable.

That war is morally wrong and that the structure of society is in part to blame and therefore needs fundamental change in order to prevent future wars has been a clear view held by a minority throughout history. Such a philosophy is known as pacifism.

Human nature, some suggest, contains an instinctive urge to fight, to dominate others, and to defend territory. This view has had great influence on western society and can be traced right back to the idea from the Bible of 'original sin'. Proponents of this view use evidence from the animal kingdom to show that human society is 'red in tooth and claw' like all other species. War, they conclude, is just part of human nature. Others would maintain that we are not naturally aggressive, and point to the dangers of comparing humans with other species – for a start we have language and culture and far greater abilities to be self-determining – but rather it is things in our upbringing and our society that may make us violent. According to Bronowski (1973), 'War, organized war, is not a human instinct. It is a highly planned and co-operative form of theft'. There is disagreement on the exact relationship between nurture and nature in accounting for human behaviour. But if the nature view is dominant, the prospects for a future without war are not easy to foresee. On the other hand, the nurture view does allow the potential for creating less violent futures.

In the past two centuries three broad types of warfare, by no means mutually exclusive, have emerged from the ferocity of wars of earlier periods. There are (1) pre-1914 limited war; (2) 1914–45 citizen warfare; and (3) post-1945 the nuclear age.

Limited war, such as the Seven Years War (1756–63) in which Britain, enjoying naval superiority, succeeded in its aim to take over French colonies in North America, the West Indies, and India for the benefit of private companies and monopolies, the American Civil War, and the Austro-Prussian War of 1866–7 had several similar characteristics. These were (1) relatively short set-piece battles; (2) manpower and material losses which had little impact upon the societies of the belligerents; (3) war planning was confined to the state bureaucracies and of little concern to the masses of population; (4) concomitant with the last point, through regimental structures, flags, parades, national anthems, and martial music the roots of modern militarism were being laid down.

The First World War saw the introduction of new weapons (tanks, aeroplanes, and gas) which began a qualitative change in the nature of warfare, and furthermore the huge casualties in the process of attrition in the trenches were associated with an extension of the franchise in parliamentary government. During the Second World War the bombing of cities such as Dresden and Coventry entailed the indiscriminate slaughter of civilians in an unprecedentedly appalling way. In both wars the notion of the people at-one-with-its-nation was strengthened in all combatant nations.

Whatever may be thought about the so-called nuclear deterrent on moral or other grounds, in the period since the invention of this new type of weapon, the chief protagonists – the USA and the USSR – have not launched into full-scale war upon each other. In general it may be said that armed conflict which used to be a matter between nations has, since 1945, increasingly become a matter between different social, religious, ethical, or ideological groupings *within* nations. But at the same time, in many of these internal struggles there are discernible overtones of a broader ideological conflict – the capitalist versus communist confrontation. The two most serious and long-lasting wars with international involvement (Korea and Vietnam) ostensibly arose from the desire of a divided nation to be reunited. They were wars of *reunification*. International intervention was due to the fact that one section of the divided country was communist and under Soviet influence, the other capitalist and under American or generally western influence.

The twentieth century has been the most war-torn in history. Since the turn of the century there have been over 120 million deaths resulting from war, there have been more than 120 wars since 1945, and on average in the 1980s there are twelve wars taking place every year. The most distinguishing feature since 1945 is that wars have predominantly happened in the Third World, funded and armed by the USA, the USSR, and other countries of the west including Britain. World military expenditure has gone ever upwards; in 1986 it was over £530 billion! Yet at the same time on this planet, one adult in three cannot read and write, 1 billion people are inadequately housed, and one person in five lives in gnawing poverty. Yet at the cost of less than half an hour's global military expenditure the United Nations destroyed a plague of locusts in Africa, saving enough grain to feed 1.2 million people for a year.

The USA and USSR have used wars of liberation in the Third World to stage east–west wars by proxy; they have also waged an economic, political, and propaganda war on each other. Wars of liberation in the Third World have occurred where in the past imperialist powers took it upon themselves to annex or divide territories, regardless of the cultural compatibility of the inhabitants. When these artificial creations of colonialism came to independence it was not surprising that the hidden tensions should, in some cases, turn into overt warfare.

Depending on the politics of the situation, the resources available, and the strategies adopted, wars since 1945 have been fought mainly as a revival of the limited war, or as protracted guerrilla campaigns. In western countries minority groups fighting governments have resorted to terrorism. All are linked by a common thread: they are prepared to use force and violence to right what they perceive to be a wrong. Thus the latter part of the twentieth century has seen a reinforcement of militarism (that is the notion that war is a normal and justifiable activity), and war and violence have become associated with glamour and excitement experienced (by most of us) only vicariously through television, film, and comic books.

SOME ISSUES ARISING

As a result of the preceding simplified analysis of the phenomenon of war, several key issues arise which require some comment.

Militarism

Militarism may be defined as a set of attitudes and social practices which regard war and the preparation for it as normal and desirable social activities. Examples of militarism include encouraging children to play with war toys, or taking a school outing to a military tattoo. Militarism is promoted by presenting an unbalanced, even false picture of war; by exaggerating the heroism, nobility, and glamour associated with war, and suppressing the darker realities, society is presented with a distorted picture. Add to this an insistence that we are about to be invaded at any moment and very soon war and the preparation for it becomes a 'desirable activity'. Enormous resources can thus be invested in defence with little opposition, and even the possibility of nuclear devastation can be contemplated in the name of 'defending our freedom'. To a visitor from outer space this situation might appear ridiculous, but for a society that has for hundreds of years been conditioned by militarism, this is the status quo. Any minority group that challenges present defence attitudes and therefore policies is strongly opposed by the vested interests of government and industry.

Enemy thinking

Militarism is able to maintain a firm grip on our thinking because there still exists in society the mechanism of the scapegoat which provides an outlet for moralized aggression, which is not only socially approved but also demanded. As far as behaviour towards an enemy is concerned, what in other circumstances might be described as the action of a criminal becomes morally acceptable. The enemy outside induces people to be co-operative, and indeed free from aggressive wishes towards members of their own group. Tribes, clans, and nations equip themselves with myths and symbols as well as modes and codes of behaviour in order to cement this sense of belonging. It is this process of identification which helps explain the strength of modern nationalism. Integration, however, is a two-way process, both a recognition of what a group has in common and also how it is distinguished from other groups. Differences between groups are therefore exaggerated allowing racial prejudice, xenophobia, stereotyping, and scapegoating. There is a tendency to 'dehumanize' outgroups and the enemy can quickly become less than human and an object upon which people can project their feelings of hatred, shame, and dissatisfaction. This disposition arises, it is argued, in infancy when young children are in painful conflict between love and hatred towards the same person. A common solution is unconsciously to shift the hate on to other people thus leading to interpersonal conflict, and then to extend it to political, racial, religious adversaries or enemy nations – with those people one may have little personal contact. The vicious circle within this mechanism contains a real or invented threat which keeps the whole cycle going. Both sides feel that they must never give in, hence the willingness to sacrifice everything in war, to contemplate genocide or world destruction.

The arms race and the arms trade

In order that nations should be constantly prepared for any possible threat – real or perceived – to their boundaries or interests, vast sums of money are invested in modernizing, renewing, developing, testing, and expanding their so-called 'defences'. Encouraged by the enormously powerful military-industrial complex three governments in five now spend more to guard their citizens against military attack than against all the enemies of good health. It is now widely recognized that the weapons and strategies elaborated by governments for 'defence' are largely irrelevant to the underlying threats and dangers of today. The escalating spiral of armaments expenditure, termed the 'arms race', is fuelled by the logic of 'security through strength'. In other words, the best way to prevent war is to arm extensively in order to deter your enemy. Whether this approach works is open to debate. Making armaments, however, is a very profitable business and all over the world the industry receives large sums of public money to make weapons for defence. At the same time, especially as national economies are depressed, governments encourage the arms manufacturers to sell as many weapons abroad as possible. This encourages the smaller local arms races in the Third World and explains why Third World arms spending has tripled since the early 1960s. Often purchasing governments are then unable to spend what is needed on health, education and other internal reforms which result in popular dissent which then requires more armaments to control them. This has been called the poverty-repression-militarization cycle.

The costs of war

Expenditure on armaments, deaths, and casualties – military and civilian – are the obvious costs of war. But there are many other costs just as significant yet seldom mentioned. Amongst these are the millions of people forced to pack up what belongings they can carry and flee from the war: today there are an estimated 12 million war refugees in the world.

At the end of a war a country has to recover and rebuild its towns and cities, to replant and repair its desolated countryside and to reinvest in new industries. There is often social decay and economic stagnation (particularly for the side that is defeated). Expectations and morale may be high at the end of the fighting, but quickly fall as the costs and the losses sink in. Returning soldiers are often promised a 'land fit for heroes to live in', but

Figure 7 The poverty–repression–militarization cycle

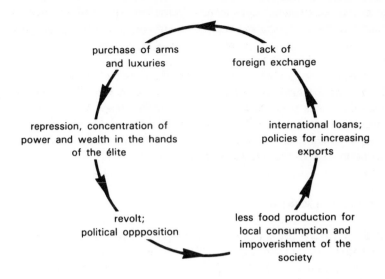

seldom is this the case. In evaluating these costs war should not be presented as an event that happens between the firing of the first and last bullets. The investment in armaments and the 'conditioning of war' all start many years before the actual fighting, and the legacy of battle lingers on for years for those who are bereaved or incapacitated for the remainder of their lives.

The Just War theory

As weapons became increasingly powerful and war became more costly and destructive Christian scholars such as Aquinas undertook the task of producing a set of principles against which any call for war could be judged. Only by fulfilling all the principles could a war be considered just. Many people still adhere to these, or similar, principles today. Thus to be just a war must:

1 have been undertaken by a lawful authority, e.g. the leaders of the state;

2 have been undertaken for a just cause, e.g. the vindication of an undoubted right that had clearly been infringed;

3 be undertaken as a last resort, all other peaceful means of settlement having failed;

4 be waged with a reasonable hope of victory for justice;

5 be waged with a right intention;

6 use methods that are legitimate, i.e. in accordance with Christian moral principles and international agreements. These are specified as being (a) discriminate (between combatants and non-combatants) and (b) proportionate (the gains from any war are proportional to likely losses).

The first five principles allow us to evaluate the justice of going to war and the sixth principle allows us to evaluate the justice in war. Accordingly on these principles it is possible for a just war to be fought unjustly, and an unjust war to be fought in a 'Christian' spirit. It is significant to note that many people would query whether such principles have any relevance at all in the context of possible nuclear war.

Pacifism and non-violence

As long as war has existed there have been people who have opposed it on moral, religious, or rational grounds. They have been known either by the name of their religion or sect – Buddhists and Quakers for example – or simply as pacifists. If the government of their country declares war on another and compels the population to take part, or even in peacetime conscripts a fighting force, pacifists will 'conscientiously object' to this by refusing to fight, even though this may result in imprisonment, or exile from that country, or simply the scorn and hatred of other citizens.

Pacifists see as illogical and inconsistent the argument that, though killing is wrong, we need to maintain armed forces to fight for us if necessary. A temporary peace maintained by the threat of violence and the willingness to kill is unacceptable to pacifists as to them 'means and ends' are inseparable.

In rejecting violent methods, non-violent alternatives have been studied and practised as means for social change. In this century the non-violent campaigns of Martin Luther King and Mahatma Gandhi have demonstrated the success of the pacifist approach as well as the need for education and training in methods of conflict resolution which do not resort to violence. With the advent of nuclear weapons the 'nuclear pacifist' has emerged who sees that the potential for total destruction make it necessary to oppose any war which could escalate into a nuclear exchange.

THE EDUCATIONAL CONTEXT

There are several important reasons why students need to learn about war.

1 Research shows that students want and need to discuss some of the issues surrounding war because they contain factors which may directly affect

their futures.

2 The issues raised are controversial and complicated and require a structured, balanced, and informed setting such as school in which to have discussions.

3 War has affected and still does affect many countries significantly. An understanding of how, why, and when this happens is an important part of political literacy, which is an essential skill in any democratic society.

4 Studying war requires an examination of our own prejudices, our own feelings of right and wrong, and encourages the development of our own personal morality.

5 War represents an extreme example of the dangers of stereotyping and scapegoating. This can be examined and the lessons learnt also applied at the personal level.

6 Whatever war has represented in the past, the evolution of weapons of mass destruction requires that underlying attitudes must be challenged and changed if future wars are to be avoided.

For many young people in Britain (excluding of course Northern Ireland) their experience of war is not first hand. War comes to them through the media (television, films, and comics) mostly in the form of 'entertainment', rather than as news or for their education. As a subject for entertainment, war is most often presented in an escapist way highlighting the exciting, manly, and heroic aspects and playing down the darker reality of war. The action for such films is often relived and played out around the neighbourhood with increasingly lifelike toys by both boys and girls. The fact that they are pretending to kill does not enter into the game. The underlying attitude is that killing is *not* wrong, provided you kill the 'baddy'. This attitude is reinforced throughout life by militaristic conditioning with few opportunities allowed to discuss the moral questions that using violence and killing obviously raise.

In addition to the images of war provided by the entertainment industry young people overhear many snippets of adult news about ongoing wars or violence. Written and aimed at adults, the information contained in the news is often confusing and upsetting for children. This confusion is added to by the apparent double-standards of adults who on the one hand tell children not to fight, yet at the same time seem to approve of military action. This may explain why research shows that young people are deeply disturbed by the apparent inevitability of war (particularly a nuclear war) and this sense of hopelessness manifests itself in the neglecting of communal and social responsibility and contributions and a concentration on personal goals and life-plans. It appears not to be the 'enemy' that young people blame, but the adult generation whose attitudes and actions have contributed to this spiral of violence. Is it any wonder that children are distrustful of a world that says it wants peace but prepares for war?

Early socialization into militarism reinforced by a competitive education system and upbringing plays on children's insecurities and encourages the ingroup/outgroup mentality which feeds a potential reservoir of prejudice that can easily be tapped into later in life. Consider the almost euphoric nationalism that broke out overnight during the Falklands War. . . . By introducing war into education, by looking at the 'realities' of battle, by presenting war as a massive failure on mankind's part to solve a quarrel and by setting children to consider the moral issues surrounding war, we encourage visions of a different future: a future without war.

Teaching about war requires a sensitivity of approach. Understanding key issues and ethical dilemmas requires at least three stages: the accumulation and clarification of factual information; the examination and consideration of different views; and the development and expression of a personal opinion. In the classroom it may not be so easy to distinguish clearly between these three stages. The teacher's role must range from being an impartial source of background information, to facilitating the student's thoughts on questions of morality. This has to be carried out in a way that empowers the student to feel that her view and contribution is important and will be listened to. It is too easy for war to be seen as a massive problem that bears no relevance to the average student's life.

If teaching about war is to cover the range of key issues identified in this chapter there are opportunities in many subjects, not just humanities and history courses; for example study the war poets in English, discuss whether Christ was a pacifist in RE, look at the social responsibility of scientists in physics, use arms race statistics in mathematics, identify trouble-spots in geography, or consider the options for an economy that wants no part in the arms trade in economics. With a little lateral thinking the possibilities for studying war, even in the existing curriculum, are plentiful.

CLASSROOM ACTIVITIES

Fighting in School

Purpose

To encourage pupil discussion about their expectations and fears in relation to fighting. To show that alternatives to fighting might offer more creative and lasting solutions.

Preparation

The teacher needs to reproduce the following statements on fighting. There should be one set for each group of four to six children. Each set of nine statements should be cut into individual strips.

1 Good, it will be very exciting.
2 I'm worried that my friend will be hurt.
3 I'm scared that if I fight I might be hurt.
4 If I fight I might hurt other people.
5 I'll see what my other friends are doing.
6 It's right that I should fight for my friends.
7 It's none of my business.
8 Fighting is a waste of time.
9 I ought to try to stop the fight.

Procedure

Explain to the children that there has been a rumour going around the school of a fight after school involving their best friend. On hearing this, what would they think? Split the class into groups of four to six and give each group a set of the statements. Ask the groups to discuss the statements and to diamond rank them, putting the most strongly agreed with at the top and the most strongly disagreed with at the bottom. Group members will have to decide how best to agree an order between themselves as a result of discussion and negotiation. As each group finishes, ask them to circulate in silence and see how the other groups are doing.

Discussion

Comparisons can be made *between* the different groups results and *within* a group's membership. Discuss similarities and differences. Who agreed with statements which encouraged fighting, who discouraged fighting? Discuss how the fight might be prevented. What information would be needed to achieve this? In particular how might a 'best friend' play a useful role in preventing a fight? In what other ways might the conflict be solved? Are 'non-violent ways' of ending conflicts better than 'violent' ones?

Images of other nations

Purpose

This activity asks students to examine critically their images of other nations and to explore where such images may come from.

Preparation

Copies of the following sheets 'The Russians are . . . ' 'The Americans are . . . ' 'The

Japanese are . . . ' 'The Argentines are . . . ' (layout as in example).

The Russians are . . .

Complete the sentences below with ten different short statements. Write the first ideas that come into your head.

The Russians ....
The Russians ....
The Russians ....
The Russians ....
The Russians ....
The Russians ....
The Russians ....
The Russians ....
The Russians ....
The Russians ....

Now look back at your statements. Write a few lines to summarize your general view of the Russians.

Students will also need poster-size sheets of paper (three per group of four to six students), marker, pens, and Blutak.

Procedure

Divide the class into four and distribute copies of the sheet so that a quarter have American sheets, a quarter have Russian sheets, a quarter have Japanese sheets, and a quarter have Argentine sheets. Explain to the class that they have to complete the sentences with ten different statements. (These instructions are on the sheets but it is important to read them out.) It is also important that the pupils do the exercise quickly, with as little time for thought as possible. Once they have completed their ten statements, they may summarize their views in a few lines of writing. Divide each of the four larger groups into smaller groups of four to six. Each of these groups is provided with three large sheets of paper to be headed *Postive*, *Negative*, and *Neutral*.

The small groups then read out their statements to each other and discuss them. They have to decide whether each statement made is positive, negative, or neutral and then write it, abbreviated if necessary, on the appropriate sheet. This is to produce a group impression of that country. Mount the American statements on one wall and the Russian, Japanese, and Argentine statements on other walls, then have the class walk round and read the statements other groups have made.

Discussion

What sort of pictures of the four nations have emerged? Was there any agreement/disagreement amongst members of each group? Where do we get these 'pictures' or images of other nations from? List all the possible sources: newspapers, books, comics, television, films, and so on. Are the groups' images of other nations accurate? How might they be inaccurate? Can pupils give examples from the media

98

of inaccurate images? Why might the media present such images? Discuss the possible dangers of having inaccurate images of other nations.

How can we find out more about other nations? What do you think American, Russian, Japanese, and Argentine people would write about (1) each other; (2) Britain, if they did a similar exercise?

Examining the Just War theory

Purpose

To understand the principles of the Just War Theory and how they are applied. To be able to distinguish between the justice of *going to war* and the justice *in war*. To evaluate the usefulness of the theory.

Preparation

Students will need to have studied at least one of the case studies listed below. Copies of the principles of the Just War theory for each student and one copy of the chart 'Evaluating the Just War Theory' for each group of four to six students.

(NB All principles must be satisfied for a war to be considered just.)

Procedure

Divide the class into groups of four to six and give each a copy of the chart. Each group should either choose one of the case studies listed below for investigation or base their work on one case study which the whole class has explored.

1 First World War.
2 Second World War.
3 The Gulf War.
4 Dropping the atomic bomb on Hiroshima.
5 Mass bombing of cities in the Second World War.
6 Using chemical weapons.

Ask the groups to apply each of the principles to their case study. After discussing whether or not the principle in question is satisfied, they should tick, cross, or put a question mark in the appropriate column. They should make a note of difficulties or questions raised in the right-hand column. After all principles have been applied, the final question 'Is the war just?' can be answered. Ask each group to report back its discussions, difficulties, and conclusions.

Discussion

Select someone from each group to explain his or her results to the rest of the class. In particular, ask the representatives to mention any difficulties they had. Which key words in each of the principles were open to various interpretations? How did this affect their decisions? What was each group's final decision – was the case study

Figure 8 Evaluating the Just War theory

Principle	Principle satisfied ✓ X ?	Difficulties and questions		
Lawful authority				
Vindication of undoubted rights				
A last resort				
Good achieved outweighs evil				
Reasonable hope of victory				
Right intentions				
Legitimate methods: discrimination proportionate				
		YES	NO	DON'T KNOW
Is/was the war just?				

just? First written down in the sixteenth century, what values does the Just War theory have for us today? How might a future nuclear war fit into the theory? Wars are more often justified today on the grounds of being 'for the greater good'. What does this mean? Who decides on the greater good? Assess whether or not your example of war was *just* basing your discussion on the principle of the 'greater good'. What problems arise out of this discussion?

RECOMMENDED READING

Barnes, R. (1983) *World Studies*, Brighton: Tressell Publications. A series of four useful student books, suitable for the secondary age range, on each of the following themes: wars since 1945; ideology of the Cold War; modern warfare: strategies, weapons and effects; arms control and disarmament.

Galtung, J. (1984) *There Are Alternatives: Four Roads to Peace and Security*, Nottingham: Spokesman Books. The eminent Norwegian peace researcher here presents detailed scenarios, with commentaries, of alternative security policies which would involve non-provocative, non-offensive forms of defence with decoupling from the superpowers.

Howard, M. (1981) *War and the Liberal Conscience*, Oxford University Press. Liberal-minded people for centuries have tried to discover the causes of warfare and the means for its abolition. Howard, now professor at Oxford, traces in an illuminating manner the pattern of attitudes from Erasmus to the Americans after Vietnam.

Leeds, C. (1987) *Peace and War: A First Sourcebook*, Cheltenham: Stanley Thornes. This practical book is intended for the 14–16 age range and covers a wide variety of issues from the nature of conflict and war to North–South issues, human rights, and the arms race.

Montagu, A. (1976) *The Nature of Human Aggression*, New York: Oxford University Press. One of the most valuable contributions to the debate about the nature of human aggression. In particular argues that aggression is as much the result of nurture as of nature.

Peace Education Project (1987) *Peace, War and Justice: Active Learning Pack*, 6 Endsleigh Street, London: Peace Education Project. By starting with, and developing, the student's own perspectives of 'war' and then relating this to meanings of 'peace' and 'justice', this pack helps students to understand the complex relationships between these concepts. It introduces issues of propaganda, Just Wars, militarism, 'means and ends', and structural violence. The pack also examines the delicate balance between the 'need for justice' and the need to 'keep the peace'.

Sivard, R.L. *World Military and Social Expenditure 1986*, Washington DC: World Priorities. A comprehensive, readable, and authoritative survey of the facts and figures in this field. Revised fairly regularly. Excellent source of quotations, figures, and comparisons, especially between military and social spending.

REFERENCES

Angell, N. (1911) *The Great Illusion*, London: Heinemann.
Bronowski, J. (1973) *Ascent of Man*, London: BBC.

7

Nuclear issues

Dave Cooke

Students should learn about a wide range of nuclear issues and be aware of key viewpoints on defence and deterrence. They should understand the effects of nuclear war and appreciate the efforts of both individuals, groups and governments to bring about nuclear disarmament.

(Table 2, p. 14)

INTRODUCTION

For many people the primary focus of concern when thinking about nuclear issues is the arms race and the attendant possibility of nuclear war. The likelihood of this happening, however remote it might seem, is increased by the nuclear competition between the superpowers and the proliferation of nuclear technology. We are living at a time when we can no longer be certain of human continuity into the future for life itself on this planet could be destroyed.

Yet life is already intolerable for many inhabitants of this planet due to needless poverty. The enormous expense of the nuclear arms race directly contributes to this for its real cost is in terms of the drain on development and thus the growth of poverty, particularly in Third World countries. One hour's global military expenditure would pay for the immunization of the 3.5 million children who die annually from preventable infectious disease (Sivard 1986).

While many see nuclear weapons as a vital element in maintaining world peace today, it can equally be argued that their existence distorts international relations through contributing to a climate of mistrust. The dangers of proliferation too are very real and there is an increasing possibility of nuclear weapons being available for use in current conflicts such as those in South Africa and the Middle East. At stake is not just the possible loss of human life but the effects of releasing high levels of radiation into the environment polluting the air, water, and soil. The tragic accident at Chernobyl illustrated

this and provided reminders, if they were needed, of the dangers also attendant on nuclear power.

When the stakes are so high the debates and their outcomes in terms of
decisions about defence, deterrence, and disarmament are clearly of crucial
importance. A variety of different interests is involved: political parties,
pressure groups, governments, military and business interests, all attempt to
influence or determine policies. The issues are often politically sensitive and
controversial in that different perspectives are based on different value positions.

In education we need to consider what our responsibilities are with regard
to teaching nuclear issues. This includes thinking about the following questions:

1 Which issues should we teach about? There is an enormous amount of
information but few readily tried frameworks in which to fit this.

2 Why should we teach about nuclear issues in the first place?

3 Are there social and cultural obstacles that may get in the way of our
understanding?

4 What teaching approaches are most appropriate?

5 How may the process of peace education help us in these matters?

These are the kinds of questions that this chapter will consider.

So what may the term nuclear issues embrace? It is generally taken to
include many, if not all, of the following:

1 Pupils' knowledge, perceptions, and feelings about nuclear weapons and
the possibility of nuclear war. What questions are *they* concerned about and
where does their information come from?

2 Basic information about the nature of nuclear weapons and the likely
effect of a nuclear war.

3 The historical context, for example Hiroshima; the Cold War and the
arms race; superpower relations and their images of each other; the dangers
of proliferation and attempts at disarmament.

4 The debates: understanding and evaluating these with regard to the
strategy of deterrence, and to multilateral and unilateral nuclear disarmament.
Who makes the decisions?

5 Interests and perspectives: political parties; the influence of the military
and of industry; the development of peace movements; the superpowers.

6 The costs of the arms race: the link between arms spending and global
social and economic problems; psychological costs – 'nuclear numbing';

Figure 9 Nuclear issues: an outline map

environmental effects of weapons testing; power station accidents; the dumping of radioactive waste.

7 Other issues: the debate about the need for nuclear power; alternatives; power sources; the link with weapons production; civil rights and secrecy in a nuclear state; civil defence plans; the nuclear-free-zone movement; morality and the bomb.

8 Futures: what governments, groups and individuals are doing about these issues; working towards non-nuclear futures.

EDUCATIONAL RATIONALE

The comments made in Chapter 1 about the teaching of controversial issues are particularly pertinent to the nuclear debate. Thus citizens in a democratic society need to know enough to understand, and to be able to consider critically, the nuclear policies that their leaders put before them.

Nuclear issues tend to be politically sensitive as well as controversial. There is some concern that they may be taught in an unduly biased way. Teachers, though, have a clear task as professionals, which is to present students with a range of differing viewpoints. This is first because the presentation of only one perspective could be construed as indoctrination. Second a crucial part of preparing young people for full participation in a democracy is to make them aware of what the controversy is about and to equip them with the skills to evaluate the arguments and evidence.

It is likely that young people are generally ill-informed about nuclear issues for schools rarely have a comprehensive programme of nuclear education. If they are covered at all, it is likely to be in the form of a short module perhaps in a general studies or a social studies course. Media coverage tends to be biased towards the case for deterrence and is also often not easily comprehensible, for the concepts involved are complex. Many parents also find the issues too painful or difficult to discuss with their children (Tizard 1984). This absence of dialogue with adults both at home and at school may convey to young people a sense of fatalism and indifference.

There is evidence that many children and adolescents experience anxiety and fear in relation to nuclear issues and that these numbers are growing (Davies 1984). Increasing numbers expect a nuclear war in their lifetime and a recent study shows that significant numbers of children from the third year in junior school upwards are afraid of nuclear war, think that it might happen at any time, perceive it to be immensely destructive, and think that their own survival is in doubt (Davies 1987). A sense of randomness about world events and a feeling of having no control over them were feelings commonly expressed by young people. The same survey suggests that a substantial proportion of young people also want more information from adults and from schools on nuclear issues.

105

There is thus a case for intervening in an already active, but flawed, learning process to provide information, to respond to anxieties, and to clarify arguments.

OBSTACLES TO UNDERSTANDING

Why is it often so difficult to think, let alone teach clearly, about nuclear issues? Lifton (1982) describes the central dilemma thus:

> It is a fact of the greatest absurdity that we human beings threaten to exterminate ourselves with our own genocidal technology. One must never lose that sense of absurdity, the madness, the insanity of it. In fact, all work in nuclear areas has to combine a sense of that absurdity with a pragmatic everyday struggle to do something about it. This struggle begins with our minds and our mental ecology, and that includes the terrible questions of the bomb's ability to impair our capacity to confront it.

Nicholas Humphreys (1982) has also described this general numbing of the mind when he writes about the 'psychology of denial'. He identifies five defence mechanisms that people use in order to save themselves from the pain of directly confronting the possibility of their nuclear extinction. They are summarized in Table 3.

Betty Reardon (1983) has also identified further obstacles to our clear thinking in this area.

Militarism

Militarism sees a secure society as one which must be based on authoritarianism and military values, and helps to legitimize the use of force and of war. The arms race is thus seen as a sensible response to outside danger. Military power is linked to the notion of national security. Good citizenship is therefore about obeying authority, while to dissent is to be unpatriotic. The growth of militarism is a global phenomenon. Internationally it is recognized implicitly, international law notwithstanding, that all nations have a right to use armed force in the pursuit of their own interests whether these be economic, ideological, or the quest to dominate. The fact that action based on such beliefs tends to be viewed as a natural and inevitable part of human behaviour should be particularly worrying.

Table 3 The psychology of denial

Incomprehension

The scale of nuclear weapons is not really comprehensible; the facts are more than the human mind can grasp: the effects, the consequences; that, for example, the nuclear stockpile today is 5,000 times the total destructive power used in the Second World War.

Denial

It is too painful to face up to the truth about the possibility of nuclear war; consciously or subconsciously we choose to be blind, it is better not to think about it; optimism is better and to be preferred; the British habit of not taking things too seriously.

Embarrassment

Nuclear issues and their possible consequences are not nice; it is best therefore to avoid plain speaking; and speaking the truth to people who do not want to hear it is often considered an aggressive act in itself.

Helplessness

And then there is the dreadful feeling that there is nothing at all that we can do anyway; feelings of total powerlessness; that our destinies are controlled by forces out of our control.

Strangelove syndrome

For some there may be a strange attachment to the technology of destruction in itself; mesmerized by the power of extinction; accepting the death of others but not the inevitability of their own also.

(after Humphrey 1982)

National identity and images of the enemy

The encouragement of national identity and national loyalty are positive in themselves, and indeed are consistent with peace education's emphasis on affirmation. However, the context for this is often a competitive one where a nation's differences are highlighted and other societies are seen as inferior. In particular images of 'enemy countries' are constructed, by governments and media, which are highly distorted and very negative.

Sexism and sex role stereotyping

Males in our society tend to be encouraged and expected to support the idea of military service and the notion that violent behaviour in certain circumstances is a legitimate way of achieving one's goals. Men are under pressure to achieve, compete, and be in control, to repress their emotional life, to deny the feminine in themselves, and to devalue women and many qualities one labels as feminine. Hence the tacit acceptance in our society of male violence towards women. The nuclear arms race itself should be seen as basically a male manifestation.

Competition

Competitive modes of behaviour are greatly encouraged in our society especially the use of force, aggressive behaviour, self-assertion, and identity. It is suggested that this forms the psychological base for the acceptance of the competitive nation-state where force or violence are acceptable against 'enemies'. The nuclear arms race itself can be seen as being fostered by competitive attitudes between the superpowers, between NATO countries, and between the military branches within, for example, the USA itself.

All these factors – militarism, nationalism, sexism, and competition – interrelate and form serious barriers to conceptualizing a disarmed world.

TEACHING APPROACHES

Six broad approaches to nuclear education have been identified by Hicks (1986) and they are outlined in Table 4.

To avoid dealing with the issues leaves pupils confused or misinformed, and possibly fearful or anxious. It's uncertain how they might contribute to any future solution if they are not helped to understand the issues while at school. Nuclear issues may be dealt with by inviting in groups who take an anti-nuclear stance and by putting forward only this point of view in one's teaching. An argument for doing this might be that pupils are probably already informed of the government perspective on defence and deterrence, and hence this approach is serving to give them a more balanced picture.

However, the concern of the vast majority of teachers is not to be unprofessional in the sense of attempting to indoctrinate their pupils through presenting only one perspective in their teaching. Even though pupils are more likely to have come across the government's viewpoint on the need for deterrence, it is still very probable that this is not very well understood.

It is clear that most pupils are in need of some straightforward and basic information. But any attempt to teach only the facts, while providing an

Table 4 Six approaches to nuclear education

Not dealt with

For various reasons nuclear issues might not be dealt with at all in secondary school. This could be by default, because no one has ever really thought about it; it could be because it appears too complex and difficult to handle or because of the teacher's own fears; it could be because the topic is considered too controversial and political. The end result is *ignorance*.

Government stance

Nuclear issues may be dealt with by using materials and speakers from the Ministry of Defence and the Foreign and Commonwealth Office who expound the government perspective on defence, nuclear deterrence, and NATO. If only this is taught the end result is *indoctrination*.

Unilateralist stance

Nuclear issues may be dealt with by inviting in speakers from CND, the Religious Society of Friends, or other groups who generally take an anti-nuclear stance. If these are the only viewpoints students meet the end result is *indoctrination*.

Teaching the facts

Students learn all the major facts about the arms race, about its history, different sorts of nuclear weapons, plans for civil defence, and other key issues. The end result of this is to impart *information*.

Understanding the arguments

Students are exposed to the major debates and viewpoints concerning defence and deterrence. They look at the arguments used by different political parties and pressure groups; the debate over the bombing of Hiroshima and Nagasaki; Soviet and American perspectives of each other. The end result of this is to develop skills of *evaluation*.

Holistic reassessment

This requires facing up to our own psychology of denial and the fears of our students. It involves working with hearts as well as minds in order to face up to the possibilities of extinction and yet to liberate energies for personal, social and political change. The end result of this should be *empowerment*.

important basis for understanding, has serious limitations. How meaningful are 'facts' without evaluation, what is a 'fact', and which facts should be included, are questions that need consideration. 'Facts' about the process of disarmament and the activities of the peace movement for instance are often omitted from textbooks. It would seem important that questions such as these are asked and considered as part of the process of learning the facts. A second drawback is that the facts alone may serve to generate further concern or deepen the sense of apathy and powerlessness. It could be argued that they need to be given in a context that leads to hopeful feelings about the future and a sense that something can be done.

Where students are exposed to the major debates and viewpoints concerning defence and deterrence, they have the opportunity to develop the skills of evaluation. They are encouraged to identify what it is that is controversial, and through experiencing a balanced programme, whereby a range of perspectives are examined, can come to their own conclusions. This approach, in combination with learning the facts, would go a long way towards providing students with 'nuclear literacy'. In particular the skills of critical thinking and awareness help to give them a sense of self-reliance and empowerment.

Holistic reassessment requires facing up to both our own fears and those of our pupils as well as developing the skills to evaluate information. Nuclear numbing is a key issue and we have seen above that significant numbers of pupils anticipate a nuclear war and are consequently afraid for the future. Holistic assessment involves helping pupils to acknowledge their fears. This can serve to liberate energies for personal, social, and political change and thus helps to empower them. This area has been admirably explored by Macy (1983). This is an ambitious approach which, while it may not be fully attainable as an objective in our teaching, can nevertheless provide us with an important sense of direction.

The way forward in teaching nuclear issues would ideally involve developing the approach labelled 'holistic assessment', I feel, as the one most consistent with the process of education for peace. Several factors then need to be taken into account.

DEVELOPMENTAL CONSIDERATIONS

Clearly we need to be very careful about both what, and when, we teach about nuclear issues. This will not be done directly with younger pupils but much work can be done with them on stereotypes, images of the enemy, developing empathy, and so on. Table 5 illustrates some of the possibilities and is based on ideas taken from *Dialogue: A Teaching Guide to Nuclear Issues* (Educators for Social Responsibility 1982). Obviously the suggestions made are flexible.

Table 5 Nuclear issues: some developmental considerations

5–8 years	9–12 years	13–15 years	16–18 years
	Help children get beyond simplifications – 'baddies' are also human beings, everyone loses in some way when fighting occurs; being stronger doesn't mean being better	Learning about stereotypes – questioning images of the enemy	Developing skills of critical thinking and analysis
	Learning about other cultures and valuing these	Developing tolerance for a range of opinions; learning respect for one another even if disagreeing with other viewpoints	Students to keep a journal and express themselves in privacy if they wish
	Media and violence – learning to think about this; questioning images	If difficult to clarify views through discussion, then individuals to do written work first	Where pupils have decided to join the armed forces, need for a sensitive and non-judgemental attitude; setting tone of tolerance and acceptance of all viewpoints and opinions
	Empathy with others – look at situations from a variety of viewpoints	Need a climate of trust and tolerance; pupils not exposed to ridicule; being listened to and supported	Building on students' idealism by providing information and skills to take a stand on how they want the world to be
Learning vocabulary for different emotions	Emphasize efforts adults are making to create a safer world	Many are afraid for the future – create opportunities for listening to pupils' ideas and worries	
If worries expressed about nuclear disaster, reassure that adults are working to end this; need a sense of confidence that adults are in control and can provide them with safety	Recognize their anxieties as real; share their concerns		
Not helpful or appropriate to educate young children about explicit details of nuclear war	A growing desire for facts – introduce to those interested		

Table 5 contd.

5–8 years	9–12 years	13–15 years	16–18 years
Causes of conflict between people and nations – begin to explore peaceful ways of resolving these	Looking at conflict at the personal level – finding non-violent solutions		Question the identification of masculinity with military strength and war
Developing a concept of 'peace' as something more than the absence of war	Emphasize co-operation		Clarifying vision of a 'peaceful' society, widening the concepts of 'strength' and 'power'
	Present ideas of thinking about a peaceful world, an attractive future	Visioning optimistic futures that they themselves can help to create	Where students have nihilistic attitudes, appropriate group action can be empowering e.g. information gathering, joining a pressure group, organizing more debate in school

Classroom climate

If our goals in educating pupils about nuclear issues are to address both their confusions and their fears, and to attempt to instil in them feelings of hope and a sense of empowerment, then it seems essential that we attempt to create a classroom climate where openness, tolerance, and trust are well developed. Some ideas for achieving this were described in Chapter 5.

Two points will be emphasized here. First, we need to create the space and security for pupils to have the possibility to express a range of opinions without fear of ridicule. If there is not sufficient tolerance and a willingness to consider viewpoints other than their own, genuine debate and the exchange of, and exploration of, a variety of ideas is unlikely to take place.

Second, as has been argued in Chapter 5, it is important for pupils to feel affirmed. Dorothy Rowe (1985) has pointed out that if people learn to experience themselves as bad in their very early years, they often feel weak, frightened, or in danger. Other people may then be seen as not to be trusted and the world full of potential enemies. Where people have low self-esteem and a poor self-concept they are less likely to be able to live at ease with others. They are more likely to fear and possibly come to hate others who are perceived of as different.

Although it is quite appropriate to identify individuals and groups as 'the stranger' in order to define ourselves more clearly ('the stranger' being that which is different), it does not follow that the stranger is dangerous or should be treated as an enemy. The distinction is a critical one for it is all too easy to categorize those who are culturally or politically different as 'the enemy'. The importance of an affirming classroom climate is crucial, then, to help pupils to accept and value those who are perceived of as different.

Creating a 'peaceful' classroom climate, where listening skills, co-operation, affirmation, and non-violent conflict resolution are well developed, is integral to the development of holistic reassessment.

Values and attitudes

Nuclear issues tend to be controversial and politically sensitive in that they are open to very different interpretations and explanations, based on different value assumptions. An exploration of competing values is therefore an essential ingredient of understanding. Young people develop attitudes, often negative, towards other peoples and countries from an early age and often prior to acquiring any factual knowledge about them. Opportunities need to be made for such attitudes to be explored and questioned, and for open-mindedness and respect for others to be encouraged.

Skills

Students need help to develop what Postman and Weingartner (1971) called their own built-in 'crap detectors' so that they can ask searching questions and detect misleading or evasive answers. They need to be able to listen and read critically and recognize bias in materials. With regard to nuclear issues this is particularly important due to the amount of propaganda and misinformation surrounding them.

A specific skill to develop in the context of expressing feelings is that of being able to listen actively to another person in a non-judgemental way. This helps provide a partner with the safety to explore their own ideas and feelings. Young people need the opportunity to hear what they themselves have to say, to hear themselves expressing their own concerns. This is a source of trust building and of improving the quality of relationships between pupils.

The question of balance

When teaching nuclear issues we are intervening in an ongoing learning process. We need to find out what pupils know, believe, and feel about the issues so that in the interest of balance a wider range of perspectives can be introduced. Pupils should not be left misinformed or with narrow simplistic points of view. Balanced learning implies that (over a series of lessons) pupils have access to a range of evidence, information, and viewpoints.

Pupils and teaching may have been exposed to one dominant viewpoint – for example that the nuclear power industry is essential to meet the growing demand for electricity in the future as well as to sustain present needs. The criteria for considering and evaluating this should be suitably broad, going beyond the purely economic to consider environmental, social, political, and moral questions as well.

Many people would argue that in our society there is not free and equal competition between alternative ideas and opinions on nuclear issues (Stradling 1987). For example, it is often difficult to evaluate the information we get, the bulk of which comes from apparently legitimate institutional sources, but which nevertheless represents particular economic interests.

An atmosphere of secrecy, purported to be in the interests of national security, surrounds some issues which, together with a largely unquestioning mass media, allows misinformation to be disseminated. This makes it all the more crucial that teachers encourage the development of the skills to detect bias, root out prejudice, and examine evidence critically.

Teaching approaches which encourage enquiry and participation, with the teacher playing the role of facilitator as much as the provider of knowledge, would seem to be most appropriate here. This would involve knowing the right questions to ask rather than providing the 'right' answers.

Emotions

Fears and anxiety, if repressed, act as blocks to learning. We need to encourage the belief that such feelings are natural and healthy; that it is quite normal to feel afraid of the nuclear threat for instance (Macy 1983).

The educational task is to help young people, first, to find constructive ways of experiencing and expressing these feelings, for the acknowledgement of them can open the way to change. When they have a chance to talk about their fears and express them, they are likely to experience a sense of relief, since this unblocking of emotion can help to release energy and clear the mind. This can help to bring a realization that their fears are part of a caring for other people and for what happens in the world. It can break down isolation and increase their sense of belonging to realize that others have similar feelings. Being given good attention and really listened to helps to overcome a sense of isolation and powerlessness.

CONCLUDING COMMENTS

Schools have a clear responsibility to meet their pupils' needs for education on nuclear issues. Consultations between headteachers, staff, and school governors could serve to assess when to introduce such issues into the curriculum, what content and teaching methods would be appropriate, what guidance and support might be needed, and what steps should be taken to maintain the confidence of parents and the community.

Parents' values and positions on nuclear issues will vary widely. It is important that these positions are supported by making all viewpoints legitimate. Many parents are concerned about how to handle their children's nuclear fears. A 'day of dialogue' might be organized so that parents can air their concerns, be kept fully informed of the school's intentions, and also become more involved if they wish (Educators for Social Responsibility 1982).

Teachers may need in-service support to help develop and implement a programme on nuclear education. Opportunities to clarify their own values and attitudes to this should be provided. In order to work with children on their nuclear fears it seems important that teachers first consider how to deal with their own 'nuclear numbing'. It has been suggested (Ornum and Ornum 1984) that effective adult–child communication in this area seems to occur only after teachers have had such an opportunity for themselves.

115

CLASSROOM ACTIVITIES

Frightening things

Purpose

To create opportunities for children to share their concerns and anxieties, and to express some of their fears about the world. If appropriate this can also provide a starting-point for exploring the fears some children may have about a nuclear disaster or the possibility of nuclear war.

Procedure

Many junior age children will have been frightened by specific episodes on films, videos, or television as well as by other incidents. Others will have heard about particular films and may be scared as a consequence. The teacher might begin therefore by describing one or two occasions, or one or two episodes, in which he or she has been frightened.

Brainstorm with the class: 'What sorts of things frighten me most' (on television or in real life)? Ask the children to give their ideas in as succinct a way as possible and also that they *don't* comment at this stage on each other's contributions.

An alternative way of getting children's responses would be to ask them to work in single-sex groups (with three or four children per group) and compile lists of what has scared them. Girls are likely, for example, to have been frightened by different things when compared with boys. This may also come out of mixed-sex groups. The teacher will need to decide which seems to be the most productive method.

The next task is for the children to draw or paint one of the events that has scared them. Ask them to sit in silence for a minute or so to focus their minds before beginning to do this. Make it clear they don't necessarily have to portray the event in an accurate way. They can be encouraged to take their time and possibly to write down first some phrases to help clarify their images.

Children complete the first part of the activity by sharing their work with a partner, in small groups or with the whole class. One way of doing this is to work in small groups of three or four. Children put their paintings or drawings face down, then take it in turn to show their work and to describe verbally what they saw and felt while they were doing it. The work could finally be displayed on the wall with everyone having an opportunity to look at the complete range of illustrations.

The next stage is to work with the class to help them categorize the various fears that have been expressed in their paintings and drawings. For example, one major classification would be between real and imaginary fears, another could be between fears which are immediate and visible and those which, while more distant, can still be worrying.

Later pupils can brainstorm, that is list as many answers as possible to questions such as: How many ways of responding to a particular fear can we think of? What are the ways in which adults can help us with this fear? How can we help each other over particular fears?

Note

There are several points to be stressed as this activity progresses.

116

1 Acknowledge that we *all* have different fears about things.

2 Some fears may be rational and others irrational.

3 Irrational fears should not be laughed at or condemned because they can be as worrying as any others.

4 Sharing fears in an open and non-judgemental way is the first step in beginning to deal with them.

5 Sharing, talking, and being well listened to are all empowering experiences.

6 Fears expressed and acknowledged allow pupils and teachers actually to support each other.

7 It is important to stress that adults, and young people too, are working to minimize the causes of many fears, whether that is to do with famine in Africa, cruelty to animals, problems over relationships, or the threat of nuclear war.

8 This activity properly sets the nuclear issue in the context of broader children's fears. To follow up the latter in more depth the appropriate references already given in the text should be consulted.

The world at war

Purpose

For older pupils to begin to consider some of the consequences of global military spending.

Preparation

Pupils require copies of Figure 10 *The world at war*. The questions suggested below require both careful consideration of the facts and statistics given in this figure as well as further individual or collaborative research. The exercise should, of course, be only one part of a more detailed scheme of work on the arms race.

Procedure

1 Using an atlas identify the twelve countries shown on the outline map of Africa.

2 What is meant by the term Third World? Mark on an outline map of the world the location of Third World countries.

3 Who do you think benefits most from such high levels of military spending?

4 Who are the superpowers and why are they called this?

5 Which superpower spent most on armaments in 1982?

6 Which superpower spent the greatest proportion of GNP on armaments in 1982?

7 What exactly is meant by the term GNP? What is *not* part of GNP (e.g, the labour of women at home caring for children or preparing food)?

8 Why do so many countries in the Middle East spend such a high proportion of their GNP on armaments? Which countries are they?

9 What correlation, if any, is there between military and health expenditure? (NB not all countries are listed in both columns.)

10 How many countries in the top twenty-one military spenders (% of GNP) are Third World countries?

The world at war

The world spent $663,120 million on arms in 1985. this affected all of us, however far we were from the nearest missile base. Military expenditure distorts economies and renders wars more likely — especially in the Third World.

DEADLY PRIORITIES

Every government makes choices about how to spend its money. Comparing the amount spent on arms with that spent on health care indicates current global priorities.

The US spends $215 million a year to operate one aircraft carrier.

This is more than the amount spent on health in 1982 by 12 West African countries combined.

The USSR spent $170,000 million on the military in 1982.

This was more than the entire Third World spent on education and health care in the same year.

The superpowers are by far the world's biggest spenders on arms. But when both military and health expenditure are calculated as a percentage of gross national product (GNP), they come much lower in the global league table.

Note that nine of the top ten military spenders are from the Middle East while nine of the top ten health spenders come from Western Europe.

Military expenditure 1982		% of GNP	Amount ($ millions)	Health expenditure 1982		% of GNP	Amount ($ millions)
1.	Iraq	29.7	8,042	1.	Sweden	9.0	10,387
2.	Oman	24.3	1,670	2.	Ireland	8.5	1,494
3.	Israel	23.9	5,061	3.	Iceland	6.7	190
4.	Iran	20.1	14,000	3.	Holland	6.7	10,413
5.	South Yemen	16.8	156	5.	Norway	6.5	3,825
6.	Saudi Arabia	16.6	26,045	5.	West Germany	6.5	49,210
7.	North Yemen	14.5	538	7.	France	6.4	40,146
8.	Syria	13.7	2,176	8.	Denmark	6.0	3,788
9.	Jordan	11.3	472	8.	Italy	6.0	22,926
10.	USSR	10.9	170,000	10.	Canada	5.8	16,187
11.	Qatar	10.1	600	11.	Switzerland	5.6	6,037
12.	North Korea	10.0	1,750	12.	Belgium	5.4	5,610
13.	Angola	9.9	1,030	13.	Finland	5.3	2,774
13.	Mauritania	9.9	80	13.	UK	5.3	28,446
15.	Mongolia	9.7	160	15.	Panama	5.2	217
16.	Ethiopia	8.8	411	16.	Aotearoa (NZ)	5.0	1,260
16.	Morocco	8.8	1,544	17.	Australia	4.9	8,216
18.	Malaysia	8.6	2,291	17.	East Germany	4.9	5,810
19.	China	8.3	25,000	19.	Austria	4.8	3,574
20.	Libya	8.1	2,202	19.	Costa Rica	4.8	129
21.	Nicaragua	7.8	200	19.	Czechoslovakia	4.8	4,050
28.	US	6.4	196,390	24.	Nicaragua	4.5	118
36.	UK	5.1	27,310	24.	US	4.5	136,830
77.	Australia	2.8	4,768	38.	USSR	3.1	48,000
89.	Canada	2.2	6,208	38.	Iran	3.1	2,184
92.	Aotearoa (NZ)	2.1	541	77.	Ethiopia	1.4	65

11 In whose interests is it to promote arms deals with Third World countries?

Note

Good back-up materials on many of the issues raised here are available from: Campaign Against the Arms Trade, 11 Goodwin Street, Finsbury Park, London N4 3HQ.

Imagining non-nuclear futures

Purpose

To help pupils develop the ability to visualize different alternative futures, in this case what a world would be like in which nuclear weapons no longer existed.

Preparation

This activity needs to take place towards the end of a series of lessons on nuclear issues. Since, inevitably, some fears will have been expressed about the dangers of nuclear accidents, as at Chernobyl, or of the possibility of nuclear war it is important to help students to go beyond those fears.

The class should be seated in groups of six, each group being provided with a large sheet of paper and some marker pens. The group should choose someone to act as a scribe. Ask everyone to close their eyes as they are going to be asked to visualize a future world which has no nuclear weapons in it.

Choose a date, say twenty or thirty years ahead, and ask the class to imagine that they have gathered together to celebrate on this day the fact that there is no longer any danger of nuclear war, for all such weapons have now been abolished. With appropriate pauses for reflection ask questions such as: There is no more danger of nuclear war. How do you feel about that? What emotions do you experience? You, your family, and friends are no longer threatened. What does that feel like? How does a future without such a threat feel? What will you plan to do now?

Using these and other questions, guide the class to feel as much a part of this imagined future as they can. Begin to ask more specific questions: Where are you living? What do you hear, touch, smell? Who can you see around you and what are they doing? It is important to help students to put themselves inside the new time, feeling that it is here and now. After helping them to build as detailed a picture as possible students should open their eyes and begin to share their images, taking it in turns for each to speak. Then they should think of different newspapers which they know and begin to create headlines announcing the news that a world without nuclear weapons has at last been achieved. This helps to make their positive future more concrete and believable. When complete, each set of headlines is presented to the whole class.

Moving backwards from the chosen date towards the present, each group thinks about what needs to have happened for such a non-nuclear world to have been achieved. These events are recorded on a time-line. The class thus works backwards from their non-nuclear future towards the present in which we live. The class then

119

thinks of what is being done in the present which will contribute to the stages they have just identified.

Note

More detailed examples of how this activity works can be found in Macy (1983) and Warren Zieglers' manual *A Mindbook for Imaging/Inventing a World Without Weapons* (1983), available from the Futures-Invention Associates, 2260 Fairfax Street, Denver, Colorado 80207.

RECOMMENDED READING

Davies, R. (1984) *Children and the Threat of Nuclear War*, St Martin's College, Lancaster: Centre for Peace Studies. A useful review of the research from several countries about children's fears in relation to the possibility of nuclear war. Cites the main surveys, quotes from young people, and generally indicates the critical nature of this field.

Davies, R. (1987) *Hopes and Fears: Children's Attitudes to Nuclear War*, St Martin's College, Lancaster: Centre for Peace Studies. One of the few surveys carried out in the UK to explore how children in the 7 to 15 age range feel about nuclear war. Drawing on other international research the survey indicates that a significant proportion of children in our schools are very worried about this issue.

Educators for Social Responsibility (1982) *Dialogue: A Teaching Guide to Nuclear Issues*, Cambridge, Mass: Educators for Social Responsibility. A comprehensive and detailed handbook which provides a wide range of classroom activities from infant to secondary level, including discussion on the developmental context. The activities are designed to develop critical thinking skills in young people as well as offering ways of dealing with nuclear fears when they arise.

Hicks, D.W. (1986) *Teaching Nuclear Issues*, St Martin's College, Lancaster: Centre for Peace Studies. This paper sets out some of the key issues and dilemmas in relation to nuclear education. It reviews various teaching materials and identifies various classroom approaches to this subject. In particular it highlights 'holistic reassessment' as ultimately the only appropriate way forward.

Macy, J.R. (1983) *Despair and Personal Power in the Nuclear Age*, Philadelphia, Pa: New Society Publishers. How do we actually work through our despair about the state of the planet today and transform our blocked energies into creative empowerment? This vital book sets out both the theory and practice via a series of detailed workshop descriptions.

Sivard, R.L. (1986) *World Military and Social Expenditure 1986*, Washington DC: World Priorities. A comprehensive, readable, and authoritative survey of the facts and figures in this field. Revised fairly regularly. Excellent source of quotations, figures, and comparisons, especially between military and social spending.

Wellington, J.J. (1986) *The Nuclear Issue*, Oxford: Blackwell. This photocopiable book contains activity sheets designed for class use with older pupils. It provides a wealth of information on the science, history, and politics of the issue, presented in a balanced and readable form.

REFERENCES

Davies, R. (1984) *Children and the Threat of Nuclear War*, St Martin's College, Lancaster: Centre for Peace Studies.
—— (1987) *Hopes and Fears: Children's Attitudes to Nuclear War*, St Martin's College, Lancaster: Centre for Peace Studies.
Educators for Social Responsibility (1982) *Dialogue: A Teaching Guide to Nuclear Issues*, Cambridge, Mass: Educators for Social Responsibility.
Hicks, D.W. (1986) *Teaching Nuclear Issues*, St Martin's College, Lancaster: Centre for Peace Studies.
Humphrey, N. (1982) *Four Minutes to Midnight*, London: Menard Press.
Lifton, R.J. (1982) 'Beyond nuclear numbing', *Teachers College Record* 84(1).
Macy, J. (1983) *Despair and Personal Power in the Nuclear Age*, Philadelphia, PA: New Society Publishers.
Ornum, W. and Ornum, M. (1984) *Talking to Children About Nuclear War*, New York: Continuum Publishing.
Postman, N. and Weingartner, C. (1971) *Teaching As a Subversive Activity*, Harmondsworth: Penguin Education.
Reardon B. (1983) *Obstacles to Disarmament Education*, St Martin's College, Lancaster: Centre for Peace Studies.
Rowe, D. (1985) *Living With The Bomb: Can We Live Without Enemies?* London: Routledge & Kegan Paul.
Sivard, R. (1986) *World Military and Social Expenditure 1986*, Washington DC: World Priorities.
Stradling, R. (1987) 'Teaching green issues' *Green Teacher* February.
Tizard, B. (1984) 'Problematic aspects of nuclear education', in *Lessons Before Midnight*, Bedford Way Papers 19, University of London Institute of Education.

8

Justice and development

Toh Swee-Hin

Students should study a range of situations illustrating injustice, on scales from the personal to the global. They should look at the work of individuals and groups involved in the struggle for justice today.

(Table 2, p. 14)

INTRODUCTION

In her moving account of poverty, hunger, exploitation, human rights abuses, and repression in Latin America, Penny Leroux (1982) helped us to hear the 'cry of the people'. Echoed around the world, amongst diverse cultures and nation-states, the cry is an urgent call for the twin ideals of 'justice and development'. It tries to make those living in the advanced industrial north, where affluence is taken for granted, realize that when a Third World child wastes away from malnutrition; when workers toil under exploitative conditions; when guns, tanks, and aid protect dictators and élite minorities; when powerful corporations accumulate their wealth without conscience; when the terms of world trade weigh heavily against poor nations; then we are witting or unwitting accomplices in those injustices and mal-development.

Justice and development education, also called world studies and global education in different countries, seeks to clarify the understanding of learners, young and old, about the global web of political, economic, and social relationships (Wren 1986; Hicks and Townley 1982). Why is it not possible for human civilization, with its abundance of natural, economic, technological, and cultural resources, to provide adequately for the basic needs of all peoples on this planet? What are the roots of world hunger and poverty? How might the over-consumption of advanced industrial states be linked with the deprivation of millions of impoverished peasants and labourers? Why, even in so-called rich societies, do Fourth World communities remain marginalized, discriminated, and oppressed?

But such questions, in the context of justice and development education, cannot merely yield academic answers. Hand in glove with objective assessment of the problems, and designs for alternative structures and relationships, the teacher and learner must also critically reflect on their values and commitment to act. If one feels empathy and compassion for the poor's suffering and injustices, what personal and social practices then need to follow to give authentic expression to those values? In short, 'conscientization', a word made so influential by Paulo Freire (1985), is integral to justice and development education: a constant rhythm of critical reflection and committed action without which all the understanding or knowledge would remain just words or policies, while the world continues to turn around the axes of injustice and distorted development priorities.

Peace educators in North environments therefore have an enormous responsibility to touch the hearts of their learners continually, to evoke the store of compassion within, to encourage commitment towards less self-centred conduct, and to seek creative opportunities for humanizing their societal and national norms and policies towards marginalized peoples. However, a sense of justice and compassion needs to be informed by, to borrow a Buddhist notion, 'right understanding'. Justice and development education requires systematic and critical analysis of the causes of and possible strategies to transcend world poverty and hunger. In this regard, learners deserve to carefully consider for themselves the 'pros' and 'cons' of alternative paradigms of theory and practice on the fate of the poor majorities of the world.

THE MODERNIZATION IMPERATIVE

Since the 1950s and through the so-called 'development decades', two major paradigms or world views on Third World 'underdevelopment' and 'development' have crystallized. One, which may be labelled the modernization paradigm, holds much sway in the academic establishment of development economists and other social scientists; the large official aid agencies; and most importantly, in the governments and bureaucracies of most Third World states (Thompson 1976). Modernization embodies a set of basic assumptions and value-orientations towards explaining and resolving world poverty which places the Third World on the same race-track as the North. The 'underdeveloped' countries and regions can try to catch up and reap the rewards of advanced industrialization, high mass consumption, and modern 'culture'. To be 'developed' is to become like a rich-world society, especially the western variant.

The recurring themes and emphases in the modernization paradigm which learners in justice and development education need to understand include:

1 The all-important yardstick of 'growth' as in indicator of development,

and the expectation that benefits will 'trickle-down' to the poor; here, even though some modernization economists have brought in the factor of 'equity' as a necessary accompaniment of growth (Adler 1977), the practices of development plans and projects largely do not match this rhetoric.

2 The stress on 'internal deficiencies' of Third World societies as prime causes of underdevelopment, such as traditional values; lack of capital, modern infrastructure, advanced technology, and education; unattractive climate for foreign investments; and political instability or 'immaturity'.

3 The concomitant belief in the beneficience of the North towards the South, as expressed in relations of trade, investments, technology/knowledge transfers, foreign aid, geostrategic alliances, and political, economic, and social role-models.

4. A positive view of transnational corporations in playing a vital role in modernizing Third World economies, bringing them needed capital, technology, employment, and expertise, and integrating them into the global market (Ghertman and Allen 1984).

5 The emphasis on export-orientation, whether in industry (e.g. free trade zones) or in agriculture (e.g. cash-crops for foreign consumers and agribusiness), which predominates over subsistence food production and distribution.

6 A faith in advanced technological solutions to problems of underdevelopment, of which the 'Green Revolution' strategy is an archetype: develop and plant the 'miracle' seeds; add chemical inputs like fertilizers and pesticides; use more machinery (e.g. tractors); and with sufficient water supplies, food production soars to pre-empt hunger or famine.

7 The reliance on aid and external borrowing to provide the capital, technology, and expertise for expensive projects and modernization schemes; a beneficient neutral image of aid agencies and experts committed to helping the world's poor (Brandt 1980) and while not always endorsed in aid circles, the provision of military aid is deemed important to preserve political stability and 'friendly' governments (Chomsky and Herman 1979).

The above themes by no means exhaust the multiple manifestations of the modernization paradigm, but they are a basic minimum worthy of careful examination by learners as one dialectical half of their justice and development curriculum. The other half may be referred to by a deliberately broad acronym PEACE, the emergent paradigm which is challenging modernization orthodoxy in academic and planning circles. Most importantly, it hears the 'cry of the people', embodies their yearning for bread and justice, and to use Capra's (1983) term, heralds a 'turning-point' for human civilization.

THE PEACE ALTERNATIVE

The PEACE paradigm reflects a set of very different assumptions, value-orientations and themes, encompassed by the concepts of participation, equity, appropriateness, conscientization, and environmentalism. Each of these terms poses critical questions for evaluating the impact of modernization ideas and strategies, and implies alternative policies that would be more responsive to the basic needs of the poor majorities in particular, and to the long-term well-being of planet earth. Table 6 provides a schematic comparison of the modernization and PEACE paradigms, in terms of assumptions, concepts, and strategies. At this juncture in world history, the PEACE paradigm receives little respect from members and representatives of the power élites and their agencies of modernization, both in the North and South. But it is making itself heard, among marginalized peoples who are struggling for bread and justice; through the tireless solidarity expressed by non-governmental organizations (NGOs) (more accurately peoples' organizations) in the rich countries active in justice and development education; and the efforts of concerned teachers to integrate justice and development issues into curriculum and pedagogy.

A PEACE perspective on world hunger and poverty would therefore clarify the following major themes, concepts, and strategies, as well as their vital interrelatedness.

Participation

Modernization schemes and projects have usually been designed by political élites, bureaucrats, and experts with little or no authentic involvement by the poor in their planning and decision-making. Such top-down imposition of 'development' not only perpetuates a passive, dependent, and powerless attitude in the recipients, but also ignores the valuable potential contributions of traditional, folk, or indigeneous knowledge, practices, and institutions. Consequently, too many such schemes have floundered for lack of understanding of local conditions, and for failing to arouse people's commitment and enthusiasm. Instead of encouraging self-reliant, grassroots, and self-determined development, modernization reinforces élitist management and control. The PEACE paradigm hence emphasizes the imperative of peoples' participation and control over their development destinies. (*New Internationalist* 1981a). Experts and development professionals need to appreciate that poor and traditional peoples also have knowledge (Chambers 1983). There should also be a willingness to learn from successful participatory projects initiated by Third World peoples themselves.

Furthermore, in many South societies, lack of popular participation has repressive and exploitative implications. Strategies of export-oriented

Table 6 Paradigms of Third World underdevelopment

	Modernization paradigm	Peace paradigm
1	Unilinear model of 'development'. Goal of advanced industrialized high consumption societies.	Historically specific development. Alternative goals of human 'basic needs' development
2	Internal obstacles to development. Lack of modern infrastructure, capital, technology, entrepreneur's values, education, economic, and political institutions.	Internal power structure determinant in poverty. Entrenched political, economic and social inequalities perpetuate hunger, oppression.
3	Concepts of traditionalism and modernity, vicious circles, and stages of growth.	Concepts of structural violence and dependency.
4	Advanced industrialized nations beneficial to development via trade, investments, and aid. Colonialism uprooted traditional barriers.	Historical/contemporary 'development of underdevelopment'. External agencies and local élites benefit disproportionately from trade, aid, and investments.
5	Trickle down theory; growth emphasized over equity. In 1970s 'basic needs' and 'growth with equity' campaign.	Growth largely fails to reach poor. Fundamental structural changes needed towards greater social political-economic equality. Piecemeal reforms avoid roots of poverty and inequalities.
6	Advanced technology essential to growth. Efficiency criteria and experts decide development processes. Poor passive recipients of ideas.	Need more appropriate technology. Participation and local knowledge of masses essential. Poor need conscientization.
7	Environment to be fully exploited.	Environmental needs must harmonize with development. Over-capital intensive agriculture inappropriate.
8	Agriculture modernized and commercialized. Cash-crop export-orientation. Green Revolution and agri-business promote development. Evolutionary land reform.	Benefits TNCs and local élites. Local food production crucial. Green Revolution and agri-business widen inequalities. Radical land reform.
9	Women's productive role de-emphasized and under-rewarded.	Women's productive role emphasized and equalized.
10	Overpopulation major cause of underdevelopment. Apolitical population control campaign.	Poverty and 'overpopulation' related. Population control should be accompanied by equitable political-economic changes.
11	Famine caused by drought or other natural causes.	Famines have political-economic bases. Inappropriate modernization causes environmental bankruptcy.

Table 6 contd.

	Modernization paradigm	Peace paradigm
12	TNC useful, transfers capital technology, expertise. Gives markets, employment. Can be regulated by code of conduct.	TNC siphons more wealth out, overcapital intensive technology, limited jobs. Exploits cheap labour and resources. Unethical conduct difficult to control.
13	New Industrializing Countries exemplary models. Export-oriented industrialization useful.	NICs limited applicability. Export-oriented industrialization does not benefit poor majorities.
14	New international division of labour useful. Mutual interests served.	New International Economic Order essential.
15	Foreign aid beneficial for modern inputs. Large-scale infrastructure, export-oriented agriculture/industry, and private enterprise favoured.	Foreign aid reinforces/widens inequalities. Benefits North exports. Neglects basic agriculture, adds to urban bias, benefits elites disproportionately.
16	World Bank, IMF, and multilateral agencies neutral and beneficial. Recognize plight of poor.	World Bank and related agencies favour North and modernization principles. Leverage exercised. 'Basic needs' rhetoric.
17	Military aid essential for political 'stability' and growth.	Political 'stability' rests on repression. Military aid maintains élites' power, protects North's interests.
18	Military aid useful, should be apolitical. Emotional appeals for public support necessary. Child sponsorship schemes useful.	Political neutrality supports unequal status quo. Conscientization essential. Appeals based on critical development-education. Avoid pity syndrome. Child sponsorship paternalistic, perpetuates 'hand-out' dependency.
19	Modern formal education helps development and growth. Overseas training useful, gives development expertise. Non-formal education for poor.	Modern formal education reinforces diploma disease, widens inequalities, irrelevant to poor. Overseas training reinforces academic élitism, modernization ideology. Non-formal education for all, otherwise perpetuate inequalities.
20	Advanced industrialized consumer lifestyle can be universalized. South societies can catch up.	Advanced consumerism not feasible for earth's resources. North over-developed, leading to environmental destruction.

industrial or agricultural modernization, whether in the mines, factories, or plantations, are often accompanied by abuses of basic rights for workers and peasants (Lernoux 1982; Bello, Kinley, and Elinson 1982). Here it bears emphasizing that lack of participation and human rights violations are present in both capitalist and prevailing 'socialist' systems, albeit with different roots, features, and sometimes consequences. The PEACE alternative seeks to redress such injustices, and to foster institutions and processes of genuine participatory democracy.

Equity

One of the most empowering concepts of the PEACE paradigm is undoubtedly structural violence. It highlights the entrenchment of social, political, and economic structures and relationships which denies the poor majorities their right to at least adequate provision of their basic needs. It is no less violent when a jumbo-load equivalent of children die daily from unnecessary malnutrition and hunger-related diseases; when toiling workers or peasants receive remuneration insufficient to provide for their families, while well-off and powerful minorities, unmoved by the suffering, accumulate more and more and divert the nation's resources and wealth into personal aggrandizement, luxury imports, and militarized apparatuses to maintain the unequal social system (George 1976; Harrison 1981: *New Internationalist* 1984a).

‘ Clearly lessons in justice and development education should bring learners into the 'shoes' of the poor peasants, forced into indebtedness or landlessness by among other things their lack of access to land and other inputs. What does it mean to be landless labourers earning a pittance, exposed to pesticide poisoning, coerced by rapacious landlords and their thugs? Can they imagine the life of an urban destitute child, surviving as garbage scavengers in over-crowded shacks lacking the most basic amenities? Not least, learners need to emphasize with the 'double' oppression suffered by countless women, from the structural violence confronting the poor as well as patriarchial and sexist inequities (*New Internationalist* 1980).

However, while rightly exposing the causes of internal inequalities, exploitation, and repression underlying poverty, the PEACE paradigm also recognizes the global dimensions of structural violence (Dumont and Mottin 1983). The highly unjust world trading system permits the overdeveloped North to monopolize resources and under-remunerate the Third World, while the international debt trap extracts an ever-increasing outflow of capital from poor to rich nations (Cavanagh 1985). Transnational corporations, in collaboration with South élites, reap super-profits from cheap labour, resources, and infrastructure under very favourable investment terms. Northern powers, anxious to preserve their geostrategic influence and interests, find no compunction about supporting, if necessary, dictatorships and repressive regimes with economic and military aid, or engaging in various forms of political intervention (Chomsky and Herman 1979; Kidron and Smith 1983: pt 3).

Justice and development education hence also asks learners to consider their moral responsibility as North citizens in this system of global inequities. If Third World poverty has historical and contemporary linkages with their affluence, then would not values of compassion and justice arouse them to work for a more just world economic and financial system, such as embodied in calls for a New International Economic Order (*New Internationalist* 1981b)? Or to question the rationale of 'national security interests' invoked to justify military and other aid to dictators and oppressive élites, as well as to examine closely bilateral or multilateral aid programmes and projects to evaluate if the benefits are really reaching the poorest (Hayter and Watson 1984; Goodenough 1976)? And, while not easy, to challenge the power of transnational corporations, as the campaign against infant formula marketing in the Third World illustrates (*New Internationalist* 1982a)? Furthermore, justice and development pedagogy also reminds North learners of the structural violence within their own midst, suffered by indigeneous communities like the Australian Aborigines and North American Indians. Their experiences of racist colonialism and ongoing internal colonialism, which has so marginalized them into 'Fourth World' status within rich societies, are as equally relevant for the theme of 'equity' in the PEACE paradigm (Roberts 1978).

Appropriateness

With the collaboration of governments, aid agencies, and local or foreign experts and corporate interests, modernization strategies brought with them knowledge, methods, and technology which by PEACE criteria are inappropriate for the needs of the poor majorities. Nowhere is this more apparent than the agricultural sector, upon which most South citizens rely for their survival. The introduction of 'hi-tech' agricultural packages (e.g. Green Revolution) has meant an excessive dependence of peasants upon chemical and other costly inputs. Apart from the environmental consequences discussed later, this technological dependency has in the context of rural inequalities even accentuated structural violence (George 1976; 113–32). The production of more food does not automatically mean a higher level of sustenance, unless equitable redistributive structures exist. Similarly when transnational or local agri-business impose their imported capital-intensive technology on huge tracts of fertile land for export-oriented agriculture (e.g. cash crops, cattle, flowers), the rural poor benefit little and subsistence food production suffers (Burbach and Flynn 1980; George 1976). The equally inappropriate and harmful marketing of transnational products like pharmaceuticals and infant formulas in the South has also affected the poor most (Chetley 1979; *New Internationalist* 1986a). Last but not least, foreign experts and consultants who bring 'knowledge' to the Third World can often be insensitive to the culturally and socially inappropriate nature of their values, theories, and techniques (*New Internationalist* 1981c; Chambers 1983).

In contrast, PEACE paradigm believers argue for a critical audit of any technology or knowledge claimed to be 'useful' for development. Not only should the poor understand how any technology works, but also they must have participatory control over and truly benefit from its use (de Pury 1983). Self-reliance as a guiding principle protects poor communities from being locked into technological dependency and maximizes a constructive synthesis of traditional technologies, local conditions, and modern agro-ecological knowledge. It also means judicious delinking and reorienting current trade dependence upon rich countries. The growth of an 'intermediate technology' movement among North and South scientists and technologists is also an important reflection of the appropriateness theme in the PEACE paradigm (Harrison 1980). Likewise, the work of some people-to-people aid groups (e.g. OXFAM, Freedom from Hunger, Community Aid Abroad) should be presented to justice and development education students as laudable attempts by North citizens to support appropriate, participatory, and self-reliant development.

One other aspect of appropriateness worthy of detailed consideration is in the field of 'tourism' (*New Internationalist* 1984a). Can learners become more sensitive to the culturally, socially, and economically inappropriate methods and technologies embodied in conventional 'tourism' to the Third World, such as five-star hotels towering over poverty-stricken slums; excessive consumption; sex-tours; and the like? Are there not alternative, more dignified and equitable ways of meeting Third World peoples, and understanding the daily realities of their struggles for survival?

Conscientization

The modernization world view of poverty has tended to 'blame the victim': the poor lack modern values and orientations; traditionalism poses obstacles on the path to progress; if only they would save and work harder, take more entrepreneurial initiative rather than be passively content with their lot. While acknowledging that certain aspects of modernity will be constructive towards people-oriented development (e.g. preventive health-care, intermediate technology, literacy, numeracy), the PEACE paradigm highlights the political context of poverty. Where structural violence exists, 'passivity' and 'resistance to change' are quite rational responses for those living on the margins of survival.

130

Hence education, in the modernization paradigm, is seen as a 'neutral' vehicle for transmitting modern values, knowledge, and skills. For PEACE advocates, however, education should not be the 'banking' of expert-determined knowledge into passive recipients. As the inspirational work of Paulo Freire (1985) demonstrates, education is never politically neutral. Often, it only reinforces the social status quo, thereby leaving the poor unaware of the roots of their marginalized existences. The PEACE paradigm hence is grounded in the necessity of conscientization (*New Internationalist* 1985), the process whereby the oppressed awake to the structural violence underlying their suffering, and begin to struggle creatively towards equitable, participatory, and appropriate communities and societies. The conscientized break their 'culture of silence', and develop courage to challenge unjust power-structures.

In this regard, the examplar of people-to-people aid projects mentioned earlier demonstrates to North citizens how they can express solidarity for the poor and oppressed by supporting projects which embody conscientization. In contrast, modernization schemes and some forms of non-governmental aid (e.g. child sponsorship) avoid issues of critical consciousness, content to work within the political status quo. By intent or default, such allegedly 'neutral' interventions leave the roots of structural violence untouched, in effect siding with the rich and powerful. Here justice and development lessons should carefully consider the impact of recent public fund-raising campaigns for the starving in Africa. How much conscientization was embodied in, for example, the enormously visible and financially successful Live Aid concerts?

Environment

The environmental crisis is now acknowledged widely as posing serious short-term and long-term threats to the quality of human life, indeed of planetary survival itself (*New Internationalist* 1982b). Unlike the scourge of mass poverty and hunger, being industrialized and affluent has not prevented the North from the consequences of environmental breakdowns and disasters, including pollution, poisoning, erosion, acid rain, and nuclear radiation (e.g. Weir and Schapiro 1981). In the Third World, however, such mismanagement and destruction of the environment has not just been equally bad or worse. It is often integrated into their modernization strategies. Thus the capital-intensive and chemical-intensive modes of agriculture and agribusiness have caused poisoning of peasants, workers, rivers and water supplies; more resistant pests; traditional gene depletion; plant disease epidemics; soil degradation and erosion; salinization and waterlogging (Bull 1982; Kang 1982).

The massive rates of deforestation throughout the Third World – as governments and élites extract quick profits from logging; as ill-thought colonization schemes replaced forests with ranches and farms; as the poor are pushed by poverty and inequalities to over-exploit fragile ecologies – inflict severe environmental damage which compound the suffering of the poor majorities, and undermine long-term sustainable development (Eckholm 1982; 155–77). Indeed, when African famines occur, inclement weather is but a trigger. The root causes are élitist mismanagement of economic and agricultural resources which engender environmental bankruptcy (Timberlake 1985). And modern industrialization, pursued by South élites and encouraged by North interests, has been accompanied by hardly any pollution and environmental controls, with consequent injury to health, despoiling of basic resources (e.g. fisheries), and disasters like Bhopal.

In sum, the PEACE paradigm calls for urgent consideration of environmental principles in understanding world poverty and designing people-oriented development strategies. How can Third World societies build social and economic systems which will provide for the basic needs of all its peoples while maintaining environmental balance? What learners in justice and development lessons need to appreciate deeply is the interconnectedness of the earlier themes of participation, equity, appropriateness, and conscientization with environmental well-being. As structural violence decreases and more justice prevails, the conditions for more environmentally sound development will improve. While belatedly some agencies like the World Bank have responded to environmentalist pressures to be more ecologically sensitive, the modernization imperative is still very powerful, and justice and development educators must certainly continue to play their role in increasing environmental literacy.

CONCLUSION

Peace curriculum and pedagogy which focus on justice and development issues has the task of raising the critical awareness of learners until they can hear the 'cry of the people'. Children crying from hunger and disease; women, youths, and men, old before their time, toiling for pittances; people screaming in the torture chambers of dictators and repressive élites; farmers or workers shot by the military for demanding their basic human rights; and the list goes on. Most importantly, contrary to the modernization world view, they know that North societies play a significant part in perpetuating that vast human tragedy. Hopefully, so conscientized, they will begin to search for ways to help dismantle the unjust and inequitable structures and relationships underpinning the present global order. Many Third World peoples, communities, and societies are already engaged in self-determined efforts towards sustainable people-oriented development. Education for justice and development, in Northern contexts, fosters solidarity for those indigeneous struggles, whether through dialogue and collaboration in participatory projects, or more importantly, by removing external obstacles posed by North interests, including unjust trade, support for repressive élites, and the excessive power and agreed of economic agencies. Essentially too, learners and teachers confronting the enormity and complexity of justice and development problems must cultivate hope – a committed vision that human beings can learn to live justly and compassionately with one another in this one world.

CLASSROOM ACTIVITIES

While the following classroom activities have their specific focus and levels appropriate for use, they should be seen as 'entry points' to the wider interrelated issues of justice and development raised in this chapter. Fragmented understanding arising from looking at only a few issues needs to be avoided. The exercises have also been written to suit the higher grades of each level, but can be easily reduced in scope and complexity for the lower grades. It bears noting too that there is now an expanding number of publications which offer useful and creative guidelines for similar activities in justice and development education (Fyson 1984; Fisher and Hicks 1985; Development Education Project 1986).

Sharing the World's Resources

Introduction

This is a simulation activity designed to explore how the world's resources are shared, and might be otherwise shared if principles of justice and equity prevail in global development. As described, it is most suitable for the junior (7–11) classes, but may be easily reduced in scope and complexity to suit infants.

Purpose

1 To illustrate the extent of world hunger and poverty, and how the world's resources are shared among North and South peoples.
2 To develop an understanding of the inequalities and injustices which underlie such resource distribution, including issues of internal structural violence and disparities in global power.
3 To evoke a sense of compassion and justice for the poor majorities, and to clarify relative values and life-styles of North and South.
4 To encourage exploration of possible strategies of world resource sharing which are more just and equitable.

Preparation

1 Ask class members to bring to school on the day of the lesson at least a sandwich each plus some other items of food (e.g. biscuits, juices, milk, sweets, fruits, peanuts, etc.). Collect these items in advance and add to the collection pieces of dry crackers, plain bread slices, and cups of water.

2 Before the lesson starts, divide the total food collection into four piles of diminishing quantity and cost: pile (A) would comprise, for example, the elaborate sandwiches, juices, fruits and fancy biscuits, plus other basic items so that its proportion is at least one-third of the total; piles (B) and (C) would each have another quarter of the items, but predominantly of basic variety (e.g. sandwiches, biscuits, milk); the last pile (D) contains only old crackers, plain bread slices, and water.

3 Have available a world map based on the Peter's projection, which is less 'eurocentric' than Mercator's map (New Internationalist 1983a), handouts of comparative North and South statistics on development indicators like GNP per capita; infant mortality rates; life expectancy; calorie/protein supply; per cent population with safe water (see Sivard 1986); and copies of the Food First comic (New Internationalist 1983b).

Procedure

1 Explain to the class that the piles of food represent both food available to eat in the world, as well as other consumer resources used (e.g. energy, minerals, etc.). Point out the composition and size of each pile.

2 Distribute the four piles as follows, assuming a class size of twenty (adjust numbers according to class size): randomly pick out two students to share pile (A): repeat for pile (B) and (C) to be shared among three and five students respectively; then ask the remaining ten class members to come up to take food items on a first come first served basis, so that a few may have nothing at all.

3 Prompt representatives of each of the four groups of students to state what food items they have and how much per person. Next, gather the groups spatially around the classroom. Group (A) sits comfortably at the teacher's table in front; Group (B) remain at their desks or tables; Group (C) sits on the floor; Group (D) is crowded standing up at a back corner of the classroom.

4 With the groups as they are situated, encourage discussion of the problems and issues. Explain that the distribution of resources symbolized by the food items reflect world patterns of consumption. Ask the students in different groups to clarify their feelings about having plenty and little or nothing, as well as the level of comfort experienced.

5 Ask Groups (B), (C), and (D) to try to exchange their food items for the 'better' items possessed by Group (A); allow a process of 'bargaining' and 'exchange'. The 'exchange' exercise illustrates to students the bargaining power exercised by the wealthy, as occurs in the unequal world trading system.

6 Allow the students to resume their seats, and provide more information on world distribution of resources, indicators of poverty and hunger, and unequal terms of trade. What would the students believe to be the major causes of hunger? Counterpose PEACE paradigm perspectives where modernization ideas are presented, as happens often. Draw on the students' appreciation of hunger or poverty in their own societies and communities. Extend the discussion to intranational inequalities, especially the gross disparities between élite minorities and poor majorities in many Third World contexts, that is the groups are equally applicable at the global

level as well as inside countries. The extra burdens faced by women and ethnic minorities also need explaining.

7 Stimulate the class to think creatively of possible ways of distributing the world's resources so that justice and equity prevail (e.g. New International Economic Order; more economic aid; reduced military expenditure). Explore in particular North life-styles in terms of obsolescence, waste, over-consumption, and the general concept of over-development central to 'green' philosophy (see Trainer 1985; *New Internationalist* 1987). What would be necessary for a decent 'quality of life'? Encourage the class to reflect also on food, dietary patterns, and health (*New Internationalist* 1984b).

8 In follow-up lessons explore in greater depth the obstacles in the path of greater justice in resource distribution. Have the class read the *Food First* comic as a basis for the discussion. Examine, for example, the role of transnational corporations and the power of ruling élites. What can North citizens do to promote solidarity? Explore examples of Third World communities and groups striving to achieve self-reliant participatory development. Utilize the many films and games now available on development education, as interesting pedagogical tools for making the Third World more real to students (for a useful guide to such resources see Fyson 1984).

The Politics of Land Reform

Introduction

This simulation activity examines the controversial issue of land reform in the Philippines. As in many other Third World societies, the chronic lack of access to agricultural land and resources, reflecting very inequitable land tenure and distribution patterns, is a root factor behind the grinding poverty of Filipino peasants. In the post-Marcos period, President Aquino has obliged the Congress to enact a Comprehensive Agrarian Reform Programme. The simulation, which enables students to explore structural injustices in the context of land reform politics, is based on a congressional committee hearing where senators and several social groups discuss their views on the land reform bill.

Purpose

1 To understand the differing values, motivations, and interests of major social groups involved in the land reform issue.

2 To see how structural injustices underly rural poverty.

3 To appreciate the interconnections between different sections of the power structure.

4 To explore possible strategies which may resolve the problem peacefully and equitably.

Preparation

1 Prepare role descriptions for the different groups represented at the congressional committee hearing on agrarian reform, namely senators; wealthy landlords; poor farmers and landless labourers; Department of Economic

135

Development; Basic Ecclesial Communities.

2 Make available large-sized display paper and marker pens.

3 If possible, borrow a copy of the BBC's Third Eye Series film on the Philippines, *To Sing Our Own Song*.

Procedure

1 Explain to the class the context of the role-play, and divide the class into five approximately equal groups to play the roles. Allow each group time to discuss their role description, and how they would put their case at the congressional hearing. Have the groups summarize their views on large paper, to help them during the role-play and to use for later discussion.

2 The wealthy landlords constitute a traditionally powerful group in the Philippines. They are a minority élite owning most of the best lands; their estates or haciendas run into hundreds and thousands of hectares. They live sumptuously, surrounded by servants and material comforts. Filipino landlords do not see anything unjust about paying their farm workers extremely low wages, or expecting high rents from their tenant farmers. The typical landlord's view of the rural poor is that they are responsible for their own plight, unable to take initiative, lazy, irresponsible, and unintelligent. The landlords at the hearing openly criticize land reform, feeling that it is unjust to their families' many generations of 'hard' work and investment. Some argue that if land reform occurs, landlords must be fully compensated immediately and in full for the loss of their lands. The landlords view the radical poor farmers' and labourers' organizations or unions as 'communist'-inspired and 'fronts' for the New People's Army, the insurgent group fighting the Philippines government.

3 The poor farmers and landless labourers are among the poorest and most exploited members of Filipino society. For example, sugarcane workers receive only $2 for a day's toil. Poor tenant farmers are constantly in debt to survive from day to day, and charged high rents for use of their plots. Workers on the large plantations run by various transnational agri-business corporations (e.g. bananas, pineapples) suffer exploitative working conditions. However, militant unions of poor farmers and labourers have been actively organizing to improve their situation, and assert their basic human right to decent wages, safe work environments, and democratic unionization. Over the years, such unions and the rural poor in general have also suffered brutal repression at the hands of the military and private armies of the landlords. At the hearing, the poor farmers and labourers strongly argue for immediate and radical implementation of authentic land reform accompanied by governmental support to help new poor landowners to develop co-operative agricultural schemes independent of landlord or corporation control and exploitation. Poor farmers and labourers also generally have little trust in the government, as previous official schemes of land reform and development have provided little or no benefits.

4 The Department of Economic Development plans and implements the government's agricultural development programmes. Because of their training at home or abroad, officials and experts in the department tend to believe in the modernization framework for developing Filipino agriculture. Hence, the department supports the import of advanced technology and other capital-intensive inputs into the countryside (e.g. Green Revolution, tractors). Officials also welcome the role of the transnational corporations in agri-business. While supporting the idea of gradual land reform, the department believes that the new poor landowners would gain most benefits if they accept the department's planning and management advice.

5 The Basic Ecclesial Communities in the Philippines are church-based communities which gather together poor rural or urban Christians to help them better understand their daily problems of poverty and hardships. Community members assist one another to find ways of resolving those problems, such as developing new skills, and undertaking co-operative agricultural projects. At the hearing, representatives of the Basic Ecclesial Communities strongly argue for urgent land reforms, as one basic tool in increasing rural justice and development. Community members also believe in self-reliant participatory rural development, and cast doubt on the benefits of foreign investment in agri-business.

6 Senators at the hearing have the role of asking the various groups to state their views and to ask for details of the groups' approaches to resolving the land reform question. Senators, however, are also often wealthy landowners themselves, or come from landlord families. Some senators therefore are not too keen personally to enact radical and immediate land reform. They appear quite sympathetic to the concerns of the wealthy landlords represented at the hearing, but do not respect the poor farmers and labourers' union representatives. Other senators are concerned about rural poverty, and support land reforms but only in a gradual way.

7 After each group has had sufficient time to rehearse their role, the mock congressional hearing is held. The senators chair the hearing and allow each group first to state their views concisely on the pros and cons of land reforms. The senators then ask more specific questions of each group based on their presentations. Through the questions and answers, the whole class should begin to see the interests, motivations, values, and strategies of the various groups represented at the hearing.

8 When the discussion time is up, ask the role-players to derole and consider several key questions pertinent to understanding the politics of land reform. Pin the large paper of notes from the groups around the classroom to help reference and analysis. For example, how do the role-players feel about being a wealthy landlord, a poor farmer, and so on? Is it possible to indicate which group or groups have a stronger claim to justice? Should the landlords receive fair compensation for their land? What happens if the Filipino government is unable to pay for the huge costs involved in compensating wealthy landlords? How much hope and trust can the poor farmers and Christian communities place in Congress to enact authentic land reforms, given the social class background of many politicians? Why are the rural poor so critical of transnational agri-business firms and government departments? In exploring such questions, students will begin to appreciate the mechanisms of structural violence, and hence the need for conscientization, as exemplified by the struggles of the poor farmers and labourers union, and the Basic Ecclesial Communities. Assist the class by drawing on critical analyses of justice and development in the Philippines (e.g. Bello, Kinley, and Elinson 1982; Anti-Slavery Society 1983).

9 The post-role-playing discussion will also be assisted considerably by the class watching the film *To Sing Our Own Song*. While made before Marcos's downfall, many of the issues and problems of poverty, injustices, and even human rights abuses portrayed are still occurring. The film also brings up the growth of the insurgency movement, which in follow-up classes deserves to be examined. Why has insurgency and armed revolutionary struggle emerged? Are there possible non-violent routes to justice and equity in the Philippines or other poor Third World country? In this regard, the world headlines story of persecution and imprisonment of Australian priest Fr Brian Gore and Irish priest Fr O'Brien by the Marcos dictatorship also deserves to be told to the students, as it illustrates how two North citizens became awakened to social injustices and were not afraid to join Filipinos to challenge non-violently the power of corrupt and repressive élites (McCoy 1984). Finally, the

ongoing political crisis in the Philippines under the Aquino government illustrates the difficulties of overcoming 'structural violence', as well as the tasks confronting people power.

Points to watch

1 While the exercise focuses on the Philippines, the general discussion should also be situated in the worldwide experiences, problems, and urgency of enacting just and equitable land reforms (Whittemore 1981).

2 It is important not to leave students with the impression that simply giving 'land to the tiller' will resolve rural poverty and marginalization. Though indispensable, land redistribution has to be integrated with other economic, social, educational, and political transformations which devolve real power and resources to the rural poor.

Aid: Pity or Solidarity?

Introduction

This classroom exercise is designed to explore the subject of foreign aid and alternative perceptions of the motivations for giving aid, as well as strategies for delivering aid. It is helpful for demystifying assumptions and views held by many North citizens about what aid 'is' and 'ought to be'. The exercise revolves around two groups of class members, representing non-governmental aid agencies, trying to convince a public audience to support their rather different approaches to aid-giving.

Purpose

1 To appreciate that aid programmes contain many assumptions, values, motivations, and practices which differ according to varying paradigms on poverty, hunger, and lack of development.

2 To explore the impact of 'pity' or 'solidarity' strategies on the lives of poor people, and to evaluate those strategies in terms of justice and development principles.

3 To appreciate the meaning of conscientization, both in the North and South.

4 To gain a wider knowledge of different types of foreign aid, and to assess their desirability for people-oriented development.

Preparation

1 Prepare two groups of about ten slides each: Group (A) slides contain pictures of hungry or starving children pleading for food and help, as well as desperate poverty conditions in the Third World; pictures of media advertisements reflecting similar symptoms and appealing to the public to pity the poor with donations (e.g. child sponsorship); pictures of western aid experts or volunteers handing out food supplies or directing villagers in aid projects, and of smiling fed children who have received sponsorship aid. Group (B) slides contain pictures of Third World people or scenes, minus the 'starving, hopeless' image; pictures of media advertisements

which also reflect this view and explicitly refer to structural violence in their appeal for public support of projects (not child sponsorship); and pictures of projects where western volunteers are not prominent and villagers are engaged in co-operative self-reliant projects.

2 Handouts based on articles in special issues of *New Internationalist* (1982c; 1983b; 1985) on various types and problems of aid-giving. For role-playing, give a few selected handouts to the two aid groups relevant to their approach (e.g. sample letters from sponsored children to their sponsors; description of style of modernization expert; descriptions of aid projects from such organizations as OXFAM and War on Want).

3 Handouts of role descriptions for the two aid groups and public audience group.

4 Large writing paper, marker pens, slide projectors.

Procedure

1 Divide the class randomly into three approximately equal groups: Group (A) represents the 'Feed the Starving' NGO aid group; Group (B) puts the case of the 'Aid for Self-Reliance' aid group; Group (C) represents the public audience whom each aid group will try to convince to support its projects.

2 Allow the aid groups to view in separate locations the slides they will be presenting, followed by group discussion of their respective roles.

3 For Group (A), the role-card states that the 'Feed the Starving' group emphasizes media advertisements showing poverty-stricken children, in order to evoke public pity for the hungry. Group members believe that the poor are trapped in their cycle of destitution, and the affluent should be moved to donate some money to pull them out of the trap. The causes of world hunger are largely seen in individualistic deficiency terms, and the North as beneficient providers of modern inputs; in short, Group (A) embraces the modernization paradigm. In their aid projects, western experts and local élites manage and direct the poor, who largely passively accept directions from above. Above all, 'politics' should be kept out of aid activities.

4 For Group (B), the role-card emphasizes a PEACE paradigm approach to aid-giving. Raising public funds for its work is based on justice and development principles; hence advertisements boldly identify inequities and exploitation as roots of poverty, and views the Third World poor as able to join hands in self-reliant, dignified, and participatory development struggles. The aid projects reflect this orientation, and aid volunteers work side by side with the poor, who exercise co-operative responsibility in planning, managing, and implementing the projects. Child sponsorship schemes are rejected as inappropriate. Raising political awareness is seen as important in the poor's struggles for justice and equity.

5 For Group (C), the public audience group, their initial discussion allows them time to brainstorm various questions they would like to ask the aid groups during their presentations. The group is helped by the teacher to identify a list of major questions, which should include, for example, 'What are the causes of hunger and poverty?'; 'How do we know if our donations are well spent?'; 'What projects will receive priority?'; 'Who will plan and manage projects?'; 'Should aid agencies stay out of the local politics of recipient communities or countries?'

6 After the group discussions and role-familiarization are over, the groups come together for the presentation session. Group (A) first briefly presents its case for aid, based on the slides, and appeals for funds from the audience. Group (C) members then ask their predetermined questions of Group (A). The exercise is repeated with

Group (B) presenting, then answering the same questions from Group (C).

7 At the conclusion of the presentations and questioning, Group (C) members are asked to choose individually whose cause they would prefer to support. This is followed by general class discussion about the reasons for such choices, and a careful analysis of the issues and values raised in the role-play. How would they feel if they were the hungry children depicted in Group (A) advertisements, and obliged to write 'thank you' letters to their sponsors? What is the relative validity of causes of hunger portrayed? Is it dignified and just for aid recipients to be merely passive followers of expert directions and control? What benefits can flow from greater participation of the poor? Is staying out of 'politics' being really 'neutral'? What is the importance of conscientization? How should the recent Live Aid compaign be assessed? How does giving aid relate to questions of global inequalities and structural violence?

8 For follow-up analysis, class members should read the special issues of the *New Internationalist* (1982c; 1983b; 1985); relevant chapters on aid from authors like George (1976) and Lappe, Collins and Kinley (1981) as well as reports of such NGO groups as OXFAM, Community Aid Abroad, and War on Want for descriptions of PEACE paradigm-oriented aid. A variety of interesting simulation games are now available from groups like Christian Aid ('Giving and Receiving') and OXFAM ('Aid Committee Game'). Guest talks can be arranged if possible for representatives of a range of aid agencies, governmental and non-governmental, to explain their approaches and attitudes. After further discussions, the class should be able to distinguish between the value-orientations of 'pity' and 'solidarity' which underly the major paradigms of development. Hopefully some members will be moved to join and support community activities more reflective of solidarity and justice principles, perhaps by forming school branches of those groups.

Points to watch

1 If possible, run the preparatory and role-familiarization part of the exercise in one discrete lesson, so as to allow sufficient time for each group to feel confident about its role.

2 A double period lesson would be ideal for the role-play and analysis portion of the exercise.

3 Students should not emerge from this exercise viewing solidarity merely in terms of appropriate kinds of aid involving the North in the South. Solidarity is equally important in terms of aware North citizens trying to change their countries' foreign policies towards greater justice and equity (e.g. challenging the validity of military aid; support of the New International Economic Order; regulating conduct of transnational corporations; reducing the debt burden; devolving official aid programmes and projects towards increased participation and control by the poor majorities who really benefit rather than élites).

REFERENCES

Adler, J.H. (1977) 'Development theory and the bank's development strategy – a review', *Finance & Development* 14, 4: 31–4.

Anti-Slavery Society (1983) *The Philippines*, London: Anti-Slavery Society.

Bello, W., Kinley, D., and Elinson, E. (1982) *Development Débâcle: The World Bank in the Philippines*, San Francisco, Calif: Institute for Food and Development Policy.

Brandt, W. (1980) *North–South: A Programme for Survival*, London: Pan.

Bull, D. (1982) *A Growing Problem: Pesticides and the Third World Poor*, Oxford: OXFAM.

Burbach, R. and Flynn, P. (1980) *Agribusiness in the Americas*, New York: Monthly Review.

Capra, F. (1983) *The Turning Point*, New York: Fontana.

Cavanagh, J. (1985) *From Debt to Development*, Washington, DC: Institute for Policy Studies.

Chambers, R. (1983) *Rural Development: Putting the Last First*, London: Longman.

Chetley, A. (1979) *The Baby Killer Scandal*, London: War on Want.

Chomsky, N. and Herman, E.S. (1979) *The Washington Connection and Third World Fascism*, Boston, Mass: South End.

de Pury, P. (1983) *People's Technologies and People's Participation*, Geneva: World Council of Churches.

Development Education Project (1986) *Teaching Development Issues*, Manchester: Development Education Project.

Dumont, R. and Mottin, M. (1983) *Stranglehold on Africa*, London: André Deutsch.

Eckholm, E.P. (1982) *Down to Earth*, New York: W.W. Norton.

Fisher, S. and Hicks, D. (1985) *World Studies 8–13*, Edinburgh: Oliver & Boyd.

Freire, P. (1985) *The Politics of Education*, New York: Macmillan.

Fyson, N. (1984) *The Development Puzzle*, London: Hodder & Stoughton.

George, S. (1976) *How the Other Half Dies*, Ringwood: Penguin.

Ghertman, M. and Allen, M. (1984) *An Introduction to the Multinationals*, London: Macmillan.

Goodenough, S. (1976) 'Unit 23 Part B: Aid–Assistance or Exploitation?' in S. Goodenough (ed.), *Patterns of Inequality*, Milton Keynes: Open University.

Harrison, P. (1980) *The Third World Tomorrow*, Ringwood: Penguin.

—— (1981) *Inside the The Third World*, Ringwood: Penguin.

Hayter, T. and Watson, C. (1984) *Aid: Rhetoric and Reality*, London: Pluto.

Hicks, D. and Townley, C. (eds) (1982) *Teaching World Studies*, London: Longman.

Kang, D.S. (1982) 'Environmental problems of the Green Revolution, with a focus on Punjab, India', in R.N. Barrett (ed.), *International Dimensions of the Environmental Crisis*, Boulder, Colo: Westview.

Kidron, M. and Smith, D. (1983) *The War Atlas*, London: Pan.

Lappe, F.M., Collins, J., and Kinley, D. (1981) *Aid As Obstacle*, San Francisco, Calif: Institute for Food and Development Policy.

Leroux, P. (1982) *Cry of the People*, New York: Penguin.

McCoy, A.W. (1984) *Priests on Trial*, Ringwood: Penguin.

New Internationalist (1979) 'Growing inequality — peasants, landlords and businessmen', *New Internationalist* 81, November.

—— (1980) 'More to lose than their chains', *New Internationalist* 89, July.

—— (1981a) 'By the sweat of their brows', *New Internationalist* 106, December.

—— (1981b) 'Out of the picture North-South: the Brandt Report and after', *New Internationalist* 104, October.

—— (1981c) 'Wisdom from above', *New Internationalist* 96, February.

—— (1982a) 'Stop the baby milk pushers', *New Internationalist* 108, February.

—— (1982b) 'Assault on the Earth', *New Internationalist* 114, August.

—— (1982c) 'Please do not sponsor this child', *New Internationalist* 111, May.

—— (1983a) 'This land is my land, part 2: a new map of the earth', *New Internationalist* 124, June.

—— (1983b) 'Food first: a cartoon voyage of discovery', *New Internationalist* 125, July.

—— (1984a) 'Visions of poverty, visions of wealth', *New Internationalist* 142, December.

—— (1984b) 'Trick or treat: the sticky world of food', *New Internationalist* 135, May.

—— (1985) 'Can you help? Charity and justice in the Third World', *New Internationalist* 148, June.

—— (1986a) 'A pill for every ill', *New Internationalist* 165, November.

—— (1987) 'What if the Greens achieve power? The politics of ecology', *New Internationalist* 171, May.

Roberts, J. (1978) *From Massacres to Mining*, London: War on Want/CIMRA.

Sivard, R. (1986) *World Military and Social Expenditures*, Washington DC: World Priorities.

Thompson, G. (1976) 'Unit 20: processes of development – Orthodox models', in G. Thompson (ed.), *Inequalities Between Nations*, Milton Keynes: Open University.

Timberlake, L. (1985) *Africa in Crisis*, London: International Institute for Environment and Development.

Trainer, F.E. (1985) *Abandon Affluence*, London: Zed.

Weir, D. and Schapiro, M. (1981) *Circle of Poison*, San Francisco, Calif: Institute for Food and Development Policy.

Whittemore, C. (1981) *Land for People*, Oxford: Oxfam.

Wren, B. (1986) *Education for Justice*, London: SCM Press.

9

Power

Jane Williamson-Fien

Students should study issues to do with power in the world today and ways in which its unequal distribution affects peoples' life chances. They should explore ways in which people and groups have regained power over their own lives.

(Table 2, p. 14)

INTRODUCTION

The inclusion of a chapter on power in a book on peace education assumes two things: first, that the issue of power is central to any debate on peace and peacelessness, and second, that education is an important medium through which the nature of power can be understood and, if necessary, challenged. It is doubtful if anyone would dispute the first assumption. It is hardly possible, for example, to investigate questions of injustice, poverty, conflict, or rivalry without reference to the patterns of power that support particular social relations and structures. What does become problematical, however, is the exact nature of power and where it is located. Differing perspectives on these issues have obvious ramifications for the second assumption and raise serious concerns about the efficacy of education as an agent for change. This chapter suggests that it is all too easy to skirt around or overlook some of the problematical aspects of power and, as a consequence, assume that education, and schooling in particular, will readily provide the necessary insights, skills, and processes to challenge the unjust use of power.

Such a provocative position requires elaboration. Power is commonly defined in Weberian terms to mean the ability of individuals or groups to impose their will even against the resistance of others. The connotations of such a definition of power are overwhelmingly negative, particularly when combined with the belief that 'power corrupts and absolute power corrupts absolutely'. Against this version of power, many peace educators (see

R. Sharp 1984) and others (Ferguson 1982) have counterpoised the notion of personal or individual power, thereby stressing alternative sources of power. Unlike the Weberian idea of public power, embodied in the dictator, the general, the bureaucrat, and so on, personal power is seen to have positive qualities which, once recognized and activated, are capable of challenging and changing the existing configurations of public power. Peace education can thus become, at least in part, the means by which students can be 'empowered'. Their consciousness of issues of peace can be raised and they can be persuaded of their ability, as individuals, to influence events. Ultimately, it is thought, if enough people can be educated in this way, a more peaceful world must eventuate.

Unfortunately, while such simple idealism conforms with the dominant, liberal ideology, it raises a number of complex questions. For example, how do we respond to our students when they ask us why, if it is all so simple, we have failed to eliminate or even reduce peacelessness in the world? Does the process of empowering our students run the risk of creating idealistic and individualistic people who become alienated, insecure, or power-hungry adults when their vision of personal power fails to provide them with the sort of peaceful life they had thought possible? To what extent is the process of empowering merely inducting students into existing structures of power and powerlessness? What purposes are served by the assumption of a dichotomy in the nature of power such that the power of 'others' (notably governments, trade unions, big business, for example) is potentially nasty or manipulative, while personal power is essentially good or liberating? Clearly peace education needs to adopt a more critical analysis of power in both the content and context of schooling. This chapter begins this process by considering the nature and sources of power and, in particular, the thorny issue of personal power. The second part of the chapter considers the implications of such an analysis for peace education.

THE NATURE AND SOURCES OF POWER

One of the major contributions of peace educators to the understanding of violence and its roots has been their recognition of structural or indirect violence in addition to direct violence (see Burns 1981; Hicks 1983). One implication of the addition of a structural explanation of violence is that power can also be identified as both overt and covert. Against the notion of naked, direct power can be ranged other types of power including those associated with the 'art of persuasion' as utilized by agencies such as the media and schools. The existence of multiple bases of power has tended to encourage the assumption that these alternative power sources are somehow separate from each other and ultimately malleable. Thus, many people may be seen to have access to power from a variety of sources. Additionally there may also be a tendency to accept that structural violence and direct violence are unconnected, except in so far as they both create peacelessness. As a consequence, links between overt and covert power are not readily made, and neither is there any suggestion that one type of violence may precede the other, instead they are perceived to have parallel existences (see Figure 1, p. 6). The validity of these assumptions requires careful analysis.

Conventionally a number of different bases of power have been identified. For example, Tronc (1970) suggests that power stems from six different sources. These sources provide the powers of reward, coercion, authority, reference, expertise, and charisma. Tronc identifies reward power as the belief that particular individuals have the 'ability to mediate rewards'. Thus students who work hard for good marks are, in part, responding to their teacher's reward power. Coercive power, on the other hand, is the 'perception that someone else can mediate punishments'. Authority is based on the notion of legitimate power and the belief that particular individuals have the right to demand certain behaviours of others; while referent powers are associated with the power of the group to mould the behaviour and expectations of individuals belonging to that group. People with expert knowledge may enjoy power as a result of that knowledge, and individuals possessing particular capacities that inspire devotion may be said to have charismatic power. Tronc utilizes this analysis to argue that 'subordinates can flex their muscles' since power is not merely delegated by superordinates to subordinates, but is also granted from below each time we make the choice to grant various powers to others. No individual, for example, has charismatic power until others recognize it and accord it to him or her.

Tronc's position accords well with the liberal notion of personal power and the sort of approach by peace activists such as Gene Sharp (1973) in his text *The Politics of Non-Violent Action*, but it fails to address three important and closely related issues. First, although Tronc recognizes that teachers may have reward, authority, and coercive powers, he nevertheless fails to explore the extent to which the acquisition of one type of power may lead to the accumulation of other powers. It could be argued, for example, that the charismatic power of Hitler provided the basis for the development of his expert power on the nature of German problems and allowed him to acquire both legitimate authority and coercive power over the German people. Power may create or breed further power. Hence, rather than there being many people with access to power, there may, in fact, be only a few. The extensive range of potential sources of power does not necessarily mean that many people occupy positions of power.

Secondly, Tronc fails to acknowledge the extent to which the accumulation of power is sanctioned and rewarded in our society. Given the widely held assumptions that human nature is inherently bad and that life is a competitive struggle for existence, the desire to accumulate power and use it is not only fundamental for survival, it is also perceived as worthy of emulation and reward. Gaining power, whether it be via expertise, election to formal office, or charismatic leadership, is seen as a worthwhile achievement in our society and, not infrequently, the most manipulative and exploitative of power seekers have received the ultimate accolades of honours, wealth, personal status, and adulation, all of which provide the basis for the acquisition of more power.

Third, Tronc fails to consider the extent to which our society is built on and perpetuates unequal power relations. As Hutton (1987) has noted, the current world view 'sees the domination of some human beings over others as a necessary pre-condition for human progress'. One outcome of this world view is the institutionalization of inequitable power relations. Such relations not only create the means whereby people can be coerced, but also, as Diaz (1981) argues, they may promote direct violence when desperate or starving people see no alternative avenues for change. The use of direct power is often promoted or caused by underlying structural inequalities and, thus, overt conflict between nations or the arms race are but symptoms of deeper social ills. Understanding the nature of power, therefore, requires an awareness of the structures that have created it. Simply identifying various types of power does not help us to understand who has access to particular powers and why such powers should accrue to them. Similarly the concept of personal power and the role of education in empowering students also need to be considered in the light of structural conditions.

PERSONAL POWER

The notion of personal power has wide currency in western societies: it lies, after all, at the heart of democratic theory and capitalist ideology. Personal power implies choice, the ability to make decisions about a range of things including mundane matters, such as what to wear or what to do at the weekend, and more complex issues relating to attitudes to others, political philosophy, and so on. It is important that the significance of personal power is not understated or derided since to do so encourages surrender, passivity, and the avoidance of individual responsibility. As Marilyn Ferguson (1982) has argued, we often 'become attached to the factors that imprison us: our habits, customs, the expectations of others, rules, schedules, the state' and, as a result, we may deny personal responsibility and become 'seduced by pain-avoidance' behaviours.

However, it is equally important that the importance of personal power is not over-emphasized and that the 'warm inner glow' produced by raising consciousness on the issue does not lead to false expectations about how existing power structures may be changed. At the same time, it is important to maintain a critical eye on the perceived nature of personal power and the extent to which theoretical models of politics and economics operate in reality. Clearly the concept of personal power, however attractive it might be, presents dilemmas for peace educators. Its efficacy in our personal lives and in social transformation as well as the constraints that limit its potential require amplification.

Consider the following story presented by Tronc:

You are driving at 40 miles per hour in a 30 mile per hour zone. You see a policeman standing on the corner. Immediately, you reduce speed. Why? It is not because of what the policeman has done – he just stood there. He may not even have noticed you. If it had been a person dressed up as a policeman going to a fancy dress ball you would still have slowed down. The effect would have been the same, if you had seen something you thought was a policeman – even a cardboard cut-out shape.

Tronc's purpose in describing this situation is to suggest that it is the individual's choice to slow down when he or she sees the policeman. Thus the policeman does not have power unless it is granted to him. Clearly such a scenario is very empowering. It implies that individuals are important, that they can take control of their lives and that ultimately power lies with them.

Marilyn Ferguson (1982) develops the significance of personal power further by arguing that awareness of personal power can have implications for social transformation. She argues:

Just as personal transformation empowers the individual by revealing an inner authority, social transformation follows a chain reaction of personal change.

(Ferguson 1982)

According to Ferguson, the process of social transformation is achieved by the creation of networks of transformed individuals and the recognition of alternative centres of power that can be utilized. Amongst the new sources of power, she identifies:

1 The power of paying attention, of facing and transforming conflict.

2 The power of self-knowledge, of letting go and refusing to engage in competitive power games.

3 The power of process, every step along the road to transformation makes the next step easier.

4 The power of uncertainty, the need for imagination, ambiguity, flexibility.

5 The power of alternatives, recognizing the range of choices.

6 The power of intuition, not charting activities solely by logic but seeking consensual intuition.

7 The power of vocation, a collective sense of destiny.

8 The power of withdrawal, we can take back the power we give others.

9 The power of women, the adoption of female qualities of nurturance, affiliation, and a fluid sense of time.

10 The power of the radical centre, a willingness to synthesize, to recognize the contributions and errors of all political persuasions, to respect friendship and empathy, not money and status.

Ultimately Ferguson sees the change to a more caring and peaceful society by a process that is itself caring and peaceful, with means and ends in tune. In the same vein, Gene Sharp (1973) presents a case for peaceful political transformation as the strategic withdrawal of consent to a repressive regime by its constituent people.

The theses of Tronc (1970), Ferguson (1982), Gene Sharp (1973), and others (see R. Sharp 1984) are obviously attractive to peace educators, because the implications are that students can be empowered by the knowledge of personal power and can be taught the necessary skills to utilize that power in the transformation to a more peaceful society. Such an approach has the added attraction of being potentially transformative while initially being set within the confines of the status quo. Persuading students of their individual power is, in theory, no more subversive than undertaking classes on civics or citizenship. Nevertheless, there are problems with this approach and peace educators need to be aware of them if they are to avoid accusations of idealism and naïvety.

A major difficulty relates to the distinction that is drawn between personal power and the other forms of power, such that personal power is perceived to be independent of and qualitatively different from other types of power. What this distinction suggests is that all people regardless of race, gender, class, position, wealth, or education have similar access to a particular power, personal power, which they, as individuals, are free to use or abuse. Furthermore, there is something rather special about personal power because when individuals utilize it in concert, it may be depicted as potentially good or liberating, whereas the other types of power, the reward, coercive, or authority powers of teachers, for example, may be categorized as potentially manipulative. Personal power embodies the positive aspects of power, while the other types of power incorporate its negative elements.

Unfortunately this neat dichotomy between individual power and the other types of power cannot be sustained. Personal power cannot be divorced from the social context in which it is created and consequently it cannot be considered apart from the other types of power. Consider the story of the driver and the policeman. In truth, the extent to which the driver is prepared to grant power to the policeman depends on how powerful the driver feels vis-à-vis the policeman. If the driver is a wealthy, white, articulate middle-aged male with a well-maintained recent model car, he can afford to ignore the policeman (that is grant him no power) because he knows that even if the officer stops him, he may be sufficiently articulate to avoid a fine. Alternatively the driver may be unconcerned about the fine as he can afford to pay it and, also, he knows that he is unlikely to attract further police attention because his motor vehicle is in good condition. The same cannot be said if the driver is poor, black, semi-literate woman driving an old car with a range of minor mechanical problems. She must grant power to the policeman and slow down because she cannot afford the fine, she is unlikely to be able to avoid paying, and she may even find her means of transport impounded for mechanical checks! These examples suggest that choices about 'granting' power are not based on some abstract idea of personal power along, but depend on the extent to which an individual's sense of power is buttressed and supplemented by other forms of power. Personal power is thus inextricably linked with other forms of power and is constrained by the social structures within which it is exercised.

Recognition of the complexity of social reality and, in particular, the role of social structures in determining effective personal power, severely compromises the emphasis placed on the individual by the proponents of the personal power/social transformation approach. Societies are not merely aggregations of individuals and the suggestion that social transformation can be achieved by the simple acts of tapping into self-knowledge, networking, seeking intuitive consensus, and so on, is appealing but facile. Ultimately focusing on the individual as change agent is fruitless unless social structures are also being addressed. As Holland and Henriot (1980) have argued:

> Social justice itself is a structural question, not simply a personal matter. For example, I may not personally be a racist, or a male chauvinist. I may treat women and people of other races as equals, in speech, attitudes, and behavior. However, this personal action does not address the deep justice issues of racism or sexism-unemployment, lack of educational opportunities, discriminatory pay or lack of access to decision-making positions. These are structural questions.

Furthermore, structural relationships are unlikely to be changed by consensus or cooperation for, as Brian Wren (1986) points out, 'power is never shared or surrendered by moral persuasion alone'. The transformation to a peaceful society implies, therefore, an element of struggle, although any such conflict need not necessarily imply physical violence.

One further problem of the personal power/social transformation approach is that while its overt messages emphasize personal power, freedom of choice, and positive change, its hidden agenda embodies an element of 'blame the victim'. Put bluntly, if individuals have similar powers and can use these powers to effect change, it follows that those individuals who fail to effect change can blame only themselves. This position, which has much in common with the reactionary conservatism of the nineteenth century (see

Smiles 1859, cited in Donaldson and Pollins 1981), has been utilized by the peace activist, Gene Sharp (1973), to explain how tyrants have been 'allowed' to stay in power and why people get the governments they deserve. For example, citing Leo Tolstoy (1937), Sharp claims that the British Raj never enslaved Indians, but the Indians enslaved themselves. Sharp's argument of course, is that people should withdraw their support from evil regimes, but if it is possible for a scholar like Sharp to be seduced with the idea that people might consciously enslave themselves, it is not difficult to imagine that school students might also be so persuaded, particularly in the absence of structural explanations. If the message is that the poor are poor because of their failure to use their power effectively, what impact will this have on the wealthy students and how will it make the less wealthy feel? Thus while the purpose of adopting the personal power/social transformation approach in peace education is to empower students, its implicit effect may be to reinforce existing social structures by confirming the range of choices and freedoms of the élite, both within and between schools, while reminding the others of their limited potential effectiveness.

THE IMPLICATIONS FOR PEACE EDUCATION

What then are the implications for peace education of this analysis of power? If power cannot readily be extracted from its social context, how is it possible to come to terms with it and undertake the struggle for a more just, a more peaceful society? This section suggests that three steps are necessary. The first of these involves the need for a change of emphasis from the consideration of types of power and the process of empowering, to an examination of the structures that create, promote, and maintain power, with the aim of identifying and joining the struggle against powerlessness and oppression. The second step consists of an evaluation of our role as teachers and, in particular, the extent to which we are committed to change and able to promote it within the educational system. Finally, the third step, which cannot be undertaken until the other two have been completed, involves facilitating our students' understanding of the structures of oppression and the means of challenging those structures.

Step one: focus on structures

The first of these three steps is integral to the other two and, probably, the most difficult to undertake. It involves, after all, the challenging of many taken-for-granted assumptions, including the reality of equality and the power of the individual, which many people hold dear. It also implies painstaking inquiries into the historical development and current status of the visible structures that affect people's daily lives, for example economic and political systems. Additionally it involves the uncovering and questioning of the invisible aspects of the structural web that legitimize and buttress the visible institutions, for example the ideological structures of capitalism and patriarchy.

Once these visible and invisible structures are recognized and examined, however, they yield answers to the question of *why* some people have more power than others and *how* such people are able to sustain and increase their power. Thus the power of the wealthy, white, male driver, in the earlier example, sprang from his wealth, his gender, and his race which were backed by the ideological structures of capitalism, patriarchy, and institutionalized racism. These ideological structures not only sanction particular patterns of power, but also promote the continued subordination of particular groups by ensuring the latters' socialized acceptance of the naturalness of the existing state of affairs. Additionally, as Wren (1986) has noted, the beneficiaries of social injustice are rarely aware of their relationship to the victims. He continues:

> In such a position, we find it hard to realize, much less accept that our privilege might be held at the cost of other people's suffering, or that the structural relationships could be different or more just.

For those of us committed to the development of a more peaceful society, recognition of the nature and process of oppression demands that we align ourselves with the oppressed, the powerless; we seek to understand from them the meaning of their oppression; we struggle with them and we constantly monitor our own positions as potential oppressors.

Step two: teacher commitment and the possibilities for change

Lining up with the oppressed implies, of course, that as teachers we must be prepared to take sides and recognize that neutrality gives tacit support to the powerful. Brian Wren (1986) demonstrates this point using the example of a multinational company wishing to build an oil terminal on the Scottish coast. The local people can support the venture, claim neutrality or oppose it, but as Wren notes, 'whatever the rights and wrongs may be, the first two courses have the same effect – they can support the company's efforts by encouragement or default'.

Adopting a committed stance (see Stradling 1984) on the issue of injustice and powerlessness is not without its difficulties, however. In the first place it may embroil individual teachers in controversy, since such a stand challenges the status quo (R. Sharp 1984) and more particularly the liberal doctrines of teacher neutrality and a balanced approach to issues. Second, teacher commitment also entails an acceptance of the necessity of conflict and struggle which may be difficult to assert in the face of the enormous value that western society places on consensus (Wren). As Specht (1974) has argued, people prefer 'cooperation, no matter how spurious, to conflict, no matter how necessary'. Insisting on the necessity of conflict and struggle may seem, furthermore, to be at odds with community notions of *peaceful* change. In order to overcome these difficulties, individual teachers may need to develop specific coping strategies to understand the conflict within themselves and become accepting of themselves (Wren). Ultimately however the success of a committed stance depends on a realistic appraisal of the nature of the education system and at what points and in what places the struggles of committed teachers are likely to bear fruit.

The primary purpose of the education system, and schools in particular, is to reproduce existing social relationships. As Huckle (1986) has noted:

> By conveying skills and beliefs which support the economic and cultural status quo, [schools] serve mainly to sort, label and socialize future workers and citizens.

The education system is, therefore, an integral part of the broader social structures. As a consequence, the activities of teachers committed to justice and peace cannot be divorced from the wider political struggles of peace activists and other pro-justice groups outside schools. Committed teachers need to involve themselves in the struggles of such groups in order to develop a sense of collective solidarity, to learn from others some of the means of resistance to unjust structures, and to obtain a support system for activities undertaken in schools. Teacher links with political activists outside schools also help to ensure that students do not have to start from scratch when it comes to mobilizing politically (Watson 1985).

In addition, teachers are well aware that the education system reproduces social relations imperfectly. Identifying the sites of imperfection may indicate opportunities, therefore, where intervention and change can occur. Huckle (1986) argues, for example, that student resistance to schooling provides opportunities for teachers to adapt critical and democratic forms of teaching. A democratic and critical pedagogy challenges both the content and form of schooling and consequently the nature of existing power structures. It may include strategies of deconstructing 'reality' such as those outlined by Shor (1980) and Alvarado and Ferguson (1983). A further possible site of intervention occurs in the hidden curriculum. Citing the work of Apple (1980) and Giroux (1981), Whitty (1985) notes that the hidden curriculum is not only part of the system of social control, 'but also the grounds on which ideological and political struggles [are] fought and hence a potential site of interventions for change'. Identification of the exact areas for action and change is difficult, however, since these may vary according to the social and historical context. Furthermore, as Anyon (1981) has pointed out, the extent to which opportunities for change achieve change will partly depend on the pedagogical strategies used to exploit them. Nevertheless, there are grounds for believing that contradictions within the educational system provide scope for intervention and change, particularly where any actions are undertaken collectively in the context of broader community actions.

Step three: facilitating student understanding

In many ways facilitating student understanding of power structures and the means of contesting them mirrors the steps taken by committed teachers. One implication of this is that what teachers and students are able to achieve together in the context of the classroom may be limited. Instead, as with teachers, students should be encouraged to join the wider political struggle and obtain a fuller 'education' about power, powerlessness, and justice within the social justice movements. This will not only enable students to get a feeling of collectivity and the sense of power that comes from solidarity, but also enable them to begin recognizing the way that power structures operate to oppress a range of groups both within their own community and outside it.

Nevertheless, such activities are unlikely to be effective unless students have developed some awareness of the nature of the power structures in their own lives, have started the process of struggle against any unjust power structures in their own lives, and have begun to appreciate how such power structures may unjustly affect others. As Burns (1981) reminds us, 'education should be a process of leading out – of present realities to something new'. This process also implies, of course, that the strategies used by teachers and the nature of classroom climate must also be open to challenge.

The activities found at the end of this chapter are designed to promote such student awareness. While it may be argued that they tend to emphasize the difficulties of achieving a more equal distribution of power, it must also be said that wresting power from the powerful is not going to occur without a struggle and, furthermore, such a contest needs to be undertaken on a broad front. No doubt the children of British miners and British printworkers, along with the children of Australian Aborigines, are well aware of this. Certainly there is room for investigating the tactics and strategies of groups that have achieved some success, for example the tree-hugging activities of the Chipko women in India, the 'Green Bans' of the Australian Builders Workers' Federation in Sydney in the 1970s, and the redevelopment planning initiatives of the Anti-STOLport campaigners in the Royal Docks, London. However, it is important not be too sanguine about the extent of such victories because, unless and until the power structures that created the problems are challenged and undermined, success on one day often only means the chance to fight the same battle again next week. Rather than praising or emulating their successes, such groups require that we understand their problems, the causes of those problems and that we campaign with them for complete justice.

If peace education is to address the issue of power it must recognize that existing distributions of power and the structures that support them are major obstacles to justice. Our schools, our classrooms, and even our relationships with our students are all, to some extent, governed by current configurations of power. We are doing our students no favours, therefore, if we suggest that achieving justice is merely a matter of will, that individuals only have to know about their power and use it for a peaceful society to be magically created. Indeed, we may in fact be reinforcing the existing structures. Instead, education for peace must adopt a critical perspective and challenge unjust power structures. This approach implies a willingness, a commitment, on the part of both teachers and students to contest injustice. It implies courting controversy and seeking out points where intervention and change occur. It means 'going political', joining the wider struggles and using them to inform the educational process. Such an approach has no expectation that a peaceful society will be easily won, but neither does it believe that peace and justice are impossible goals.

CLASSROOM ACTIVITIES

Status and power in an Australian country town

Purpose

To explore the relationship between status and power in the context of an Australian country town.

Preparation

1 This activity is based in part on data collected by Wild (1974) in his study of Bradstow, a small Australian country town. It explores status groupings and the relative power of those groups in the context of Bradstow. Please note that the role-play is based loosely on Wild's work, but the map in Figure 12 is completely fictitious and not designed to represent any particular Australian town.

2 Each student will need to be provided with copies of Figures 11 and 12, and you will need one copy of each of the role-cares, Table 7 (see pp. 160–2).

3 You may feel it necessary to provide a brief introduction on the nature of status before beginning this activity. This could be done by brainstorming about the sources of status in your community, e.g. education, type of job, location of home, and so on.

4 Prior to investigating status in Bradstow, students need to be told that Wild located six status groups in the town and that they can be ranked. The groups are in order of rank from top to bottom: the gentry, the Grange-ites, the local bosses, the trades people, the workers, and the no-hopers. The following information on each of

the status groups should *not* be provided to students at this stage, but you may find it useful in the debriefing and discussion sessions following the exercises.

The gentry

This group have been established in the Grange area of Bradstow for several generations and although not all of them are very rich, many of them have substantial wealth. The gentry are proud of their pedigree and devoted to what they perceive as a genteel, rural English way of life. They seek to prevent any changes in Bradstow that might threaten their life-style (e.g. industrialization) but, in general, they prefer to remain behind the scenes rather than act as political front-runners.

The Grange-ites

As the name implies, these people live in the Grange area of Bradstow; however they have none of the important ancestral associations with the area that the gentry have. They are a wealthy group. The Grange-ites consist of two major subgroups: business people who wish to legitimatize their recently acquired riches by living in the Grange; and professional people who have retired to the Grange. Both groups often have extensive and influential contacts with people outside the Bradstow area. This group is more active politically, more visible, and often more ostentatious than the gentry, but members will have to wait for several generations to achieve the higher status of the gentry. The Golf Club is the exclusive preserve of the gentry and Grange-ites.

The local bosses

Established in town, these people are active in local politics and–or local business. They may aspire to be Grange-ites and their life-style certainly mimics that of the Grange-ites with their penchant for big houses in their own suburb of Harris Hill and the formation of their own association – the Country Club.

Tradespeople

One of the bigger status groups in Bradstow, these people may have moved up from the workers' status group and may have designs on being in the local bosses group. Most tradespeople were educated locally and they constitute the main support group for many of the sporting clubs in town, particularly the bowls, cricket, rugby league, and soccer clubs. Their homes are smaller and often more old-fashioned than those of the bosses. The tradespeople resent the patronizing attitude that the Grange-ites display towards them.

Workers

This group constitutes nearly half the population of Bradstow. All attended government schools and many left school early. Most workers are wage-earners or former wage-earners. The workers live on the northern–industrial side of town and their homes are modest dwellings with small patches of lawn as gardens. The most popular workers clubs are the rugby league club and the Returned Servicemen's League, but few workers hold any offices in them.

No-hopers

A small group of desperately poor people who rent their dilapidated homes on the northern outskirts of the town. Most of the group have limited education while some are illiterate. When they are employed, they generally hold only semi-skilled or unskilled jobs. Few no-hopers are members of any clubs or organizations. Rather, the males of the group tend to frequent the public bars of a couple of pubs close to their homes. The Bradstow town-dwellers tend to look down on the group, hence their name. In return, the no-hopers have considerable contempt for the other status groups.

Procedure

1 Provide each student with a copy of Table 7, which features eight role-cards, and ask eight volunteers to read the roles. Then discuss the roles and make sure that students comprehend the information on the role-cards.

2 Provide each student with a copy of Figure 11. Students use the information in Table 7 to work in groups of two or three students to complete the table in Figure 11. This will provide them with a summary of the status characteristics of the individuals on the role-cards.

3 Ask students to answer the following questions from their completed tables:
- Into which status groups would you fit the individuals in roles?
- Although you have fairly limited data, can you identify the common life-style of each status group? Pick a number of words to describe the life-style of each group.
- What factors provide the basis of Bradstow's status ranking?
- Do these factors provide the basis of the status ranking in your own community? why–why not?

4 Hear the responses from the groups and debrief carefully. Issues that should be discussed at this stage include:
- The range of status groups in Bradstow, and whether this range is typical of communities generally;
- Whether the status groups that Wild located were appropriate for the women in the role play, e.g. is Mary Conway a member of the workers' status group because her husband can be located there?
- The way that pedigree and Englishness, in addition to wealth, seem to provide the basis of status in an Australian country town, and the extent to which this might be typical of other communities.

5 Organize students in groups of two or three to examine Figure 12, which is a map of the Bradstow area, and complete the following exercises:
- Indicate where you think each of the individuals featured on the role-cards lives. This can be done by looking at the legend at the bottom of Figure 12, and placing the number allocated to each individual where you think that person lives. For example, you will place (1) on the map where you think Mary Conway lives, (2) where you think Lady Legge-Smith lives, and so on.
- List the reasons for your placement of the individual's homes.

6 Hear the responses from the groups and discuss the reasons presented for the placements. A number of quite different responses are possible, but the class should decide on definite placements.

7 Divide the class into six groups. Each group is to represent one of the status groups of Bradstow. The groups can be of roughly the same size or you could make each group's size proportional to their actual size in the town. Thus the workers will constitute the largest sized group (40 per cent of the population), followed by the tradespeople (23 per cent), the Grange-ites (18 per cent), the local bosses (12 per cent), the no-hopers (4 per cent) and the gentry (3 per cent). Explain that an engineering firm is seeking permission to establish a plant to manufacture irrigation sprinklers in the Bradstow area. At this stage it is not clear where such a factory might be sited, but a river frontage is necessary for testing the products.

8 Students discuss the proposed factory with the other members of their status

group. They may use the appropriate role-cards to aid them. Each status group should then consider the following:

- Should the proposed factory be allowed to go ahead? If so, provide a list of at least three reasons supporting the proposal and indicate on your map (Figure 12) where you think the most appropriate site would be. If not, make a list of at least three objections you have to the plant.
- What actions might your group take to follow up on your decision about the factory? In thinking about this, you might consider these questions: What 'tools' you have at your disposal, e.g. do you have local government politicians or officials in your group who could influence the planning–zoning regulations in one way or another? Could you get assistance from powerful individuals and groups located outside the Bradstow area? Whether any of the other Bradstow status groups might support your position on the factory? If you believe this is the case how would you approach those groups?
- How successful do you expect your group to be in having the factory accepted or rejected? Provide reasons for your answer.

9 Allow each group to present its case and follow this with an analysis of its ability to influence the final decision about the factory. The relative power of the various status groups should become obvious at this stage. Discussion on the following points might also be useful:

- Whether some students felt alienated and–or frustrated by the lack of power in their status groups;
- Whether other students were concerned about their ability to wield so much power;
- Whether the majority of people were going to get what they wanted, i.e. whether power automatically lies with the majority;
- Whether status groups would be likely to act consciously and in concert over such an issue;
- What factors other than similar status might encourage people to band together to promote or reject change.

Follow-up

Make a study of an environmental issue in your area. Identify the people who have been campaigning for and against the issue, and consider whether any of the people concerned can be associated with a particular status group. Analyse the outcome of the issue, that is identify the 'winners' and the 'losers' that result from the decision and consider why some people lost and some won.

Source

Adapted from J. Williamson-Fien (1987) 'Power and status in an Australian country town', in J. Fien and P. Wilson (eds *Living in the Australian Environment*, Canberra: Curriculum Development Centre.

Figure 11 Analysing status in Bradstow

Name	Mary Conway	Lady Legge-Smith	Tom Elliott	Joseph Page	Rose Jones	Bill Goff	Mrs Forsythe	Ted Bell
Home location								
Type of home								
Education								
Clubs								
Work								
Clothes								
Car								

Figure 12 Map of Bradstow

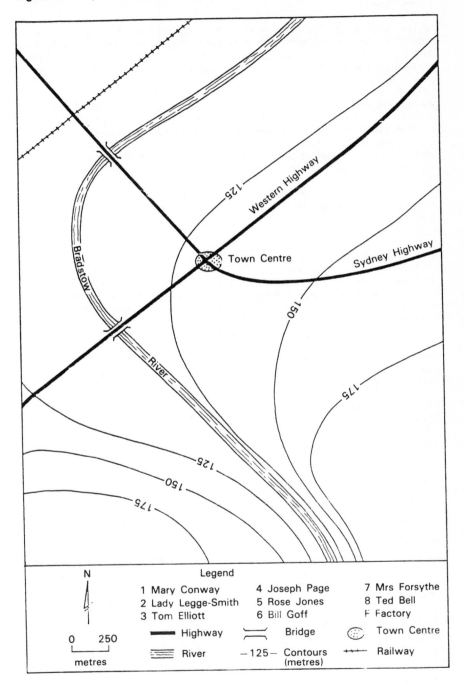

Table 7 Bradstow Role Cards
1 Mary Conway

I'm Mary Conway. My husband is a worker at the cement factory and we live in a small fibro cottage on the north side of the town, close to the industrial area where my husband works. We are hoping to pay off our home before Jack retires next year. We have three daughters, one at home, she works in the milkbar in town, and the other two are married and living in Sydney.

We like Bradstow. It's a nice country town. I don't think we would want to retire anywhere else, but sometimes I think it would be good if there were more jobs here and then our married daughters might be able to live closer to us. Still, I wouldn't want too much more industry close to my place! I would really like to have a nice garden, but I can't afford to buy too many shrubs. I don't bother with clubs – it's difficult for me to get into town. I enjoy watching TV at home.

I don't remember the last time we had a holiday or I bought some new clothes – money really is a problem. Our old VW can only just get us to the RSL or Jack to the Pigeon Racing Club.

2 Lady Legge-Smith

My name is Lady Legge-Smith. My family and that of my husband have been living at the Grange, a high-class part of Bradstow, for three generations. My home is like a little piece of England, eleven acres of gardens and lawns surround my stately, white, colonial home, In my garden, I grow English flowers – foxgloves, primroses, azaleas and camellias. We employ a servant and a gardener.

My husband has retired from our grazing property which is now managed by our elder son. Our other son is at Cambridge University in the UK studying law. I went to finishing school in Switzerland myself.

I belong to the Bradstow Golf Club, the Liberal Party and the Red Cross (Bradstow Branch). My husband and I don't enjoy assisting with the administration of these associations, although we do like to feel that we can influence things when necessary.

Bradstow has always been a charming, rural town with a gentility not found elsewhere and we like to think that we can keep it that way.

3 Tom Elliott

My name is Tom Elliot. I'm the Mayor of Bradstow. This is my second term. I'm also the President of the Chamber of Commerce and the Bradstow Lion's Club. Bradstow is my life and I really want to see it expand. I went to the local schools and was active in local politics from an early age because both my father and my uncle have been mayors of Bradstow.

We already have a small tourist industry here as Bradstow has some great beauty spots and the houses and gardens in the Grange attract visitors. However, perhaps

Table 7 *contd.*

we should also encourage some light industry into the area.

My wife, Mavis, and I live in a pleasant four-bedroomed house with a swimming pool on Harris Hill, our answer to the Grange! Mavis, I'm proud to say, is a full-time mother of our four kids and she does all the shopping, food and clothing, locally.

We enjoy a night at the Country Club, our version of the Golf Club, and at weekends I like to take the family for a drive in my new Volvo.

4 Joseph Page

I'm a self-made man, the name's Joseph Page. I own an imposing two-storey mansion in the Grange where I have lived for five years. I've furnished my home with French provincial furniture and I own my own plane and fly to Sydney three or four days a week. I went to a Sydney state school which I left at fifteen and I've made my money manufacturing plastics. I drive the latest model Mercedes Benz and I employ two domestics and a gardener.

I belong to the exclusive Bradstow Golf Club, where I expect to be elected President next year, the Picnic Race Club and the Aero Club, as I own both a racehorse and a plane. Most Saturday mornings, I like to go into town and pick up a few interesting things to eat at the local delicatessen, for example, tinned pheasant, imported biscuits etc. I feel part of the town that way and I make a point of talking to some of more important local leaders so they know how people in the Grange feel about things.

I came to Bradstow to get away from the noise and crowds of Sydney and to mix with a nice class of people. If people can't find jobs here, they should push off to Sydney. Don't let's spoil this beautiful area with anything more than the local tourist industry.

5 Rose Jones

My name is Rose Jones and my husband and I own three delicatessens and a quality food restaurant in Bradstow. We employ ten people in all, including three people to manage our various businesses. Bradstow could use more people, but I wouldn't want it to become too big and full of fast food joints. We believe in quality of life, like quality food! My husband likes to be well-dressed, dark suits, and I like tailored clothes which I get on my half-yearly trips to Sydney.

We have the biggest house on Harris Hill, five bedrooms, a pool room etc. I've just bought a new car – the latest model Mazda – and my husband has a new Ford, but we also own a number of vans and utilities for the shops.

My husband enjoys a game of golf at the Country Club two days a week, but he is also active in Rotary, Apex, and the Bradstow Swimming Pool Committee.

Table 7 *contd.*

6 Bill Goff

Bill Goff is my name and I've a wife and four kids. We live close to the railway line out on the edge of town. We rent a little timber house and right now we have got me brother and his wife living with us. It's a bit hard on the kids with home work and that.

I don't have much education. In fact, neither me wife or meself can read and write too good. I'd like a steady job, but all I can get is casual labouring at the cement factory. It would help if the local council did more to get jobs for people like me.

I like to go down the RSL and the Railway Hotel but money's low and the old Holden's nearly had it. I dont belong to no organizations and I think the people in town are lot of bloody stickybeaks. They've got piles of money and they all talk posh.

7 Mrs Forsythe

My name is Mrs Forsythe. My husband was a very high-ranking public servant in Sydney and we have just retired to a comfortable home in the Grange. It has just six bedrooms. Bradstow is a delightful place to live: we were attracted by the peace and quiet here. My husband was educated at one of Sydney's better private schools and we met at university where we were both studying. We have one son who is a diplomat with the Department of Foreign Affairs.

We have joined the Golf Club, and local branch of the Liberal Party, the local Anglican church and the Gardening Club, but every month we like to travel down to Sydney, in our Rover, to attend the opera, theatre, or a concert. I can also keep up with Sydney fashions that way and my husband can maintain contact with his former colleagues. We are planning to entertain many of our Sydney friends at home when the weather gets warmer – the Grange is a perfect area for such things. I enjoy working in my garden, although we employ a gardener part-time, and I look after the house work myself.

8 Ted Bell

I'm Ted Bell. I was born in Bradstow and, like my Dad, I became a plumber after leaving school at fifteen. My wife and I live in a medium-size brick veneer home on the eastern side of town. I've got a good lawn growing out the front of the house and we are getting together some pretty modern furniture. We have just put down wall-to-wall carpets in our bedroom and, with my wife's pay as a clerk, we expect to be able to replace our old Ford Falcon next year.

Dad belongs to the Bowls Club and he wants me to join, but right now I'm in Apex and we enjoy a night on the poker machines down the RSL. In winter I like to play a bit of football and, in summer, I'm the captain of the cricket club.

Sometimes I feel I would like to leave Bradstow. It's a bit small and when you do work for those people out at the Grange, they tend to treat you like dirt. Still, if we could get a few more people up here, there would be more work for plumbers and we might get better facilities in the town.

Australian Aborigines and power

Purpose

To alert students to the plight of Australian Aborigines in their struggle to maintain their control over their traditional lands and to encourage students to consider what actions they can take to promote awareness of and justice for Australian Aborigines.

Preparation

Obtain background information on the dispute between Australian Aborigines and mining companies. Jan Robert's (1978) book, *From Massacres to Mining*, is useful. Also Dave Hicks's (1987) minority experience exercise which specifically addresses the situation for Aborigines could be used as an introductory activity. Wren (1982) provides a helpful section on the tactics of the powerful which may be useful for Section 4 below. Make copies of the two cartoons (Figures 13 and 14, pp. 165–6) for each student. Try to ensure that the second cartoon is copied towards the top of a large sheet of paper so that additional frames can be added by students.

Procedure

1 Use Hicks (1987) and Roberts (1978) to introduce students to the conflict in Australia between Aborigines and mining companies.

2 Discuss with students the importance of the land in Aboriginal culture. Ask students to write a paragraph on each of the following:
- How they would feel if land that was important to them was to be used for large-scale mining operations.
- What actions they might encourage their community to take to prevent such mining operations taking place.

3 Give each student a copy of the first cartoon (Figure 13) and organize them into small groups to:
- Identify the sources of power of the mining company.
- Outline the tactics the mining company plan to use to undermine the objections of Aborigines.

4 Hear the responses from the groups and debrief by:
- Questioning students about the significance of the clothes, sex, race, age, etc. of the mining company executives and what this might mean in terms of their ability and willingness to understand the Aboriginal position on land.
- Considering the range of tactics open to the powerful to promote decisions they desire and prevent changes they see as unacceptable.

5 Give students a copy of the second cartoon (Figure 14) and ask them to continue working in their groups to consider the following:
- How is the powerlessness of Aborigines depicted in the first eight frames of the cartoon?
- What strategies do you think Australian Aborigines would have undertaken to develop the solidarity with their cause that is evident in frame 9?
- Draw 4 to 6 additional frames of the cartoon in order to illustrate the likely outcome of this issue. Think about the reactions of the mining companies and further actions that Aborigines and their supporters might take.
- What actions might your group take to support the Aboriginal campaign? The

community actions you suggested earlier may be helpful here.

6 Hear the group responses and discuss the range of outcomes suggested by the groups. Discuss the actions proposed by each group, list these on a chart, and hang the chart in a prominent place so that further ideas can be added to it when students have completed the follow-up activities.

Follow-up

Students could be organized into three groups to undertake research on the following;

1 The extent of the investment of British mining companies in Australia, whether any of these companies mine on Aboriginal land and the extent of Aboriginal concern about such activities.

2 Mining operations in other parts of the world where mining companies are in conflict with native people over mining operations, the nature of the conflict, the anti-mining activities of the native people and the means used by the mining companies to legitimize their activities.

3 The extent and nature of activities undertaken by groups, both native and others, at local, national, and international levels which are concerned about the treatment of native peoples with respect to their land.

The information gathered by the three groups should be shared with the whole class and further ideas for action considered and added to the list. Students should be encouraged to continue their activities in this area.

Figure 13 Company power

Figure 14 Aboriginal power

ABORIGINAL POWER

REFERENCES

Alvarado, M. and Ferguson, B. (1983) 'The curriculum, media studies and discursivity', *Screen* p. 24, 3.

Anyon, J. (1981) 'Social class and school knowledge', *Curriculum Inquiry* p. 11, 1.

Apple, M.W. (1980) 'The other side of the hidden curriculum: correspondence theories and the labour process', *Journal of Education* p. 162, 1.

Burns, R. (1981) 'Can we educate for disarmament in the present world order?', in M. Haavelsrud (ed.) *Approaching Disarmament Education* Guildford: Westbury House in association with the Peace Education Commission of the International Peace Research Association.

Diaz, J. (1980) 'The arms race and the role of education', in M. Haavelsrud (ed.) *Approaching Disarmament Education* Guildford: Westbury House in association with the Peace Education Commission of the International Peace Research Association.

Donaldson, P. and Pollins, H. (1981) *Capitalism*, Melbourne: Nelson.

Ferguson, M. (1982) *The Aquarian Conspiracy*, London: Paladin.

Giroux, H. (1981) *Ideology, Culture and the Process of Schooling*, Lewes: Falmer Press.

Hicks, D.W. (1983) *Studying Peace: The Educational Rationale*, St Martin's College, Lancaster: Centre for Peace Studies.

———— (1987) 'The minority experience', in J. Fien and P. Wilson (eds) *Living in the Australian Environment*, Canberra: Curriculum Development Centre.

Holland, J and Henriot, P. (1980) *Social Analysis: Linking Faith and Justice*, Washington, DC: Center of Concern.

Huckle, J (1986) 'Ten red questions to ask green teachers', *Green Teacher* p. 2.

Hutton, D. (1987) 'What is green politics', in D. Hutton (ed.) *Green Politics in Australia*, North Ryde: Angus & Robertson.

Roberts, J. (1978) *From Massacres to Mining*, London: War on Want/CIMRA.

Sharp, G. (1973) *The Politics of Non-Violent Action*, Boston, Mass: Porter Sargent.

Sharp, R. (1984) 'Varieties of peace education', in R. Sharp (ed.) *Apocalypse No*, Sydney: Pluto Press.

Shor, I. (1980) *Critical Teaching and Everyday Life*, Boston, Mass: South End Press.

Specht, H. (1974) 'Disruptive Tactics', in *Readings in Community Organisation Practice*, Englewood Cliffs, NJ: Prentice-Hall.

Stradling, R. (1984) 'Controversial issues in the classroom', in R. Stradling, M. Noctor, and B. Baines, *Teaching Controversial Issues*, London: Edward Arnold.

Tolstoy, L. (1937) 'A letter to a Hindu', in *The Works of Tolstoy*, Vol. 21, *Recollections and Essays*, London; Oxford University Press.

Tronc, K. (1970) 'Subordinates flex their muscles', *Quest*, May.

Watson, I. (1985) *Environmental Education and Community Action*, Canberra: Canberra and SE Region Environment Centre.

Whitty, G. (1985) *Sociology and School Knowledge*, London: Methuen.

Wild, R. (1974) *Bradstow*, Sydney: Angus & Robertson.

Wren, B. (1986) *Education for Justice*, London: SCM Press.

10

Gender

Stefanie Duczek

Students should study issues to do with discrimination based on gender. They should understand the historical background to this and the ways in which sexism operates to the advantage of men and the disadvantage of women.

(Table 2, p. 14)

INTRODUCTION

Is a focus on gender important and legitimate in the field of peace education? I believe it is because the patterns of domination by the male of the human species over the female, and myriad forms in which male oppression manifests in women's personal and professional lives, denote a fundamental state of unpeacefulness in human relationships and organizations that should be neither overlooked nor underestimated by educators concerned with issues of peace.

The past two decades have seen the re-emergence of a women's movement of international dimensions and links which has focused attention on the injustices suffered by women from individual men as well as from a male-dominated world system, often referred to as patriarchy. A mid-term statement issued during the United Nations Decade for Women (1976–85) encapsulates the injustices that women are experiencing world wide:

> Women make up half the population of the world, perform two thirds of all the world's work, receive one tenth of the world's wages and own one hundredth of the world's resources.

Ruth Leger Sivard in her report *Women . . . A World Survey* (1985) comes to the conclusion that throughout the world women are disproportionately represented among the poor, the illiterate, the unemployed and the underemployed and remain a very small minority at the centres of political power. Her investigations showed that whether in the economy, education, health, or government, there is no major field of activity and no country in which women have attained equality with men.

When we begin to allow ourselves to comprehend what these global statements entail in terms of personal suffering, broken dreams, thwarted talents, and unrealized potential, then the enormity of the damage to the whole of the human species becomes visible. The oppression of women by men in its personal and institutional manifestations is a global factor that is underlying all other forms of oppression, such as those based on race, class, nationality, colour, or religion.

I had the pleasure to attend the end of the Women's Decade Conference held in Nairobi, Kenya, in July 1985. Thirteen thousand women attended this event, more than twice the expected number, which in itself shows the growing awareness and awakening of women on a global scale. I was very moved when talking to some of the rural Kenyan women who had defied tradition and walked hundreds of miles to the country's capital because they were determined that nothing and no one would keep them from attending this international women's gathering. Lasting memories that remained with me since then are the sense of courage, humour, and sharing that permeated the event, as well as an awareness about the diversity of women's concerns that are none the less interlinked at many levels. So called 'women's issues' are fundamentally human issues the creative solution of which affects humanity as a whole. Leger Sivard (1985) introduces a note of hope into her report when she writes:

> Yet the 'silent revolution' is slowly gaining in strength. Women are more educated, more active economically, more successful politically than they were a few decades ago. There is an undercurrent of confidence and co-operation among them that is new to the world and has great promise.

GENDER SOCIALIZATION AND THE PATRIARCHY

Ann Oakley (1972) defines 'sex' as a biological term whereby a person's identity as male or female can usually be judged through reference to biological evidence. 'Gender', however, is a psychological and cultural term. It refers to learned characteristics that constitute supposedly feminine and masculine behaviour patterns which may vary over space and time. She argues that every society uses biological sex as a criterion for the ascription of gender roles, but beyond that simple starting-point, no two cultures would agree completely on what distinguishes one gender from the other.

The learning of what is socially accepted gender behaviour for girls and boys, men and women, occurs within an overall system of patriarchy. Patriarchy – the rule and supremacy of the fathers – is at its root a system

169

of male domination and male power, that is controlling women through economic dependence and the threat and use of violence, and which assigns women to the private sphere of home and family, and directs males to the public spheres of work and decision-making. And if we take a look at the institutions that surround us, the government, industry, the business and financial sector, the judiciary, the police force, the universities, the media and churches, we can perceive this rule of the fathers: everywhere the key decision-making positions are largely occupied by men. Few women have found their way into high positions of the patriarchal power structures and those who have will often exhibit male gender behaviour of authoritarianism and dominance. At this time in history, military men have access to a nuclear arsenal which once unleashed in fear, anger, or stupidity can extinguish all life on the planet. Hence, patriarchal rule has made the survival of the human race an open question.

Patriarchal values and attitudes not only are embedded within our institutions, but also permeate our language (Spender 1980) and our very ways of thinking; they provide the male perspectives from which history has been written and rewritten, making the struggles, sufferings, and contributions of women largely invisible (Rowbotham 1973). Patriarchy infiltrates the very way we make sense of our world, how we view reality, how we organize our relationships with others and how we relate to ourselves as men and women; thus it informs not only our outer structure but also our mind structures. The predominant form of structuring and organizing is that of the hierarchy and within a hierarchical system of thinking and organizing the notion of power is always related to having power *over* something or somebody; it is the power of domination, of authoritarianism backed by the implicit or explicit threat of violence and punishment.

The learning of specific gender roles in our society is a complex and intricate process that starts from the very day we are born. Through the rewards and punishments we receive for certain types of behaviour, the toys, books, and stories that are available to us, the images we see in the media, the role models that are around for us to imitate, we receive a barrage of messages of what is supposedly appropriate behaviour for us as boys and girls. Boys are socialized towards aggressiveness, dominance, independence, and competitiveness, girls towards submission and dependence. Competitiveness in girls is tolerated and encouraged as long as it is geared towards finding and holding a male. Gender roles in our patriarchal society are deeply sexist; they are, in fact, the inevitable outcome of a sexist belief structure that provides the motor and the justifications for the continuing 'rule of the fathers'.

At its most basic level sexism is a belief system based on the assumption that the male of the human species is biologically and intellectually superior to the female. This mistaken belief is embedded in male behaviour patterns and attitudes often termed male chauvinism, and it finds expression in many forms from subtle gestures and use of language to overt harassment and assault on women. Encountering sexism in its attitudinal form is irritating and annoying for women; at its worst it can be life threatening. Sexism is also embedded within the forms and structures of patriarchal institutions, from the family to multinational corporations. Attitudinal and institutional sexism are the corner-stone of a patriarchal society and we need to focus attention on both, if we are concerned about creating a more equal and peaceful society.

Reardon (1985) suggests that sexism is damaging to all human beings as it reduces the significance of non-gender criteria in the self-development and definition of both men and women. She further suggests that the socialization of boys in a patriarchal society is more rigid than for girls, that they are subject to more pressure to reject the human attributes that are traditionally associated with the other sex, and that their roles and behaviour repertoires are less flexible. She argues that the experienced frustrations on account of the rigidity in the male gender role is an aspect that might lead to the greater aggressiveness in men and boys.

It is the case that over the last decades women have begun to examine, question, and transcend what has been traditionally regarded as appropriate female gender behaviour. This process of personal growth and growing political awareness has led to a wealth of publications, research, and strategies for action. A comparable re-examination and questioning of the male gender role by men has not, as yet, taken place. I suggest that this is necessary if, as a human species, we are to transcend the limiting gender roles that the patriarchy imposes on us.

INSIGHTS FROM PSYCHOLOGY

Patriarchy is a system of dualisms: mind over body, thinking over feeling, heaven over earth, spirit over flesh – dualisms in which women are identified with the negative side, argues Zanotti (in Reardon 1985). This conceptual mode of dualistic thinking, where in order to advance we have to strive towards the one and deny the other, has had a powerful hold over us being strongly supported by the Judaeo-Christian tradition and the development of so called rational, objective, scientific thought. This thinking pattern, which divides the head from the heart, reason from emotion, has led to the development of a mentality that has created the most devastating weapon systems in human history and the destruction of the planet on an unprecedented scale. Psychologists have argued (Keen 1985) that this dualistic conceptual mode is deeply damaging our development towards mature, loving human beings, that both aspects of the imagined dualities belong to us and that the subjugation or denial of one in favour of the other does not make the former disappear; we merely relegate it to our subconscious where it becomes that which we do not want to look at. It then becomes our 'shadow side', that part of our psyche that we fear. Normal adult character organization is a form of inter-psychic warfare between the reigning ego and the guerrilla forces of the repressed anti-ego, says Keen (1985), where the dark and forbidden qualities are disowned and projected on to an enemy, the opposite sex, or nature. Hence, it seems that the creation of scapegoats, of an outside enemy whom we can imbue with all that we fear and dislike in ourselves has its root in our distorted psychic development that occurs within an overall system that supports, and is in turn dependent upon, dualities of thinking.

Schierse Leonard (1982), a Jungian analyst, explores the damage that is done to women's psychological development under patriarchy, she refers to this as 'the father–daughter wound' that women experience not only from their actual fathers but also from the cultural fathers of society. Jungian psychology has suggested that all human beings have male and female aspects to their psyche and that a development of both, and their integration, is essential for our psychological well-being. If the psychological development of women is hindered under patriarchy, through a distorted relationship to the male aspects of their psyche, it follows that the psychological development of men too is damaged and distorted through their inability to relate to the female aspects of their psyche. We are all 'wounded' by a system that insists on dualities.

How can an inner healing take place? Macy (1982) warns us that it is not through a reversal of the dualities, of valuing emotion over reason, intuition over intellect, women over men, that it is not through a return to a matriarchy. She suggest that the challenge of our time lies in the breaking through dualistic mind structures, and in the integration and honouring of the male and female aspects within ourselves. How might this be done? Miller (1983), a psychoanalyst who has written about the damaging effects of authoritarian child-rearing practices which she believes are the 'roots of violence' within our society, argues that we need to remember the hurts that have been done to us as children, re-experience the pain and anger that we were not allowed as children to express towards adults, and that the re-experienced and acknowledged feelings of rage can make room for deeply felt sorrow and grief that can then lead to forgiveness, thus breaking the vicious circle of repetition whereby we pass on our own hurts to our children.

What does this mean for us as men and women, who are socialized in a sexist and authoritarian culture, and where we are valued differently because of our sex? It might mean that, against all the odds, we have to come together, listen carefully to each other with a non-judgemental mind, sharing our hurts and emotions openly without the defence mechanism of blaming the other, so that through our common grief we might be able to become allies in the struggle towards overcoming patriarchy, a struggle that cannot and should not be fought by women alone.

Reardon (1985) suggests that an emphasis on the need for personal and relational change is important as, in her view, authentic transformation of the global order is as much a matter of emotional maturity as of structural change, and that structural changes within the public order without significant inner psychic changes in human beings will be ineffective.

MILITARISM

Militarism is a belief system which is based on the assumption that human beings are by nature violent, aggressive, and competitive and that the social order needs to be maintained by force. Societies with militaristic tendencies socialize their young into accepting conflict and its 'solution' by force and repression as the 'natural' order of things. In short, might is right (Reardon 1985), and the military itself, a hierarchical, authoritarian, and sexist organization can be regarded as the distilled embodiment of patriarchy.

Militaristic values of what 'real' men should be like pervade our culture. Supposedly 'real' men are aggressive, repress emotions, and have no fears, or if they have fears and doubts, they certainly do not admit to them as this would be regarded as feminine and weak. Enloe (1983) argues that militarism plays a special role in the ideological structure of patriarchy because the notion of 'combat' plays such a central role in the construction of concepts of 'manhood' and in justifications of the superiority of maleness in the social order. The reality of being a soldier of the state means, of course, to be subservient, obedient, and almost totally dependent on the authority structures. However, this mundane reality is hidden behind a potent myth: to be a soldier means possibly to experience 'combat' and in this lies the ultimate test of a man's masculinity.

Militarism despises any characteristic in men that might be termed feminine, such as gentleness, sensitivity, or caring; it is a deeply misogynistic belief system. Military training of soldiers in the US Marine Corps, as reported by those who have come back from Vietnam to tell their tales, embodies a constant assault on the soldiers' sexuality by using misogynistic terms of abuse. Gilder (in Daly 1979) states:

From the moment one arrives, the drill instructors begin a torrent of misogynistic and anti-individualist abuse. The good things are manly and collective; the despicable are feminine and individual. Virtually every sentence, every description, every lesson embodies this sexual duality, and the female anatomy provides a rich field of metaphor for every degradation. When you want to create a solitary group of male killers, that is what you do, you kill the women in them. That is the lesson of the Marines. And it works.

The more militaristic a society the more sexist it tends to be, where the 'macho' image of the male is valued as the highest ideal of manhood. This of course stands in stark contrast to the military myth of the noble soldier who trains and goes to fight to protect women and children against an evil enemy. Enloe (1983) suggests that there are aspects of the military institution and ideology which greatly increase the pressure on militarized men to 'perform' sexually in order to conform to the standards of 'masculinity'. Having constantly to prove that one is a 'man' and not squeamish in the face of violence may well lead to rape and can make it especially hard to say 'no' to gang rape. The connection between militarism and aggressive male sexuality, that is the development of a rape-mentality, is exemplified by the slogan 'This is my rifle, this is my gun, one is for killing, one is for fun', a chant that is used in Marine Corps training. Brownmiller (1975) gives numerous examples where the mass-rape of enemy women has been consciously employed as a military strategy of retaliation in order to weaken the enemy's resolve to fight. Although it is women that suffer, these attacks are deemed to get at the men, via the desecration of their 'property'.

A militarized society not only increases sexual abuse and harassment of women, but also affects them economically. The military commands vast financial resources, and in times of economic recession, it is the social rather than the military expenditure of the state that tends to be cut. Women are especially vulnerable to welfare cuts, and some might even enlist in the military services in order to compensate for the loss of jobs and economic security resulting from spiralling military spending. This, Enloe (1983) argues, may help to explain why, by 1981, 42 per cent of all enlisted women in the US Army were black women, who are doubly vulnerable because of their sex and colour. Increased military spending at the expense of social expenditure contributes significantly to what is called the feminization of poverty.

As peace educators then, we need to be aware of the connections between militarism and sexism and how militaristic values about 'masculinity' can influence the behaviour patterns of boys to the detriment of girls who are on the receiving end of 'macho' behaviour. And we need to be aware of the social and economic costs of militarized societies, which are largely borne by women who are totally excluded from the decision-making processes concerning the military.

QUESTIONS FOR EDUCATORS

If peace education is to be more than a focus on specific content areas, that is if it is to inform also how we as teachers interact with pupils and how pupils interact with each other, then it is obvious that sexist attitudes, language, and behaviour patterns exhibited either by teachers or by pupils are dysfunctional to a peaceful classroom.

Having ourselves been socialized within a patriarchal and sexist culture, it is of vital importance that we as educators become aware of and sensitive to our own sexist assumptions and behaviour patterns in the classroom. I know of teachers who actively enlist the help of their students in doing so, whereby students measure the time spent by the teacher engaging with boys or girls, note sexist language used by the teacher or by fellow students, and investigate written materials for sexist bias. Such approaches of awareness raising in co-operation with students seem to me more peaceful and in the long term possibly more effective than authoritarian approaches by teachers' forbidding the use of sexist language or sexist behaviour in the classroom.

A concern for the transformation of sexist attitudes, discriminatory behaviour patterns, and institutional practices is of course not only confined to women; many men and male educators have become concerned with these areas. It can be said, however, that the initial impetus and energy that have led to sexism and sex discrimination becoming visible issues have origniated from the efforts, struggles, and campaigns of the women's movement throughout the past two decades. These struggles have been admirably described and analysed by Coote and Campbell (1987). The setting up of anti-sexist working parties within schools has often been preceded by a women's group of teachers within those schools. These efforts by women teachers to put sexism on the agenda has, at times, exacerbated sexist behaviour in their male colleagues. A friend of mine related her experience of setting up such a women's group in her school which in turn led to the most blatant sexist behaviour by some of her male colleagues who would gather outside the windows, making faces and silly noises in order to inter- rupt the meeting. One can only speculate on the positive advances that could have been made, if those male teachers had the courage to form a men's group and began to explore openly their own sexist socialization patterns and the fears that arise when confronting these.

I have argued that the oppression of women under patriarchy is a global factor that affects all areas of our lives. It follows that every issue of peace and conflict that we may chose to study will have a gender perspective to it if we are prepared to look for it and to search for the relevant questions to ask. David Hicks outlined in Chapter 1 five broad problems of peace and five corresponding values underlying peace. Below I have sketched out some of the questions we might ask if we take a gender perspective on each of these problems and values.

Violence and war – non-violence

May we investigate the 'private' violence that is perpetrated against women and children in the home, such as wife-battering and child abuse? What about the violence of rape and incest (the latter being in nearly all reported cases a form of father–daughter rape)? May we include sexual harassment as a specific form of male violence against women? What about pornography with its objectification of women as pleasure objects and that has produced in its most extreme and sickening form the notorious snuff movies where female actors are actually murdered on screen? What are the effects of warfare on women? United Nations statistics show that more than 80 per cent of refugees in the world are women and children. What about the rape of enemy women as a distinct military strategy? And, on a more positive note, what are the non-violent movements and strategies that have been instigated and led by women, and what were the obstacles they had to face?

Inequality – economic welfare

What are the inequalities that women suffer in their often dual roles as wage-earners and carers for the family? What are the mechanisms and structures that hinder women gaining access to skilled and professional work? What about the growing 'feminization' of poverty? Is it true, as Glendinning and Millar (1987) argue, that poverty is not gender-neutral and that the causes for this lie in the persistent division of labour that marginalizes women's involvement in the labour market?

Injustice – social justice

What are the specific injustices that women suffer because they are women? What are the limitations on the movement of girls and women because of the threat of male violence on the streets? What injustices have women faced under the patriarchal legal system? Are there instances where men and women have been treated differently for similar offences? What are the injustices which women suffer through their portrayal in a sexist media?

Environmental damage – ecological balance

To what extent is growing environment damage a result of patriarchal values and attitudes operating in industry and business whereby nature and the planet are seen as dead matter to be dominated and exploited for profit? What are the similarities and links between the treatment of the planet and the treatment of women under patriarchy? To what extent can ecological values of care and concern for the environment be identified as female values as Reardon (1985) has argued?

Alienation – participation

What is the damage done to our development of self in a patriarchy which is based on authoritarian and dualistic modes of organizing and perception? How does this alienation from self manifest itself psychologically in men and women? What are the mechanisms and structures within our social, political, and economic arenas that hinder and discourage women's participation? What strategies and policies need to be developed to enable and support women's participation? Would an equal participation and sharing of women and men in the private as well as in the public sector lead to the eventual transformation of patriarchy, that is a transformation not only of our outer but also of our mind structures?

I presume that for many of us, the above questions are not only uncomfortable but also painful to consider. I am not suggesting that in their sketched-out form above they are easily transferable to the classroom. What I am arguing for, however, is that we as educators concerned with peace should begin to explore these questions and related ones within ourselves and with the supportive help of others. Disconcerting and controversial though these questions may be, they all point to aspects of our deeply unpeaceful patriarchal society, a society that is divided into winners and losers and where women are disproportionately represented amongst the latter.

As teachers concerned with peace and gender issues in schools it is important that we establish a support network of colleagues within our school, possibly in the form of a working group, where we can share our experiences, discuss and identify areas of special concern, and develop strategies for action. Advice and resources are available from the Equal Opportunities Commission in Manchester, LEA Advisory Services, and from teachers' unions.

As gender is an issue that pervades the whole school, the hidden as well as the open curriculum, school organizations as well as teacher and pupil attitudes, there are many starting-points. Many schools have begun to re-evaluate their resources and reading materials eliminating those with sexist bias. Others have formed departmental working groups investigating sexism in the subject syllabus, course books, and examination papers. Does, for example, the history we teach reflect and incorporate the experiences of women in history? Are we aware of the achievements and contributions of women to the sciences? On examining mathematics textbooks, are the exercises and examples given of interest mostly to boys? How is geography presented? Are we aware of the adverse effects of aid programmes on women in Third World countries who produce, store, and prepare most of their families' food supplies? How many of the texts studied in English are actually written by women? All these are basic questions but we need a close examination of 'what is' as a starting-point from which to move towards change.

It is important to investigate not only what we teach but also how we teach it, that is we need to be aware of our relationship to pupils in the classroom. Concerning gender awareness, one might begin by asking some of the following questions. Do I relate differently to girls and boys in the classroom, and if so why? Do I tolerate behaviour from boys that I would not tolerate from girls? How much of class time is taken up by responding to boys or girls? What kind of classroom organization would facilitate all pupils participating, for example pair work or small group work? What language do I use in the classroom? Do I use the terms 'man', 'mankind', or 'he' generically? Do I praise girls more for appearance and neatness rather than for competence? Do I punish boys by making them sit at a girls' table or vice versa? Do classroom displays and posters show images of women and if so in what kinds of roles are they portrayed? How do I react to sexist comments from pupils or colleagues? Again, these are basic questions which can help us explore our assumptions and attitudes regarding gender issues in the classroom.

On another level, we might investigate the leisure spaces and recreational facilities in the school. Do girls have equal access to these spaces and facilities or are they largely occupied by boys? Some schools have established 'girls only' rooms or areas in order to redress the balance. An area of growing concern in schools is that of verbal and physical sexual harassment and abuse of girls and women teachers. Pat Mahony (1987), who has done extensive research into gender and education, thought at one time that girls lacked equal opportunities mainly because they were marginalized from classroom talk, physical space, high-status jobs, and from large parts of the male-orientated curriculum. The solutions, though not easy, she thought at least straightforward, including the production of non-sexist teaching material and the development of strategies to distribute class time fairly. She now suggests from her research that the real problem is sexual harassment and violence experienced by girls and women teachers, to which schools responded inadequately. This then poses a dilemma for teachers concerned with gender issues; on the one hand verbal abuse and sexual harassment of girls by boys are issues for peace education and should be explored openly, on the other hand, such exploration can take place successfully only in a classroom where basic trust and co-operation between pupils and their teacher have already been established. It might be that schools need to develop clear and unambiguous policies on sexist behaviour that will give teachers support and a framework in which to act. Male teachers will need to explore their own relationship to the masculinity models provided by patriarchal society and examine how they themselves may represent other models of maleness to students.

In an odd sense, the recognition of male violence in schools as a problem is a positive step. I do not believe that it is a new problem, as male violence towards women is so much a part of patriarchal society. Its very recognition as being unacceptable and in need of change is a sign of movement, even though as educators we are struggling with the questions of how to respond and act adequately.

Oakley (1981) suggests that the rise of the second sex demands a new language and new structures of thought, to gestate a completely different society. I believe that a focus on gender and peace and the interrelationship between these issues are helping such a gestation process to come about. As men and women we have to find ways of becoming allies in the struggle of transforming the deeply unpeaceful and limiting system of patriarchy, a transformation which to my mind is essential if we, as a human species, are to have a future into the twenty-first century and beyond.

CLASSROOM ACTIVITIES

Hearing each other

Purpose

To encourage students to reflect upon their own gender socialization, to develop listening and discussion skills, and to explore how both boys and girls can support each other in the struggle against sexism.

Preparation

This activity is for groups of four or five pupils of the same sex. Each group needs to have a set of the questions (see p. 180), with every pupil having pen and paper to note down his or her individual responses, and a large sheet of paper for the groups' combined response, which is later used for feedback to the whole class.

Procedure

The class is divided into single-sex discussion groups of four or five pupils. Question sheets containing questions 1 to 4 are handed out and students should have some time to consider their individual responses. These responses are then shared with the other members of the group. Supportive listening is vital and every group member should have an equal amount of time to share his or her thoughts and feelings. Group discussion follows and the groups' responses noted down for the report back session.

During the report back one might want to alternate between boy and girl groups. Attentive listening is required. It is useful to note the responses to question 4 on a large sheet of paper for further reference. It is this question that is likely to raise feelings and it is important that what the other gender group has to say is heard. After the reporting back pupils reflect in their small single-sex groups on what has been said, especially with reference to question 4.

179

Question 5 is handed out for discussion in the single-sex groups, taking into account what has been said by the other gender group on question 4. Again, a reporting back session is needed, and positive suggestions and strategies emerging from the different groups are noted on a large sheet.

From the outcomes of question 4 and 5, which are displayed on large sheets for reference, pupils might want to come to certain agreements concerning behaviour or actions that can be tried for a week and be reviewed in the next lesson.

Points for consideration

The above activity has been adapted from an exercise used in co-counselling that is concerned with building supportive relationships across the boundaries of sex and gender. This activity cannot be done successfully as a one-off exercise, but *only* as part of a longer-term structured programme on gender issues in the classroom.

Questions

1 What do I really like about being a girl/boy?

2 What experiences make me sad or angry about being a girl/boy?

3 As girls/boys, what difficulties do we have with people from our own gender group?

4 As girls/boys, what do we never want to hear or experience again from people of the opposite gender group?

5 What can we do as girls/boys to understand and support the other gender group and to create better relationships between us?

Will the Army make a man out of you?

Purpose

To investigate the masculine model presented by the Army and to compare this with an actual account of training experienced by an American soldier.

Preparation

Copies of the soldier's statement need to be available for all students, as well as a selection of advertising materials for joining the military, which can be found in Sunday paper magazines.

Procedure

In small groups students brainstorm attributes and characteristics that are traditionally associated with being a soldier.

Students investigate the advertising materials and search for clues in the text and pictures of how the military presents itself to prospective applicants. What is offered: excitement; adventure; training? What qualities in people are they looking for?

180

They then read the training account of the American soldier. Some clarification of terms might be necessary. Many questions arise from this text. How does this kind of training dehumanize soldiers? What methods are used? How do they affect the soldier? After training like this, how might he relate to other men? To women? To people in general? How does this account of training relate to the Army recruitment material students have been looking at earlier? What are the discrepancies? The account is by an American soldier training for the Vietnam war; is training in the British Army likely to be similar or different?

Points for consideration

Information of this kind needs to be handled sensitively and with care. It should be part of a longer-term study into male and female socialization.

A US Army Paratrooper writes:

Basic training encourages woman-hating (as does the whole military experience), but the way it does it is more complex than women sometimes suppose. The purpose of basic training is to dehumanize a male to the point where he will kill on command and obey his superiors automatically. To do that he has to be divorced from his natural instincts which are essentially nonviolent. I have never met anyone (unless he was poisoned by somebody's propaganda) who had a burning urge to go out and kill a total stranger.

So how does the army get you to do this? First you are harassed and brutalized to the point of utter exhaustion. Your individuality is taken away, i.e. same haircuts, same uniforms, only marching in formation. Everyone is punished for one man's 'failure' etc. You never have enough sleep or enough to eat. All the time the drill instructors are hammering via songs and snide remarks that your girl is off with 'Jody'. Jody is the mythical male civilian who is absconding with 'your' girl, who by implication is naturally just waiting to leave with Jody.

After three weeks of this, you're ready to kill anybody. Keep in mind there is no contact with the outside world. The only reality you see is what the drill instructors let you see. I used to lie on my bunk at night and say my name to myself to make sure I existed.

(H. Michalowski (1982) 'The Army will make a "man" out of you', in Pam McAllister, (ed.) *Reweaving the Web of Life*, Philadelphia, PA: New Society Publishers.)

REFERENCES

Brownmiller, S. (1976) *Against Our Will: Men, Women and Rape*, Harmondsworth: Penguin.

Coote, A. and Campbell, B. (1987) *Sweet Freedom*, 2nd edn, Oxford: Blackwell.

Daly, M. (1979) *Gyn–Ecology: The Metaethics of Radical Feminism*, London: Women's Press.

Enloe, C. (1983) *Does Khaki Become You? The Militarisation of Women's Lives*, London: Pluto.

Glendinning, C. and Millar, J. (eds) (1987) *Women and Poverty in Britain*, Brighton: Wheatsheaf Books.

Keen, S. (1985) *The Passionate Life: Stages of Loving*, London: Gateway Books.

Leger Sivard, R. (1985) *Women . . . A World Survey*, Washington, DC: World Priorities.

Macy, J. (1982) *Women and Power*, lecture given in London, no printed source available.

Mahony, P. (1987) *Times Educational Supplement*, 23 October.

Miller, A. (1983) *For Your Own Good: Hidden Cruelty in Childrearing and the Roots of Violence*, London: Virago.

Oakley, A. (1972) *Sex, Gender and Society*, London: Temple Smith.

—— (1981) *Subject Women*, London: Fontana.

Reardon, B. (1985) *Sexism and the War System*, New York: Teachers College Press.

Rowbotham, S. (1973) *Woman's Consciousness, Man's World*, London: Penguin.

Schierse Leonard, L. (1982) *The Wounded Women: Healing the Father–Daughter Relationship*, Boston, Mass. and London: Shambhala.

Spender, D. (1980) *Man Made Language*, London: Routledge & Kegan Paul.

11

Race

June Henfrey

Students should study issues to do with discrimination based on race. They should understand the historical background to this and the ways in which racism operates to the advantage of white people and to the disadvantage of black.

(Table 2, page 14)

RACE AND SOCIAL CONFLICT

Many modern societies are racially and culturally complex, consisting of larger or smaller aggregations of communities of ultimately diverse origins within a single political and socio-economic structure. Sociologists, and others with an interest in studying human society, have been fascinated by this diversity and at pains to analyse and explain it, all the more so since it rarely presents itself as being unproblematic. On the contrary, the tendency has been to ascribe to this diversity a major role in the creation and the reproduction of social conflict.

It has sometimes been tempting to see this conflict as inherent in racial and cultural difference itself. The nineteenth century developed elaborate notions of natural and hierarchical distinctions, in terms of ability and worth, between the various human phenotypes. Modern science has discredited such theories but remnants of them remain active, more especially at the popular level of inter-group relations and even in the mainstream ideologies of some political systems. The apartheid regime of South Africa comes to mind as a prime example of the latter case. However, while prejudice, bred of ignorance, lack of familiarity, and fear, plainly exists, it has been the task of sociological method and analysis to probe behind the surface manifestations of mere bigotry to uncover the deeper structures which underpin their persistence.

One body of sociological theory has defined racially diverse societies as plural. It suggests that such societies consist of a number of racially different segments, each complete in itself, in terms of language, religion, and customs and internal social structure, meeting other segments only for the purpose of conducting business and commercial relations. Such societies are held together by some external force. In the original conception (Furnivall 1948), this external force was the colonial power, and when it was weakened or removed, competition and conflict between various segments ensued. What this theory does not explain is why there should necessarily be conflict in the first place, kept at bay only by the presence of strong, not to say authoritarian, government.

Other theorists have seen race relations in terms of competition for territory, sometimes geographical and sometimes social. Looking at societies as diverse as Brazil, the USA and USSR, Park (1950) saw this ecological competition as leading to a race relations cycle going through four phases of development: contact, assimilation, competition, and accommodation. It is evident that the optimism which this line of analysis implies failed to be borne out by the historical experience of certain groups, especially black people of African descent in the USA. Their original status in that society as slaves, rather than voluntary immigrants, effectively prevented them from competing on equal terms with other groups and excluded them, up until the very recent past, from the American ideal of a rich and healthy diversity of cultures and ethnicities. These forms of exclusion were all the more effective since it was the very blackness of black people which set them apart. Distinctive physical appearance acted as a badge of low status, providing easy and highly visible cues by which the group's social location could be accurately fixed.

In modern complex societies, social location is also a question of class. All such societies are stratified in socio-economic terms, and the over-representation of black people in the lower strata of many societies has led to wide-ranging discussion and analysis of the interaction of race and class factors. Within these discussions there are a number of distinctive strands. Some see race relations as nothing more than class relations, and it has even been suggested that the term 'race' be abandoned altogether by sociologists, since its continued use only serves to give credence to the discredited notion of biologically different human types (Miles 1982). From this perspective, the existence of racism as a structured system of beliefs and practices, while not denied, is underplayed, with much more emphasis being placed on economic factors.

A second perspective gives far greater weight to ideologies of race and racism (Hall 1978) and stresses the tight interlocking of race and class disadvantage in the lives of black people. It is significant that, in Britain at least, this line of analysis has been principally adopted by commentators who are themselves black, and who might thereby be credited with having certain insights into the black experience as a lived reality. One of the most valuable insights deriving from this perspective has been the recognition of the capacity of ideologies of race to reform and reconstitute themselves to meet changing social and economic conditions. This helps to explain both their potency and their persistence.

Looking at race and class together has enabled and even compelled us to examine not only structures but also processes. This represents a considerable analytical advance since one of the significant features of racial disadvantage is its generational reproduction. Looking at processes also helps us to focus on the ways in which differential access to economic and political power has been acquired and maintained, creating entrenched systems of advantage and disadvantage. Finally, it opens the way for a discussion of racial conflict which can be located with some precision within the material conditions in which it occurs.

This analytical framework does not place great stress on factors such as linguistic or religious differences. It acknowledges that they exist and that they have some significance. Undue concentration on them, however, deflects attention from the real issues which are those of economic power and political control. It is not meaningful to describe a privileged élite, however small and even when culturally distinctive, in terms of its minority ethnic status. Significantly this terminology is almost exclusively reserved for relatively powerless social groups.

Race relations occupy an important place in social interactions from which they cannot be abstracted. Attempts to do so falsify social reality and historical fact. The specific experience of racial disadvantage is as undeniable as the broader socio-economic inequalities with which it overlaps.

RACE RELATIONS IN THE GLOBAL CONTEXT

The current global situation with respect to black and white people is a consequence of the last 400 years of world history, the single most important fact of which has been European domination of the world. The outward thrust of European development, beginning in the sixteenth century, brought the white-skinned peoples of Europe into contact with other human groups, all of whom could be distinguished phenotypically from Europeans by means of their skin colour. The technical advantages which Europe possessed led to the overthrow of local systems and to the imposition of colonial rule involving structures of inequality and patterns of dominance. At their crudest these entailed slavery and forced labour, backed up by mechanisms of control, both military and political.

It is important to see these processes in the context of the emergence of capitalism as a world economic system. This phenomenon coincided with and was fuelled by the colonial expansion which resulted in a significant European presence in virtually every corner of the globe. The needs of developing capitalist economies – for capital accumulation, for raw materials, for

185

markets and, above all, for labour – were fully met only by Europe's ability to mobilize and deploy resources not only from within its own continental space and populations but also on a world-wide basis. The consequences were traumatic and, at times, disastrous for many non-European peoples and systems.

The incorporation of most of the rest of the world into the European empires was accomplished in a number of stages from simple trading contact to total control. Off-shore island and coastal toe-holds, precariously held at first, became the vantage points from which entire continents were exploited. This was sometimes achieved by the introduction of European populations as happened in the Americas, Australasia, and, later on, in parts of Africa. Where this occurred the effect on local populations was immediate and destined to be long term, involving both geographical displacement and severe dislocation, or even destruction, of socio-economic systems. Here too questions of 'race relations' presented themselves as the conflicts resulting from new forms of economic competition took on a racial dimension. The direct legacy of these early 'race' issues are still evident in countries like Australia and New Zealand and, most notoriously, in South Africa.

The area of economic and social affairs in which race featured with greatest prominence was that of labour relations. The labour requirements of the new economic mode were enormous. Moreover, because of the generally alienating nature of the work and the conditions under which it was performed, it soon became necessary to coerce that labour. To begin with, this was accomplished in a way that did not discriminate between low-status Europeans and persons of other racial groups – indentured labour in the Americas was, in the first instance, white – but the sheer pressure of demand changed this in a manner which was to be crucial in its consequences.

The nature of the change and the developments that ensued from it is most graphically exemplified in the enslavement and trans-shipment of millions of Africans. It is worth remembering, however, that there was forced labour of various kinds and of a wide range of populations, throughout the European empires, and at all stages of imperialist expansion. This allowed for almost total separation of Europeans from others within colonial labour markets. This state of affairs has tended to persist in post-colonial times and is still visibly operative in the contemporary, neo-imperialist world of the multi-nationals.

Broadly speaking, the pattern which emerged was one of managerial, supervisory, and administrative work for Europeans and of back-breaking, physical labour for others. Lower-status whites were incorporated into the higher-status group as racial lines of demarcation hardened and as it was increasingly perceived as necessary to expand and consolidate European settler communities. Thus race and colour came to denote social and economic status with blackness and other indicators of African descent becoming the badge of slavery. These primarily economic arrangements were held in place by a system of ideas and beliefs which were racist in the extreme. In particular, the relative ease with which it was possible to enslave and retain in servitude so many millions of Africans was seen as proof of their inferiority and of Europeans' right to dominate.

The ideologies which developed to underpin and sustain slavery were transferred to other contexts. Kiernan (1972) notes this with reference to British rule in India, and certainly the notion of African inferiority was deployed to good effect in the unceremonious annexation of the African continent in the early years of this century. Furthermore, these belief systems have persisted with some force into our own time and have been mobilized to thwart the forms of resistance which have everywhere and increasingly evolved to fight European domination.

These forms of resistance have a long and distinguished history, and range from the maroon movements and slave rebellions of plantation America, through the anti-colonial movement to the more recent wars of national liberation. One constant ideological thread which has run through all these instances of confrontation has been a white presumption of privilege and a corresponding black sense of injustice.

It might be argued that in terms of the global politics of race, we have reached a stage when the old colonial order has formally passed and when many of the more overt forms of racial oppression have been dismantled. The conscience of the world, it could be said, has been awakened to inequalities of racism. However, the history of black struggle demonstrates quite clearly the danger of relying on any sense of moral imperative in these matters. The political independence of much of the previously colonized world barely masks its continued economic dependence. It is neither accidental nor wholly ecological that most of the world's rich and comfortable are white and of the west, while nearly all the hungry are black and of Afro-Asian origin. The lines of economic privilege can still be racially traced.

RACISM IN BRITAIN

Britain's role in the imperialist, expansionist phase of European history was a central one. Of all the European empires, Britain's was the largest and the most powerful and the fact of empire indelibly marked the conduct of British affairs, not only abroad, but also within Britain itself. The empire had to be militarily defended and politically administered and this meant equipping ordinary Britons with the skills and, more importantly, the attitudes appropriate to these functions. At home, the ideology of empire was an essential element in maintaining national pride and minimizing the importance and extent of social and economic divisions. Domestic tensions were also eased by the export of unwanted or surplus populations to overseas territories where, in time, they too, miraculously cleansed and readmitted into

Britishness, could wave and defend the flag.

British attitudes to race were formed in the crucible of empire and while most imperial subjects remained scattered around the globe, imperial connections inevitably led to the arrival and settlement of some black people in Britain. The attitudes and procedures to which they were subjected in the colonies were reproduced in Britain itself, as is shown by the histories of long-settled black communities in places like Cardiff, Liverpool, and South Shields. The fact that such histories have been largely hidden and are only now being unearthed, itself bears testimony to a form of racism which persists in believing that black residence in Britain is a recent, post-war phenomenon, and that the disadvantages which black people suffer can be explained away by reference to factors such as newness and cultural or linguistic differences.

The evidence is otherwise. What is significant is not that black communities when new might encounter some of the same difficulties as other recent arrivals, but that even when long-established their experience of disadvantage is worse. Black people in Liverpool in the middle years of the nineteenth century are described as 'keeping together for fear of slights'. There is also some discussion of the difficulties they experience in finding work, despite their willingness to take any available job (Mayhew and Dickens as quoted in Lorimer 1978). In 1987 levels of unemployment in work-hungry Liverpool are still significantly higher for black people than for white, and the city council, the area's largest employer, still has a work-force less than 1 per cent of which is black although the city's black population is about 8 per cent. This is a scenario which the usual explanations do not fit and which needs to be seen as the product of deeply ingrained and well-established patterns of discrimination (Ben-Tovim 1980).

The discussion of race relations in Britain has often been weakened by a failure to include this particular strand of the historical perspective. While most commentator and strategists have been alive to the nature of Britain's long-standing links with black people abroad, few have satisfactorily explored the implications of the equally venerable domestic racism. This has had serious consequences most notably in allowing space in which both the white establishment and some black groups have engaged in playing the 'ethnic' game, a device which by focusing on language, custom, religion, and other 'cultural' factors, serves to obscure the true nature of racism.

Nevertheless, the most recent wave of black settlement has had a number of important consequences. It has triggered a crisis in domestic race relations which, in retrospect, will prove to have been a turning-point not because racism is any less present but because the resistance to it is stronger and better co-ordinated. The reasons for this are interesting – a certain strength in numbers, and especially in the numbers of young black people born and bred in Britain and having no other national allegiance, and the heightened political awareness which has marked black and anti-racist struggle in the second half of the twentieth century. The recent history of urban Britain has been noteworthy for the saliency which race has acquired in local social relations, and the inner-city disturbances have signalled both the depth of racism and a determined rejection of it.

Meanwhile this domestic crisis in race relations has had significant repercussions in the education system. There is no other area of British social life where the issue of race has been discussed so long and so earnestly. There has been a plethora of well-intentioned initiatives whose success can best be described as no more than partial.

RACE AND EDUCATION

It is usual to consider this issue from two main perspectives. The first is the effect on black children of a system permeated by racist attitudes, criteria, and procedures. If the system is thus defined, the next step is to consider which measures are most likely to effect real change in it. The second perspective focuses upon the need to inform all children about the realities of race and racism in both the global and the local context. It will be evident that in any rational construction and delivery of an anti-racist education strategy these two perspectives will be taken as being interdependent.

Nevertheless this was not the understanding on which the earliest initiatives were based. On the contrary, their starting-point was very often a notion of cultural deficit which characterized black children and their communities as failing to measure up to a number of British cultural norms, principally in terms of linguistic skills. Narrowly focused at first, these initiatives were subsequently broadened to meet the perceived need for the school to reflect the cultural diversity of the local community which it served. Great store was set on the potential of the multi-cultural curriculum to solve the problem of race and education, and as it has increasingly failed to deliver, a measure of disillusionment has set in among practitioners. Black critics (Stone 1981; Dhondy 1974) were among the first to point out that initiatives were missing their target and a conceptual shift occurred from multiculturalism, seen as a liberal soft option, to anti-racist education, defined by its protagonists as having a cutting political edge and as going beyond the high-minded celebration of cultural diversity to tackle the problem of structural and institutionalized racism.

The contention is that anti-racist education strategies redress the previous reluctance of education policy-makers to address racism directly. To do so involves confronting the issue of where power lies, as between black and white communities, and having done so to introduce mechanisms which allow for a more equitable spread of control. As the debate has gathered momentum, it has become more and more fashionable to vilify the multiculturalists and to declare oneself an anti-racist.

We must in all conscience wonder how real the terms of this debate are. It is instructive that the new anti-racist tide has done little to stifle the calls coming from the black community for separate black schools, and it was only ever the most naïve multiculturalists who supposed that their curricular initiatives would achieve very much unless they were set within a political framework which recognized the need to fight racism. At the same time it would be idle to pretend that the content of the school curriculum, or its mode of delivery is neutral especially with regard to the black experience. In addition, the categories and forms of knowledge with which we currently operate are far from being value-free, and the values on which they have traditionally been based are more likely than not to distort or misrepresent the lived experience of certain, unempowered groups.

The task for education is to show how racial inequality has been constructed, how it continues to be exemplified, and to point to ways in which equality might be achieved. At the level of the classroom this will require the exploration of specific, sometimes new or unusual, areas of knowledge, employing methods which encourage discovery and leave room for reflection and assessment. Looking at issues of race within the framework of peace education allows for reiteration of the point that racism is unjust and that, without justice, there is no peace.

An anti-racist school is one in which it is recognized that race is not a marginal or peripheral issue but one which is central to young people's understanding of their society and of the modern world. The gross racial assumptions of the imperial age may have disappeared, but they have been replaced by a 'new' racism which sees black people as alien and undesirable if not straightforwardly inferior. This attitude is an important sub-text in many aspects of contemporary British life. It has to be the function of anti-racist education to address the implications of this belief system.

At the level of school organization, this requires the development of structures which challenge the expression of racism. It has been too easy in schools which are totally or nearly all-white to collude surreptitiously with racism, simply because facing up to it is uncomfortable. Schools with black pupils must ask themselves the simple question: 'Is this a safe and comfortable environment for all our children including those who are black?'

At the level of the curriculum, the need is to avoid content and approaches which are unidimensional and ethnocentric. The perspectives and experiences which the curriculum includes are those which it validates and marks out as valued knowledge. Those which it excludes are correspondingly not valued, if only by omission. The manner and style of the inclusion are important, however, for much damage has been done by those initiatives which have presented the life-styles of black populations as exotic, or over-simplified and therefore stereotyped. This is because the tendency has been to insert superficial 'facts' about black people into an otherwise unchanged curriculum, with little or no attention paid to contextualizing them or integrating them fully into the learning process. They have been tokenistic and therefore dangerous.

In my own search for appropriate examples for classroom activities, I have looked for instances of black experience which illustrate at least some of the following qualities, that is they are readily understandable because of their contemporary relevance, they are not set in ritual aspic but relate to real issues, and though black-specific, they speak to the general human condition. Above all, they raise questions and encourage the search for answers.

CLASSROOM ACTIVITIES

The purpose of these activities is to show the potential for change and peaceful resolution by exploring identified situations of race relations. The struggles waged by black people against racial injustice have taken many different forms. These are themselves instructive since they illustrate how relatively powerless groups are forced to bring into play whatever resources they possess when they find themselves struggling against much greater odds.

Marcellus

Purpose

To explore with young children the meanings and reasons behind the Rastafarian look, belief, and life-style. These beliefs and forms are much misunderstood and even shunned by some people as being sinister.

Preparation

Teachers will need to familiarize themselves with some of the beliefs and concepts of the movement, its history and symbolism, its music and other cultural products. Appropriate resources are listed below.

Procedure

Through the story of *Marcellus* (see resources list below) allow children to investigate the reasons why Marcellus and his family might want to wear their hair in this way. Draw and colour Marcellus themselves. Talk positively about differences in hair type and skin colour. Use reggae music as the basis of expression through movement and dance. Discuss its origins and meaning.

Resources for teachers

Barrett, L.E. (1982) *The Rastafarians*, 3rd edn, Kingston, Jamaica: Sangster–Heinemann.
Clarke, S. (1980) *Jah Music*, London: Heinemann Educational.

Patterson, O. (1986) *The Children of Sisyphus*, 3rd edn, London: Longman Caribbean Writers.

For use with children

Hersom, K. (1985) *Maybe It's a Tiger*, 2nd edn, London: Macmillan Children's Books.
McKee, D. (1983) *Tusk Tusk*, London: Arrow.
Simeon, L. (1986) *Marcellus*, London: Akira Press.

Black women in the struggle
___

Purpose

To explore the specific role of black women in the struggle for racial justice. This special contribution has been underplayed in the past but presents rich possibilities for individual and group learning.

Preparation

Teachers will need to acquaint themselves with the major themes in the historical and contemporary experience of black women from the list of resources given below. This is best communicated to children of this age range through a series of pen portraits of outstanding black women, for example Nanny of Accompong, Sojourner Truth, Claudia Jones, Winnie Mandela.

Procedure

Use the extracts given below to stimulate oral discussion and to generate written work.

> On this, my 37th birthday, I think of my mother. My mother, a machine worker in a garment factory, died when she was the same age as I am today – 37 years old. I think I began then to develop an understanding of the sufferings of my people . . . and to look for a way to end them.

Claudia Jones, who made this statement in a speech, went on to prove herself a great fighter for just causes. Among other things, she founded a newspaper called the *West Indian Gazette*, the first independent black newspaper in Britain in modern times.

> 1 Why did Claudia's mother die so young?
> 2 Why is it important for groups of people to have their own newspapers?
> 3 Produce a special 'Black Girls and Women' issue of your class newspaper.

> Paulette was the only black child there. So much so that before she went to school the whole school was briefed about this child coming from a different country . . .

She didn't complain . . . but when she was nineteen, I found out that this teacher told her that because she is from Trinidad she should be good so that she would be an example to others.

(Adapted from Dodgson 1984: 58)

1 Was the teacher being fair to Paulette?

2 Do you think Paulette would have been happier in a school where there were more black children?

3 Imagine that you are Paulette and that you keep a diary. Write about your first day at school in your diary.

Points to note

1 The importance of community contacts especially for black groups and others of 'minority' status.

2 The special role that black women have played in reshaping communities in different parts of the world.

Resources for teachers

Davis, A. (1982) *Women, Race and Class*, London: Women's Press.
Dodgson, E. (1984) *Motherland*, London: Heinemann.
Johnson, B. (1985) *'I Think of My Mother': Life and Times of Claudia Jones*, London: Karia Press.
Mandela, W. (1985) *Part of My Soul*, Harmondsworth: Penguin.
Mathurin, L. (1975) *The Rebel Woman in the British West Indies during Slavery*, Kingston, Jamaica: African-Caribbean Publications.
Nichols, G. (1982) *I'se a Long-memoried Woman*, London: Karnak House.
Walker, A. (1985) *Horses Make a Landscape Look More Beautiful*, London: Women's Press.

The life and work of Marcus Garvey

Introduction

Garvey is an interesting and controversial figure who ran foul of officialdom in his own time and has been something of a conundrum for subsequent generations. Yet his impact on ordinary black people has always been strong and the popular memory of him curiously 'alive'. A century after his birth, he is now being more rationally assessed and the relevance of his thinking to the process of achieving racial equality is being re-examined.

Purpose

To look at his life and work in the context of its own time and to assess its contemporary relevance. To present students with an opportunity of examining in detail some of the ramifications and contradictions of black political struggle through the focus of a central figure.

193

Preparation

Teachers will need to acquaint themselves with the details of Garvey's life and work, by consulting some or all of the texts listed below, and present these to students as structured inputs of information under a number of headings:

1 The Jamaican background and anti-colonialism.
2 Pan-Africanism.
3 Garvey in Britain.
4 Garvey in the USA.

Procedure

Two key statements by Garvey, which are worth studying to elaborate on these themes, are given below. Obviously there are many others teachers could use:

> The Psalmist prophesied that Princes would come out of Egypt and Ethiopia would stretch forth her hands unto God. We have no doubt that the time is now come. Ethiopia is now really stretching forth her hands. This great kingdom of the East has been hidden for many centuries, but gradually she is rising to take a leading place in the world and it is for us of the Negro race to assist in every way to hold up the head of the Emperor Ras Tafari.
>
> (*Blackman* 8 November 1930)

1 Why should Ethiopia have a symbolic significance for people of African descent?
2 What are the chief characteristics of Garvey's Pan-African vision as expressed in this passage?
3 What political value should we attach to Garvey's rhetorical style?

> in the absence of anything that will be more hopeful for the native it is preferable that they become communists than be entirely left to the mercy of the heartless Africaaners [sic] who have no other purpose but to deprive the people of land, of life and of liberty.
>
> (*New Jamaican* 15 October 1932: 2)

1 What light does this passage shed on Garvey's understanding of anti-colonial struggle?
2 Why might he have been considered dangerous by the authorities of his time?
3 Can you suggest more recent and contemporary parallels to the situation Garvey is describing?

Resources for teachers

Campbell, H. (1985) *Rasta and Resistance: from Marcus Garvey to Walter Rodney*, London: Hansib Publications.
Edwards, A. (1972) *Marcus Garvey, 1887–1940*, London: New Beacon Books.
Jacques Garvey, A. (1970) *Garvey and Garveyism*, New York: Collier Books, Macmillan.

James, C.L.R. (1985) *A History of Negro Revolt*, 3rd edn, London: *Race Today* Publications.
Lewis, R. (1987) *Marcus Garvey, Anti-Colonial Champion*, London: Karia Press.

Resources for students

Pan-African Congress Movement (1987) *The Honourable Marcus Mosiah Garvey – Centenary 1887–1987* (Seven Year Calendar), London: PACM.

REFERENCES

Ben-Tovim, G. (1980) *Equal Opportunities and the Employment of Black People on Merseyside*, Liverpool: Merseyside Area Profile Group.
Dhondy, F. (1974) 'The Black explosion in British schools', *Race Today*, February.
Fryer, P. (1985) *Staying Power: The History of Black People in Britain*, 2nd edn, London: Pluto.
Furnivall, E. (1948) *Colonial Policy and Practice*, London: Cambridge University Press.
Hall, S. (1978) *Policing the Crisis*, London: Macmillan.
Kiernan, V.G. (1972) *The Lords of Human Kind*, Harmondsworth: Penguin.
Lorimer, D. (1978) *Colour, Class and the Victorians*, Leicester: Leicester University Press.
Miles, R. (1982) *Capitalism, Racism and Migrant Labour*, London: Routledge & Kegan Paul.
Park, R. (1950) *Race and Culture*, (ed.) E. Cherrington Hughes, Glencoe, Ill: Free Press.
Stone, M. (1981) *Education of the Black Child in Britain*, London: Fontana.

12

Environment

John Huckle

Students should have a concern for the environmental welfare of all the world's people and the natural systems on which they depend. They should be able to make rational judgements concerning environmental issues and participate effectively in environmental politics.

(Table 2, page 14)

In the early 1980s the people of Newham in London's docklands were confronted with major redevelopment of their environment. The newly formed and unelected London Docks Development Corporation wanted the last remaining area of real estate close to the City for expansive private housing, small factory and office units, a marina and short runway airport, all designed for the rich. Local people were already facing rising unemployment, a lack of housing which they could afford, and a decline in services. They decided to fight these plans and, with the help of the Greater London Council, carried out an audit of local needs and resources. They found that unmet needs could be largely satisfied by the appropriate use of physical and human resources currently unused or underused within their community. They drew up their own People's Plan for the area around the Royal Docks showing how such development as ship repair, a riverbus, sports centre, and people's marina would create jobs, revive local services, and improve the environment for the majority. Such development would cost money, but would reduce the amount spent on welfare. Drawing up the plan raised people's awareness of wasted resources and the value of socially useful production. It fostered a mistrust of experts, cultivated a new pride in community and neighbourhood, and forged new alliances between tenants associations, trade unions, and voluntary groups.

The people of Newham are not alone in working for forms of development which meet social needs and improve environmental welfare. The People's Liberation Front in Tigray, rubber tappers in Brazil, Solidarity in Poland, the Consumers' Association of Penang, Sandinistas in Nicaragua, the Wilderness Society in Australia . . . these and other groups suggest that given power, ordinary people are capable of building environments which foster social harmony and peace between society and nature. This chapter examines the links between democracy and environmental welfare, argues the case for eco-socialism, and describes a libertarian form of environmental education which can promote peace.

DEMOCRACY, PEACE, AND ENVIRONMENT

The root cause of our present environmental predicament is the unequal distribution of economic and political power. The world's land, natural resources, and human environments are owned and controlled by a minority of the world's people. The vast majority have little control over the social use of nature or the social construction of the environments in which they live. Decisions taken by powerful minorities generally mean that it is the poor and powerless who suffer most from such environmental problems as polluted drinking water, damp housing, the shortage of fuelwood, flooding as a result of deforestation, and inner-city crime. Structural violence is built in to people's environments and fosters conflict in the home and the community. Verbal abuse, sexual harassment, vandalism, mugging, terrorism, and war, all are caused by and result from a lack of environmental well-being. Violence in many cities now condemns minorities, old people, and women in general to lives of loneliness and fear and severely limits children's opportunities for play and development. Only people's efforts to reverse the recent historical trend towards centralization, hierarchy, and the erosion of direct democracy will create environments which engender peace.

For most of their history on planet earth, people have lived in societies characterized by mutual aid, co-operation, equality, and direct democracy. The rise of hierarchical, adversarial, aggressive, and undemocratic societies can be traced to two significant periods. First, the emergence of a warrior class and the replacement of egalitarian, domestically oriented, matricentric relations by hierarchical, politically oriented, patricentric relations. Second, the discovery of the New World and the rise of capitalism which brought new forms of cruelty, destructiveness, and greed and facilitated changes in economic, political, and cultural life which continue to this day. Since economic surplus first became a regular product of society's use of nature, it has been used as the basis of hierarchy and class rule. Warriors, patriarchs, priests, slave owners, feudal lords, merchants, factory owners, company directors, state bureaucrats, and politicians have all denied the people democracy and peace. An examination of the workings of today's world suggests that wealth and power continues to accumulate in the hands of such minorities but that the ideal of a democratic, peaceful society has not been forgotten.

UNDERSTANDING THE CONTEMPORARY WORLD

The most comprehensive understanding of the contemporary world is provided by world systems theory (Harris 1983; Wallerstein 1984; Johnston and Taylor 1986). This explains the modern world order in terms of a three-tier world economy overlain by a three-tier political system. The economy consists of a network of commodity chains which link the producers and consumers of goods and services in different parts of the world. It is a capitalist economy based on production for profit and entails unequal exchange between societies variously arranged within a global division of labour, according to the kinds of production processes within their borders. The product of colonialism and subsequent imperialism, it now embraces virtually all the world's peoples and involves them in a process of combined but uneven development. The manner in which a society uses its natural resources and the nature of the environments so produced, largely depends on its past and present position within this world system.

At the core of the world economy are the richest and most powerful nation states. It is in such countries as the USA, Japan, and West Germany that multinational industrial and financial corporations, which are now the main agents of imperialism, have their headquarters. Profits they produce elsewhere in the world return to the core and it is here that research and development which leads to new product cycles is concentrated. Competition between corporations for economic power, and between core states for political power, fuels the drive for economic growth and technological innovation. During the post-war boom, corporations, governments, and workers in the core all became party to a treadmill of production and consumption which delivered increased profits, taxes, and material living standards but meant ever more damaging impacts on the natural world. The political stability which this treadmill assured in the liberal democracies was threatened from the mid-1970s when boom turned to recession. Efforts to restore profitability and growth, in such core states as Britain, led to the erosion of environmental safeguards (Goldsmith and Hildyard 1986).

The wealth and power of the core depends on the poverty and exploitation of the periphery. Countries in the South are predominantly small and powerless and continue to be actively underdeveloped by the process of unequal exchange mentioned above. They have dual economies in which an extensive subsistence and pre-capitalist sector exists alongside a modern sector oriented to the needs of overseas investors and their local agents. Heavily dependent on manual labour and the export of raw materials and cash crops, they display an urgent need for appropriate development to meet basic needs. Locked into structures of economic and political dependency, governments and people in these countries are forced to over-exploit their natural resources in order to survive. Minerals and timber are sold off to multinational corporations to increase cash income and repay national debts.

Pastures are overgrazed, soil eroded, and wildlife hunted to extinction to maintain the power and wealth of ruling élites and to meet the immediate needs of the desperately poor. Politics in these states is dominated by anti-imperialist and national liberation movements which seek to turn the economy and development to the advantage of the local majority. They have succeeded in establishing variants of socialism in some states but economic scarcity, corruption, bureaucracy, and the policies of core states have often subverted their efforts. The current crisis in Africa (Timberlake 1985) illustrates their predicament. Famine and desertification are the result of such factors as government apathy, urban policy bias, and export cash cropping, made worse by drought.

Between core and periphery are a third group of states, many of them large and resource rich. Having production processes typical of both core and periphery, these semi-peripheral states have been able to accumulate some capital locally and attain a degree of dependent development. The environmental costs, as in the case of Brazil's rainforests or Australia's soils, have generally been high and the political price of this development has often been subjugation to undemocratic and repressive regimes. A fourth and final group of states is made up of the state collectivist economies which fall within the realm of Soviet imperialism. More isolated and self-sufficient than the capitalist states, they do show increased dependence on the rest of the world where the majority have peripheral or semi-peripheral status. The felt need of actually existing socialist states to compete with the west and defend their revolutions partly explains their generally uncritical approach to technology and economic growth, excessive bureaucratic centralization, and an exploitation of people and nature which contradicts their socialist ideals. Despite China's example of communal organization and radical technology, there is now evidence that impressive improvements in social welfare have been gained at considerable environmental cost (Smil 1984).

POLITICAL SYSTEMS AND GLOBAL CRISIS

It is the world's political systems which are generally thought capable of resolving or managing the social conflicts arising from the operation of the world economy. They operate at local, national, and international levels, but a competitive state system means that there is no one political unit capable of controlling the market or tackling global problems. Nation states come into existence to manage the affairs of the dominant class within their territory and the need to protect the interests of local capital remains the major constraint on their attempts to redistribute wealth in such forms as environmental welfare. They show varied forms of government, reflecting their history, culture, and position within the world economy and they adopt different approaches to environmental management and planning. Within

199

states, politics remain characterized by class struggle which has been made more complex by the rise of other oppositional groups seeking separate identity or pursuing single issues such as peace or ecology. Across states, international politics is dominated by the struggle for power between different groups of the world's ruling class. States continually enter and leave pacts and alliances in pursuing shared aims and it is the competition between these groupings which sustains the arms race and poses the ultimate environmental threat.

To complete our understanding of the world order, we should realize it is a dynamic system. The world economy shows long-term waves of growth and decline, based on major new technologies and product cycles, in which shorter-term cycles are embedded. We are currently at the start of a new wave based on electronic and information technologies and this is leading to a restructuring of the global division of labour. The core of the world economy is likely to shift to the Pacific Basin and countries such as Britain, now in the core, may undergo further decline. A recurring result of such restructuring over the past 400 years has been an extension of the periphery bringing new workers, resources, and markets into the world system. That process is approaching the social and physical limits to growth as more of the world's people join oppositional movements and the ecological crisis intensifies. A number of recent reports point to the severity of the global crisis (World Resources/International Institute for Environment and Development 1986; World Commission on Environment and Development 1987) while two atlases provide a graphic representation of the current state of the world system (Kidron and Segal 1984; Myers 1985).

THE SOCIALIST ALTERNATIVE

Within movements opposing the anti-democratic structures and processes of the world system, socialist elements are particularly significant. Socialism offers the prospect of a society free of hierarchy and domination in which people live in approximate social and economic equality, making common use of the means available to promote social welfare. In such a society, equality is the foundation of democracy, freedom, and peace. Once people have equal rights to the material and cultural means of realizing citizenship, they are able to join with others in protecting and advancing their own interests and values within a framework of consideration for the interests and values of others. They can begin to influence the decisions of those in power, hold them accountable for social problems, and work with others to extend democracy and welfare.

Despite its promise, socialism is in crisis. The majority of actually existing socialist societies are undemocratic and controlled from above by privileged bureaucracies. They have generally applied theory and central planning too rigorously, pursued economic growth and militarism relentlessly, and failed to develop forms of technology, politics, and culture which would extend the rights of ordinary people. The autocratic and alienating nature of Eastern Bloc societies is largely a product of their history and the difficulties of building socialism in a climate of economic scarcity under threat from capitalist states. Where social democracy has been the experience in the west, it too has left a legacy of disillusionment with collectivist solutions to social problems. The bureaucratic state, nationalized industries, public sector housing, and trade unions are some of the institutions which have alienated a growing number from the labour movement. The crisis of faith in socialism is compounded by a crisis of agency as technological change displaces workers and erodes socialism's expected constituency.

Libertarian socialism

Fortunately socialism is heir to a libertarian tradition which discounts the possibility of socialism's being established by a benevolent minority from above. It looks to the mass action of ordinary people to reshape society from below, by popular political activity within their work-places and communities. Anarcho-communists and social anarchists have long insisted that once freed from structural violence, people could again organize their lives on the basis of co-operation, direct democracy, and freedom. In societies characterized by social ownership, mutual aid, and production and distribution for need, individuals would realize their freedom in conscious and reflective interaction with the freedom of others. The early anarchists saw the need to base such social organization on natural laws but it is perhaps in the writings of William Morris, Peter Kropotkin, and Murray Bookchin that social anarchism and ecology are best united. They evoke ecology to support their case for decentralized and federally organized communities in which more harmonious relations between people would be likely to lead to harmonious relations with nature. They state a preference for the simple life, austerity, and appropriate technology which is in tune with ecology and provide outlines of utopias which have had a strong influence on the modern environmental movement (Pepper 1984). Murray Bookchin (1974) regards ecology as both a critical and reconstructive science, pointing both to the dangers of simplifying natural and human communities and to the need for anarcho-socialist societies which would foster diversity. In his recent work (Bookchin 1986), he notes a growing self-consciousness of our predicament and grounds his optimism in libertarian populist movements working to exorcise domination and hierarchy and re-empower the citizenry via new forms of community politics.

Red and green

Elements of libertarian socialist theory and practice have been rediscovered in recent years particularly by the green movement. Greens stress quality of life, harmony with nature, self-reliance, appropriate technology, diversity and non-violence (Porritt 1984; Spretnak and Capra 1985; Swift 1987), but are often unaware of the historical precedents for such a philosophy and utopian in their neglect of power. They offer a somewhat naïve and unqualified critique of industrialism and adopt an essentially liberal or pluralist approach to social change (Weston 1986). In seeking to bring this about via mass conversion to new values, life-styles, and an emerging 'green paradigm' (Capra 1982), they fail to recognize the importance of transforming existing social relations through material struggle and the continuing, if diminishing, role of the labour movement in this task. Greens remind socialists of the need to transform the nature of production and consumption and to appeal to new social movements. Libertarian socialists remind greens of the value of class analysis, the power of the state, and the need for a social environmentalism which promotes peace and environmental well-being via wider programmes of social reform. Debate with the greens has been a key element in the current rebuilding of socialism (Williams 1983) with journals such as *New Ground* setting out the resulting eco-socialist perspective.

Eco-development

Eco-socialism is well represented in the theory and practice of eco-development which is taking root around the world. It has been described as development leading to economic equity, social harmony, and environmental balance (Riddell 1981), for it seeks to satisfy basic needs, encourage self-reliance, and sustain natural processes on which future development depends (Glaeser 1984). It is now possible to find more examples of societies living off the interest, rather than the capital, which nature provides, and learning much from the innovations in economic, political, and cultural life which have made this possible. In Britain, the best developed expression of eco-development is the municipal socialism which emerged in the mid-1980s. Faced with severe economic and environmental decline, resulting from global recession and central government policies, local authorities in Greater London, Sheffield, the West Midlands, and elsewhere set up local enterprise boards to enable local people to intervene in the economic restructuring affecting their lives. Local spending was used to satisfy unmet needs using wasted resources and, in the new or revived enterprises so created, opportunities were taken to improve the quality of work and management, extend industrial democracy, introduce appropriate technology, raise low pay, and positively discriminate in favour of minorities and women. Municipal socialism has brought together politicians, community groups, and trade unions to develop community resource centres and local plans. It has encouraged debate on socially useful production (Collective Design Projects 1986) and above all has empowered people at the local level. More now realize that they can make their own histories and environments and that hierarchy, violence, and domination are not inevitable. They have begun to see for themselves the logic of the present system and to work for alternatives which allow such concerns as ecology, arms conversion, human rights, healthy diets, and local culture to shape community decisions.

Socialist local authorities can do much to support one another with such development, but a national government could co-ordinate and defend local initiatives from above. It could also play a key role in the international field by working for a new international economic and information order, global disarmament and a co-operative world system based on a federation of people's states. Mrs Thatcher's government in contrast has mounted an assault on socialism and democracy in the name of freedom. Its policies to reassert individual property rights and strengthen market forces further remove questions of economic and social development from public debate and collective control, erode the powers of trade unions, community groups, and local authorities, and encourage a more unstable and divided world. Central initiatives currently put libertarian socialists on the defensive, working to preserve elements of collective provision, and defend popular democracy against attacks which link them with undemocratic elements on the left. In the increasingly divided and violent society which is being created, we should continue to press for political and economic reforms but should also realize the urgent need to fashion a new politics, addressing more numerous sites of struggle and energizing people to new demands (Beetham 1987). If the present technological revolution is to serve the majority, rather than a minority, ways should be found of constructing an alternative to the enterprise future. Such an alternative should connect with ordinary feelings and experiences, develop political imagination, and offer freedom via the deepening rather than the erosion of democratic life (Gorz 1985; Frankel 1987). Eco-socialism has a key part to play in that historic project as does libertarian education.

EDUCATION FOR DOMINATION

The growth of inequality and hierarchy within societies brought considerable cultural change. Accepted ways of relating to the social and physical environment were progressively modified and this change legitimized by changing beliefs and values. With advancing technology and control over nature, religious mysticism and nature worship gave way to scientific rationalism and secular materialism. Capitalism accelerated the rise of a competitive, forceful, and manipulative culture with an instrumental approach to the natural world. As the world economy grew, cultural imperialism destroyed much traditional knowledge and imposed life-styles and values which shaped notions of progress, development, and environmental management. Education is one agent of such imperialism. It now plays a key role in sustaining hierarchy and domination throughout the world.

Schools are primarily conservative institutions which have expanded in order to train, grade, and socialize the work-force. Their function remains that of producing young workers and citizens with appropriate knowledge, skills, and values and this continues to be done largely in environments reflecting the hierarchy and competition found outside the school. The school curriculum in Britain fails to provide the vast majority of pupils with a critical understanding of the social use of nature in different parts of the world. It fails to explore radical social alternatives and fails to provide the foundations of a critical and participatory citizenship which would enable young adults to join with others in the type of democratic social change considered earlier in this chapter. I have examined the ideological nature of much environmental education elsewhere (Huckle 1983; 1986). The remainder of the chapter will focus on radical educational alternatives.

EDUCATION FOR LIBERATION

The early anarchists attached much importance to education as it offered a means of changing society from below without the assistance of the state. Like the child-centred progressives, they favoured a non-coercive pedagogy designed to foster individual initiatives and development. For libertarian socialists, however, the primary goal of education was not the liberation of individuals but the liberation of the working class. Education was to provide a theoretical and practical understanding of the world of work, unite mental and manual labour and develop an awareness of the need to rectify the political and social disadvantages of working people as a group. While libertarians recognized state schooling as a training in subservience, and most of their early initiatives were in experimental schools marginal to the mainstream, the syndicalist teachers of nineteenth-century France attempted to change state schools from within. They encouraged pupils to examine and discuss society from a perspective which was anti-royalist, anti-militarist, and anti-capitalist and developed a form of social education which stressed co-operation and mutual aid and 'the great natural law of solidarity'. Charged with indoctrination and values imposition, their defence was a strict adherence to rationality. Reason was to be applied to all viewpoints including libertarian socialism and rationalism was itself libertarian. One cannot help but draw parallels with today's debates about peace education.

Libertarian educators suggest that education for freedom should develop independence, autonomy, and critical citizenship. It should enable the individual to assert autonomy with others in a society characterized not by individualism, hierarchy, and competition, but by co-operation and mutual respect. An extract from the final page of Michael Smith's book (1983) reminds us of its central relevance for eco-socialists.

> Education should liberate from but it should also liberate to, and what it would be liberating to in this case is to contribute to the building of a better, more equal society, a decentralised society with a great deal of individual and local autonomy, and one structured around the principles of co-operation and mutuality.

Education 'to' freedom cannot be a passive process. It requires the development of self-awareness via desocialization from dominant meanings and reflection and action on viable alternatives. The teacher can aid this process by facilitating the learner's ability to develop new meanings and apply them to the real world. Paulo Freire and Ira Shor have perhaps done most to popularize such a pedagogy which combines experiential learning with conceptual analysis. Shor (1980) urges teachers to assist pupils in re-experiencing and transforming the ordinary. They are to become aware of the location of everyday objects and events within a network of economic and political relations, consider alternatives and then act to democratically transform their world. Such reflection and action will represent both an inner and an outer journey (Greig, Pike, and Selby 1987) and both peace and environmental educators have done much to develop appropriate learning techniques. Examination of one curriculum project suggests how the approach can be applied to environmental education.

WHAT WE CONSUME

Part of the World Wildlife Fund's Global Environmental Education Programme, *What We Consume*, provides teachers of 11- to 16-year-old pupils with ten curriculum units, each linking a product which they consume to an issue of environment and development in another part of the world (World Wildlife Fund UK, Education Department 1988). By a suitable choice of products or commodity chains, it samples the major themes of the World and UK Conservation Strategies and introduces pupils to the social use of nature within the main forms of political economy found around the world. For example, a tin of corned beef links pupils to the destruction of rainforest in Brazil and the development priorities of a military regime in a country undergoing dependent development on the semi-periphery of the world economy. Buying a Band Aid record links them to Ethiopia, desertification, and the policies of a centralist Marxist government in a country being actively underdeveloped on the periphery of Soviet imperialism. While seven of the units focus on environment and development in nation states, there is an introductory unit on society and nature and two concluding units which examine attempts to ameliorate environmental problems by multilateral action from above, and attempt to create ecologically sustainable development by grassroots activity from below. The project was developed by a team of teachers in Bedfordshire and Milton Keynes and draws heavily on the philosophy and approaches of *World Studies 8–13* and the Programme for Political Education (see Porter 1984).

To encourage structural thinking, *What We Consume* makes use of a curriculum framework of key questions and concepts which was derived from the type of analysis outlined in the first part of this chapter and from ideas developed by Adrian Leftwich in his book *Redefining Politics* (1983). The questions focus attention on the social use of nature within different systems of economic production, distribution and redistribution, power and decision-making, social organization, culture, and ideology. They encourage teachers and pupils to regard the environment as socially constructed, to recognize that the environmental costs of production and development are unevenly shared and to assess critically whether a transition to ecologically sustainable development requires fundamental economic, political, and cultural change. The link between eco-development and democracy is a theme which runs through the units and each provides positive examples of people working for eco-development. The ten classroom activities provided in each unit enable teachers and pupils to pose key questions and develop key concepts while critically examining the unit's key ideas. The example at the end of this chapter suggests how they make use of experiential learning activities developed by world studies. It also shows how, by exploring systems of power and decision-making, pupils develop the knowledge, skills, and attitudes which contribute to political literacy. Readers will find more about the project's rationale in the teacher's handbook which accompanies the first unit. They should find that its materials and activities reflect guidelines on bias issued by the Politics Association (Jones 1986).

GETTING INVOLVED

This chapter has focused on global issues of environment and development and how they might be taught. It has perhaps overlooked the local studies or community focus in environmental education, so well documented in recent years by the *Bulletin of Environmental Education*. It is important that we *think globally and act locally*, working to create socially critical schools engaged in local issues and providing pupils with opportunities to improve the environmental well-being of others. Groups like *Community Service Volunteers* provide much useful help and the *Environmental Action Pack*

(Channel Four 1985) is one excellent directory of sources and ideas. The *Global Impact Project* (Greig 1987) has begun to examine the links between environmental, peace, human rights, and development education and will hopefully lead to more of the kinds of activities reflected on the pages of *Green Teacher*. European Year of the Environment has revived environmental education and the forthcoming HMI discussion document will hopefully legitimize many initiatives. Readers seeking further advice are recommended to consult the ten starting-points in *Earthrights* (Greig, Pike, and Selby 1987).

Libertarian education flowered briefly in the late 1960s and early 1970s. Since then economic and educational policy has shifted to the right and conservative school reform has meant a significant attack on surviving libertarian elements in such fields as environmental and peace education (Shor 1986). The language of peace, equality, and democracy has been replaced by that of authority, competition, and élitism but libertarian educators are not defeated and this chapter has argued that their work can play a part in the general struggle to maintain democracy and extend elements of socially useful production. The rhetoric and the new vocationalism, economic and political awareness, a core curriculum, and greater parental control, provide us with the space to do this. In difficult times, we should seek to keep an alternative vision of an eco-socialist future on the agenda. Colin Ward (1983) suggests what this future might be like. Education is based in the community and plays a major role in making it more habitable. It prepares young people for self-employment and workers' co-ops, engages people of all ages in popular planning, designs socially useful products, and helps people put wasted resources to use. It combines work and learning, enriches local culture, and slowly democratizes existing institutions and power structures from below. It empowers people to take charge of their own lives, to implement forms of eco-development, and to create a lasting peace.

For a brief moment, the people of Newham glimpsed this future. Our task is clearly to work with such groups, raise our pupils' awareness of their struggles, and develop a critical understanding of the necessary transition to eco-development. The alternatives are peace or yet more environmental poverty, more violence . . . more war.

CLASSROOM ACTIVITIES

The two activities outlined below are taken from *What We Consume*, the module of the World Wildlife Fund's Global Environmental Education Programme described on pp. 205–6. Full versions of the activities can be found in Units 7 and 8 of the module and teachers wishing to use them in schools are strongly advised to obtain these.

Figure 15 Taking care of the trees

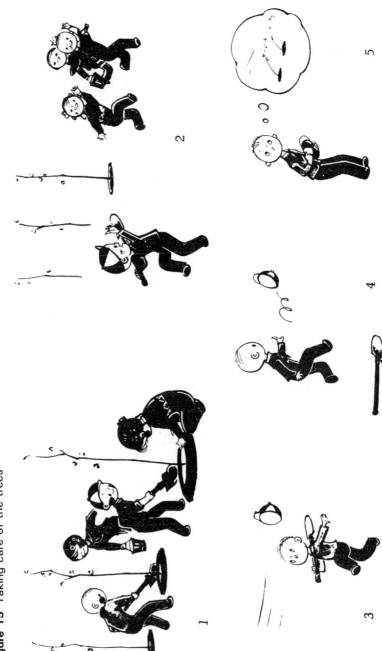

Source: Peng Kuo-Liang (1975) *Stories of Little Red Guards*, China: Foreign Language Press.

Education or indoctrination?

Purpose

To consider, through a sequencing activity, issues to do with environmental responsibility.

Preparation

Sets of the ten pictures illustrated in Figure 15 need to be reproduced, enough for each group of four children to have one set. They are taken from a children's storybook, *Good Children*, printed in China.

Procedure

Pupils work in groups of four. The pictures are dealt out face down and each individual takes it in turn to describe his or her pictures without showing them to the rest of the group. Then the group decide as a whole, still without actually looking at the pictures, the sequence they feel they should be in to 'tell the story'.

Having agreed on this the pictures are then laid face up in the agreed sequence. The group then review their decisions and rearrange pictures as they feel appropriate.

Questions that can then be posed to the class are: What is the story trying to teach its Chinese readers? Might the story be told differently in Britain? In what different ways can we each be responsible for the environment?

Mikhail Gorbachev's dilemma

Introduction

When the Soviet Union's new five-year plan was published in 1986, it became clear that ambitious proposals to transfer water from north-flowing rivers to the south had at last been abandoned. These plans represented a huge modification of the natural environment and had attracted growing opposition from Soviet scientists and writers and from environmentalists outside the USSR. The cancellation of the schemes coincided with Mikhail Gorbachev's rise to power as General Secretary of the Communist Party. This activity puts older secondary pupils in his position, making a decision on the water transfer schemes.

Purpose

The activity is designed to increase the pupil's political literacy by providing an insight into environmental decision-making within the USSR. Used within a scheme of work on the Soviet water transfer projects, it should increase both propositional and procedural knowledge of Soviet politics.

Table 8 Mikhail Gorbachev's Dilemma

It is mid-1985 and you are Mikhail Gorbachev, the new General Secretary of the Communist Party of the USSR. Under your leadership the Party has adopted a new policy of 'glasnost' or openness. It is more prepared to recognize the inefficiency in the economy, to listen to complaints, and to provide people with rewards in order to revive economic growth. As a top Party official for agriculture, you earned a reputation for economic efficiency and the careful examination of large construction projects.

For over fifty years, Soviet planners have dreamed of transferring water from north-flowing rivers towards the south. These plans were revived in 1982 and included a scheme to transfer huge quantities of water from the rivers Ob and Yenesi to the drylands of Central Asia. The water would be carried in a long canal and used to irrigate farmland and prevent the spread of deserts around the Aral Sea. The scheme would cost billions of roubles but would bring much-needed water to a fertile area. Increased food production is necessary if the Soviet people are to enjoy better diets and the many new settlers in Siberia are to be fed.

In a June 1984 interview in *Izvestiya*, Polad Polad-Zade, First Deputy Minister of the Ministry of Land Reclamation and Water Management and the chairman of the Science-Technology State Committee's Scientific-Technical Commission on Water Redistribution, said that it was impossible to imagine the south of the USSR in the near future without water from the north. Much research and survey work has been carried out on the project and construction teams are in Western Siberia ready to start work.

Before coming to power, you had argued against the water transfer projects. You were much influeced by M. Ya. Lemshev, an environmental economist, now with the Commission on the Study of Productive Forces of the Academy of Sciences. He suggests that water transfer would harm navigation, damage fisheries, increase river pollution, and drain huge areas of West Siberia's swamps. It would affect the ice cover and climate of the Soviet Arctic and the diversion canal could cause much ecological and landscape damage along its course. In his view, the money would be better spent on rural development, including soil and water conservation, in the southern drylands.

The Soviet economy is no longer growing rapidly and there is little chance of finding the money for the water transfer schemes without reducing spending on defence. If you want the schemes cancelled, you will have to persuade the Politburo, the Party's political committee, before it approves the next five-year plan. Some of its members owe their power to Leonid Breshnev, who revived the water transfer scheme in 1982. They could be removed but challenging their positions may invite an attack on your leadership and new policies.

What are you going to do: rally your support in the party and the media to get the schemes cancelled *or* hold back, let them go ahead, and hope that the schemes turn out to be a success?

Preparation

Pupils will have previously studied the economic and political system of the USSR in outline. Using suitable maps, pictures, and background information (see sources below), the teacher should inform the class of the two main water transfer projects in the USSR. She should outline the history of the projects, their supposed advantages and disadvantages, and the progress which had been made towards their construction by early 1985.

Procedure

Pupils are given individual copies of the activity sheet *Mikhail Gorbachev's dilemma* (see Table 8). The teacher reads through this with the class and they discuss any parts of the text which are causing comprehension problems.

The pupils are now asked to assume the role of Mikhail Gorbachev and decide what they are going to do about the water transfer projects. Having made individual decisions, they form small groups of three or four and discuss the reason why they made their individual decisions. What factors were most important in shaping their choices? Which least important? What other factors may have been involved?

The teacher now asks the groups to report back, summarizing their decisions and discussions. She tells them that the schemes were cancelled and that, according to commentators, Gorbachev did appear to have a major influence on the outcome. She discusses other factors which may have been significant and updates the story using the sources listed below. The activity clearly allows pupils to explore key concepts such as authority, manipulation, and bureaucracy.

Sources

The Great Powers (Jim Cannon, Bill Clark, and George Smuga, Edinburgh: Oliver & Boyd, 1987) provides a good introduction to the USSR's economic and political system for secondary pupils. Background on the water transfer projects and the decisions surrounding them can be found in 'The status of the Soviet Union's north–south water transfer projects before their abandonment in 1985–6', P. Micklin, *Soviet Geography* 27, 5, May 1986, and 'Soviet decree officially cancels north–south water transfer projects', T. Shabad, *Soviet Geography* 27, 8, August 1986. NB The dilemma technique is described in *Learning for Change in World Society*, One World Trust, 1979, p. 71.

REFERENCES

Beetham, D. (1987) 'A new democratic order', *New Socialist* 49, May.
Bookchin, M. (1974) *Post-Scarcity Anarchism*, London: Wildwood House.
——— (1986) *The Modern Crisis*, Philadelphia, Pa: New Society Publishers.
Capra, F. (1982) *The Turning Point*, London: Wildwood House.
Channel Four (1985) *Environmental Action Pack* (PO Box 4000, London W3 6XJ).
Collective Design Products (1986) *Very Nice Work if you Can Get it: The Socially Useful Production Debate*, Nottingham: Spokesman.
Crow, B. and Thomas, A. (1983) *Third World Atlas*, Milton Keynes: Open University Press.
Frankel, B. (1987) *The Post-Industrial Utopians*, Cambridge: Polity Press.
Glaeser, B. (1984) *Ecodevelopment, Concepts, Projects, Strategies*, Oxford: Pergamon.
Goldsmith, E. and Hilyard, N. (eds) (1986) *Green Britain or Industrial Wasteland*, Cambridge: Polity Press.

Gorz, A. (1985) *Paths to Paradise: On the Liberation from Work*, London: Pluto.

Greig, S. (1987) *Global Impact Project: Report of Survey*, University of York: Centre for Global Education.

Greig, S., Pike, G., and Selby, D. (1987) *Earthrights: Education as if the Planet Really Mattered*, London: WWF–Kogan Page.

Harris, N. (1983) *Of Bread and Guns: The World Economy in Crisis*, Harmondsworth: Penguin.

Huckle, J. (1983) 'Environmental education' in J. Huckle (ed.) *Geographical Education: Reflection and Action*, Oxford: Oxford University Press.

———— (1986) 'Confronting the ecological crisis', *Contemporary Issues in Geography and Education* 2,1.

Johnston, R. and Taylor, P. (eds) (1986) *A World in Crisis? Geographical Perspectives*, Oxford: Blackwell.

Jones, B. (1986) 'Bias in the classroom: some suggested guidelines', *Teaching Politics* 15,3, September.

Kidron, M. and Segal, R. (1984) *The New State of the World Atlas*, London: Pan.

Leftwich, A. (1983) *Redefining Politics: People, Resources and Power*, London: Methuen.

Myers, N. (ed.) (1985) *The Gaia Atlas of Planet Management*, London: Pan.

Pepper, D. (1984) *The Roots of Modern Environmentalism*, Beckenham: Croom Helm.

Porritt, J. (1984) *Seeing Green: The Politics of Ecology Explained*, Oxford: Blackwell.

Porter, A. (1984) *Principles of Political Literacy*, London: University of London Institute of Education.

Riddell, R. (1981) *Ecodevelopment*, Aldershot: Gower.

Sharp, R. (1984), 'Varieties of peace education' in R. Sharp (ed.) *Apocalypse No*, Sydney: Pluto.

Shor, I. (1980) *Critical Teaching and Everyday Life*, Boston, Mass: South End Press.

———— (1986) *Culture Wars: School and Society in the Conservative Restoration 1969–1984*, London: Routledge & Keegan Paul.

Smil, V. (1984) *The Bad Earth: Environmental Degradation in China*, London: Zed Press.

Smith, M.P. (1983) *The Libertarians and Education*, London: Unwin Educational.

Spretnak, C. and Capra, F. (1985) *Green Politics* London: Paladin.

Swift, R. (ed.) (1987) 'Green politics', *New Internationalist* 171, May.

Timberlake, L. (1985) *Africa in Crisis: The Causes, the Cures of Environmental Bankruptcy*, London: Earthscan.

Wallerstein, I. (1984) *The Politics of the World-Economy*, Cambridge: Cambridge University Press.

Ward, C. (1983) 'Deadsville revisited – a hope still unrealised', *Bulletin of Environmental Education* 151, December.

Weston, J. (ed.) (1986) *Red and Green: The New Politics of the Environment*, London: Pluto.

Williams, R. (1983) *Towards 2000*, Harmondsworth: Penguin.

World Commission on Environment and Development (1987) *Our Common Future*, Oxford: Oxford University Press.

World Resources Institute–International Institute for Environment and Development (1986) *World Resources 1986: An Assessment of the Resource Base that Supports the Global Economy*, New York: Basic Books.

World Wildlife Fund UK, Education Department (1986) *What We Consume*, Richmond: Richmond Publishing Company.

213

13

Futures

Richard Slaughter

Students should study a range of alternative futures, both probable and preferable. They should understand which scenarios are most likely to lead to a more just and less violent world and what changes are necessary to bring this about.

(Table 2, page 14).

WHY STUDY FUTURES?

The single most important objective of futures study in schools is to help pupils develop a genuine sense of optimism and empowerment about their own life prospects. This follows from having adequate information about their society and the world, from an awareness of their own inner vocation or sense of purpose (which is very different to a narrow vocationalism), and the opportunity to develop skills of self-mastery. I suspect this can take place fully only where students are regarded as agents rather than spectators and are given the chance to develop autonomy through decision-making and choices. The imposition of knowledge structures in the form of stereotyped subjects works against optimism and empowerment because it confronts students with pre-givens which require accommodation and acceptance rather than reconceptualization and creativity. Futures study is one of a number of interdisciplinary foci which hold out more nourishing options.

Careful person-centred futures work encourages students to be more confident about their abilities. With this confidence, and with developing insights, they can be encouraged to refuse many of the artificial boundaries which our culture has imposed upon a seamless and interconnected world (Wilber 1979). Two consequences follow. First, the removal or reinterpretation of boundaries eliminates the causes of many conflicts. The latter tend to look absurd when we perceive our common standing in the very same 'ground of being'. Second, they can look beyond ego to explore their immersion in wider networks and processes of energy, food, relationship, and meaning (Dossey 1982).

214

A related attitude is the willingness to join with others in defining and working towards shared goals and purposes. It is all too easy to drift passively towards protest and rebellion. But behind both lies the essential task of defining in positive terms just what is wanted and needed. This has become difficult in a culture which has in so many ways broken with the past and yet sustains few compelling visions of liveable futures. Futures study deals with this situation directly by providing tools and contexts for developing views of futures worth living in.

Each pupil needs to develop an image of how he or she would like to be in the future. This 'future-focused role image', as it has been called, is not just a piece of wishful thinking, or need not be. The view which people hold of themselves deeply conditions what they consider to be worth attempting in the present. Many existing curricula tend to obscure this important process but it can be made explicit through stories, time-lines, values clarification, and many other futures exercises.

Inherent in the foregoing are many different kinds of skills: self-knowledge and empathy with others: reflexivity (standing back from one's immersion in culture to reflect critically upon it); clarity about values, meanings, and purposes; a broad and holistic understanding of global processes; the ability to understand and critique the images and plans of futures as they are re-presented (brought again into the present) by powerful groups; the ability to understand the differences between possible, probable, and preferable futures.

It is important to note here that the purpose of futures in peace education is not to predict, not to say what *will* happen. That is the task of forecasters, system analysts, and the like. Our major concern is to understand alternatives. By so doing we introduce into the present a wide range of choices. The exercise of considered choice is what eventually leads us toward one future and away from others. So the term *possible futures* covers a very wide range indeed. Many things are possible, not all of which we will want to support. *Probable futures* are those that will draw on forecasts, projections, scenarios, and stories to grasp something of the range of what is now considered likely. (Note that many important issues seem to rise and fall with media coverage, so the latter cannot be used as a guide to their real significance.) *Preferable futures* are those we positively hope for and work to create. Some of the criteria available for constructing images of preferable futures are related to commonalities of human experience such as were noted above: sustainability, health, peace, justice, and so on. With appropriate help and support students of all ages and abilities find it surprisingly easy to engage in this process. Any fears and worries which arise can be acknowledged, focused, and directed towards constructive and creative ends (see below and Macy 1983).

SCHOOLS ARE ALREADY IN THE FUTURES BUSINESS

All school curricula carry a range of implicit messages. Some of the latter suggest that the past is dominant, powerful, and authoritative. By contrast, futures may seem problematic and 'speculative' if, that is, they appear at all. Most curricula comment on futures merely by leaving them out of the 'map' of significant knowledge. However, few can be unaware that this 'map' of standard subjects has become severely dated. In order to understand how futures contributes to peace education (and vice versa) we need to focus briefly on some of the deficiencies of present maps.

Specifically I want to offer three comments. First, in lacking a futures dimension, school curricula take on a repressive character. That is they elevate a concern for the maintenance of knowledge (and therefore power) structures over human concerns. To render the future invisible, not worthy of discussion or study, is to strip away much of human significance in the present. For teaching and learning do not take place simply as a result of the pressure of the past. Statements of aims and objectives usually refer to purposes, goals, and intentions which *necessarily refer forward in time*. So there is something of a contradiction involved in disregarding futures study since they are already present, already there in present-day teaching and learning.

Futures concerns are so deeply involved in creating the present that it is doubtful if we could act at all without them. Indeed the present is not a fixed span of time. It varies according to perception and need. With growing knowledge and insight we can venture out of the narrow 'here and now' into the wider spans of space and time which our technological culture already occupies. Furthermore, we can consciously choose not to use past and future simply as escape routes into reconstructed pasts and spurious 'Star Wars' type futures. By consciously engaging processes of interpretation and anticipation we may widen the boundaries of the present and discover quite new options.

The concept of future, or futures plural because there is no single-track path into a predetermined end point, is not an abstraction. Few teachers would undertake the rigours of training if it were not related to personal and professional goals. Few pupils would remain at their desks if they were not persuaded of the benefit. It is not really possible to begin to discuss careers, personal development, social change, or peace without reference to the world of the future in which all of this is supposed to happen. A futures approach ought not to suggest that we get rid of all our old maps but it does suggest some profound changes in, and additions to, them.

A second comment is that a curriculum for whole persons needs a futures dimension. For persons *require* a future to guide them in the present. But the implicit model of personhood which we have inherited from the industrial era overlooks this and much else besides. It recognizes *some* of the mental and

216

physical attributes of persons but deals scantily, if at all, with their emotional and spiritual aspects. By 'spiritual' I do not mean religious. There is plenty of religiosity in schools. But, apart from some independents such as those following Steiner's pattern, few recognize the inner person and its higher needs. That has not been a part of recent western culture in the past and it is therefore not seen as important now or in the future. Yet little can be *more* important than to have a developed view of human growth and human potential which includes notions of peacefulness, caring, and stewardship (Slaughter 1987a). This is part of the human basis for resisting the arrogance of technological overkill. It is therefore essential to incorporate a concern for human development into all peace work.

The industrial model needs replacing with one which gives due attention to the *layered quality* of persons and the world in which they live; to the way in which not only are we all grounded in the physical world but also we range upwards through emotional and mental states to levels of functioning which can only be called spiritual (Schumacher 1977). A world view based on Cartesian logic and Newtonian paradigms of enquiry simply cannot cope with that. But the fact of the matter is that as we proceed from the lower to the higher we discover *emergent qualities*. Just as a watch is more than the sum of its parts and a living cell is much more than the sum of its chemical constituents, so the highest levels of human consciousness do in fact reach the transcendent. A world view or curriculum which misses this is actually missing one of the most humanly significant features of our world. For higher levels of awareness tend to be inclusive rather than exclusive. They reach out to embrace broad spans of space and time and have therefore become essential in healing our planet, creating peace, and moving towards new stages of civilized life.

The third comment is that as they are presently constituted, school curricula tend not to offer a critical purchase on the underlying causes of the present world crisis. Schooling actually *contributes* to the problem when it unthinkingly reproduces an obsolete world view. For the sources of most world problems, including issues of peace and conflict, lie in the character of paradigms and systems of valuation and thought which support the western way of life (Berman 1981). The practical power of our technology and organizational ability has been purchased at an enormous price: pollution, conflict, alienation, social decay, ecological breakdown, and nuclear stalemate. Those features of the world are often glossed over in schools. Yet any map which omits areas of danger is hardly worth having. So ways are needed of coming to grips with the underlying belief systems and approaches to knowledge which have brought our civilization to this dangerous and unstable condition. While some groups find this essential and constructive work threatening or even 'subversive' (perhaps because of entrenched interests or dated knowledge) it cannot be overstressed that understanding the breakdown is an essential precursor to real cultural innovation and recovery.

Futures in education is most centrally concerned with negotiating and exploring new and renewed understandings about our present cultural transition beyond the industrial era. It therefore has a role to play in defining and creating a more just, peaceful, and sustainable world. Visions and views of desirable futures always come before their realization. Futures study therefore contributes directly to the central project of all peace work. It explores and defines the wider context, providing concepts, methods, perspectives, and proposals which complement the peace worker's more detailed attention to specific issues. Hence any curriculum which works towards a better and more peaceful world will have a strong and explicit futures component. The rest of this chapter outlines some of the ways this can be achieved in the context of peace education.

THE FUTURES FIELD AS AN EDUCATIONAL RESOURCE

When people ask how one can study something which 'does not exist' they are saying three things. First, that they are implicitly referring to empiricist traditions of enquiry which tend to value only the tangible and the measurable. Second, that they have not given much thought to values and meanings which are not diminished by their non-material status. And third, that they have not looked seriously at the futures field. If they had, they would know that powerful groups such as governments, transnationals, and the military spend a great deal of money of the kinds of futures work of benefit to them. Why schools have not yet done the same on any wide scale is an interesting question. In fact futures have been taught in schools for over twenty years. Hence while some of the ideas may appear recent they are not untested in practice. How, then, does one begin?

The first thing to note is that there is indeed a broad field of study, research, and practice involving futures which has three main foci. These can be arranged upon a continuum which extends from a 'hard' or 'scientific' pole mainly inhabited by professional forecasters, systems analysts, and so on, to a 'soft' or participatory pole which includes citizen action groups and social movements (such as the peace, women's, environmental, and anti-nuclear movements). In between these two poles lies the area of future studies (or futures study) which I take to be a broadly synthesizing focus drawing on work at both ends of the spectrum. Here one finds writers, commentators, teachers, and researchers who attempt to develop broad, often holistic, views, of the field and its subject matter. It is useful to see futures in education situated at this point and be able to select critically from the whole range of the field.

The subject matter of futures has sometimes given rise to quite spurious dismissals. But if one looks through any of the journals, magazines, or books associated with it, the subject matter is very clear. It ranges from forecasts, plans, surveys of various kinds, through careful analyses of particular issues to explicitly partisan statements about hoped-for or intended futures. Nor should we leave out of this sketch the branch of speculative writing (or SF) which has used the future as an imaginative backdrop. For it is often within the context of stories that the human significance of futures can be most productively explored (Slaughter 1985).

Clearly within such a diverse field there are many different interests and foci. The protestor against nuclear weapons seems far removed from the systems analyst who works on marketing strategies for a large corporation. Both would appear to be remote from the academic or teacher. But underlying these differences are certain important common interests and themes. To understand both is to grasp the central project of the futures field as a whole and its significance in education.

One of the central themes of the futures field is that underlying all human differences are certain *commonalities of interest*. These include food, shelter, companionship, a healthy environment, peace, and justice. Whatever one's position or viewpoint these underlying interests provide a basic framework for enquiry and for curriculum development. The all-too-obvious differences that arise are arguably less important than the shared fact of a common underlying agenda. But this is not all. What the analyst, protestor, and teacher have in common goes beyond this. For each, in his or her own way, and with greater or lesser clarity and awareness, attempt to plot a course through a changing world. This involves reading signals from the environment, interpreting them, making decisions, and acting.

NEGOTIATING CHANGE: A CYCLE OF TRANSFORMATION

It is regrettable that pundits, commentators, children's books, and most media productions involving futures tend to misdirect students and to focus on the external 'construction' of the future by technology (Slaughter 1987c). For underlying the surface of technical change there are important human processes. These have to do with *transformations of meaning*. In this view we can distinguish at least four stages within the wider process. To begin to be aware of specific opportunities for intervention is to open up new areas of enquiry and action. In so doing we penetrate to the core of critical futures work.

Teachers are more aware than many that uncertainty, depression, frustration, and fear often appear to be the dominant emotions of our times. Third world populations have seen the material cornucopia of the west and yet, broadly speaking, it is denied to them. On the other hand, the rich, and relatively rich, populations of the industrialized world have many of the goods but have lost a coherent view of where they are going or why. The nuclear sword hangs over us all. A large number of the values and beliefs

219

which sustained the social landscape and gave it coherence have fallen, or are falling, apart. Work, leisure, defence, gender, progress, health, and so on have lost much of their earlier significance. We are, in other words, living through a *breakdown of inherited meanings*. This is the first stage of a 'transformative cycle', or T-cycle for short (see Figure 16). The point is this. Whereas unreflective immersion in the breakdowns of unemployment, racism, crime, poverty, and meaninglessness is certainly a cause for depression and anger, it is of enormous value to see that the breakdown is structural. It is not *merely* the result of individual failure or bad luck. However well-off we may be we are all affected. So, first, we can recognize a society-wide process which affects everyone and for which we are all responsible. Second, we can begin to move out of the sense of guilt and–or depression which results because, having brought the breakdown to full consciousness, we are now open to new choices and possibilities.

In Figure 16, an example from a workshop on defence, participants have recorded their views about each of the stages. Note that the cycle is a record of interpretations and judgements. It is never simply right or wrong. The recognition of breakdown is a kind of ground-clearing exercise (though in fact it is also continuous and parallels the other stages). It alerts us to search the cultural environment for anything which might be helpful in resolving the problem. Here we reach a second stage. For a highly significant part of the futures field is engaged in evolving proposals, suggestions, practices which explicitly address these breakdowns. Many people who put forward *reconceptualizations* (or new proposals) would not, perhaps, think of themselves as involved in 'futures'. Yet that is just what they are involved in. For in elaborating possible solutions they are setting up possibilities which invite individual and social responses. This occurs in almost every conceivable area. The difficulty is that much of this solution-orientated work never makes it into the mass media which are dedicated to relatively trivial ends such as marketing and reality-avoidance (Postman 1985). Most proposals simply fall by the wayside and are lost. Some fail because they are inappropriate or impractical. In any event, this takes us on to the third stage.

Since far more proposals are fielded than can ever be taken up some kind of winnowing process is needed. At present the process is obscured by power politics, lack of knowledge, and lack of appropriate forums. New proposals often reach the stage of *negotiations and conflicts* without ever having had the benefit of wide public discussion. If you think of the sheer effort and cost of mounting opposition to the siting of nuclear power stations or cruise missiles it is immediately obvious why many other possibilities seem to disappear without trace.

Conflicts occur because the new impacts upon the old and someone always has interests bound up in the way things were (Schon 1971). The crucial capacity here is to be able to move from a position of open conflict to one of negotiation. That involves organization, support, commitment, a suitable

Figure 16 Illustrating change: the transformative cycle

Subject: e.g. Defence

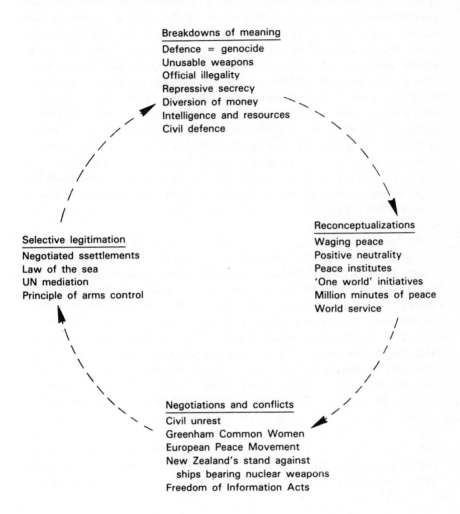

Breakdowns of meaning
Defence = genocide
Unusable weapons
Official illegality
Repressive secrecy
Diversion of money
Intelligence and resources
Civil defence

Reconceptualizations
Waging peace
Positive neutrality
Peace institutes
'One world' initiatives
Million minutes of peace
World service

Selective legitimation
Negotiated ssettlements
Law of the sea
UN mediation
Principle of arms control

Negotiations and conflicts
Civil unrest
Greenham Common Women
European Peace Movement
New Zealand's stand against
    ships bearing nuclear weapons
Freedom of Information Acts

Complete the cycle by filling in the stages of a single issue *or* locate different issues
at each of the four stages.

arena, and the equalization of power relations (if only for the purposes of discussion). To the extent that this occurs there is a chance of socio-cultural innovations to be taken up and legitimized. This is, in fact, the final stage of the cycle. *Selective legitimation* refers to innovations and proposals which are taken up and incorporated in the new pattern. Examples would be the emancipation of women, preventive health measures, smoke-free restaurants, nuclear-free zones, and real ale! However, we cannot assume that under present conditions the 'solutions' which are accepted are the 'right' ones or even the best available. Often they are not. Nevertheless this outline of the cycle does place in context many activities which hitherto may have been considered in isolation. As a workshop method, teaching tool and research approach the T-cycle has a variety of uses. Figure 17 shows an elaborated T-cycle. It suggests that individuals can act effectively at *any* stage ('autonomous recovery of meaning') and that far from returning to a notional starting-point, the process can lead on to a new synthesis and new states and stages of being. We can see more clearly how peace education and futures interact. Each supports the other in this wider process of breakdown/innovation/conflict and change.

To summarize, we can say that futures study provides a context and a foundation for forward-looking work of many kinds and is a vital element of peace education. It provides an overview of social, cultural, economic, and technical processes at all levels from the local to the global. It assists the 'mapping' of important issues and deploys a range of specimen resolutions to problems. Properly understood, it probes beneath the surface of technical change to underlying questions of world views (including commitments to particular interests and ways of knowing). At the symbolic level, futures study provides a variety of perspectives, views, and visions which are precursors of any change in social arrangements. It therefore provides access to visions and scenarios of worlds we wish to avoid and those we hope to achieve. Finally by providing access to critical concepts and skills it helps pupils and teachers alike to develop well-grounded and constructive attitudes toward change. These are among the most tangible consequences of good futures work. With these points in mind we have an outline of underlying social processes and a firm foundation for futures work in the context of peace education.

IMPLEMENTATION

Those who remain immersed in obsolescent ways of knowing and teaching will continue to doubt how, or even whether, futures can be studied. But others are now finding the past of lesser interest than the range of alternative futures now confronting us. For, historically speaking, we have never been here before. Historical parallels relevant to the present global situation are

Figure 17 An elaborated tranformative cycle

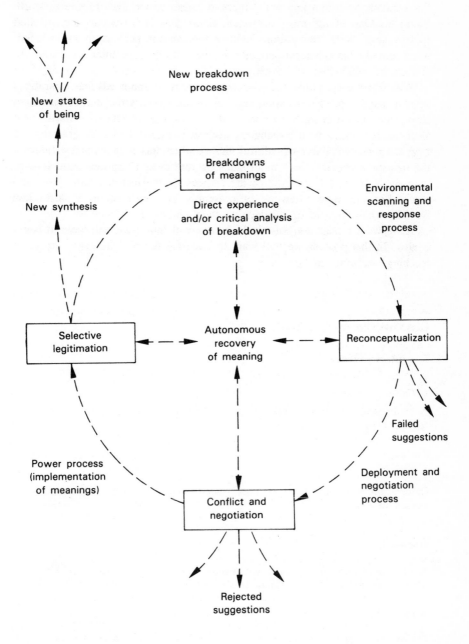

tenuous at best. Nor does it require extensive study and research to take up the available tools and join with others to negotiate and explore futures worth living in. One of the most consistent findings is that students tend to find futures study very rewarding. Neither threats nor persuasion are needed. Most already have natural interests in the unfolding of their lives and the context in which that will take place.

With other curriculum initiatives which focus on the needs and aspirations of real people, peace education can contribute towards the deeper paradigm shift which could change the nature of schools and of education itself. That shift has less to do with passing on declining culture than with grasping the new and renewed source of cultural vitality which has been suppressed during the industrial era. It is less about studying futures as a dry academic activity than about creating them through the choices we make in our daily lives and work. For the mere extension of present trends leads on to a world few would wish to live in or hand on to their children.

If we want a peaceful, sustainable, convivial future we will have to begin it now. In that process we will want to integrate futures into every aspect of teaching, learning, and research.

CLASSROOM ACTIVITIES

The futures wheel

Purpose

To help students explore the wide-ranging consequences that may follow from a specific decision made in the present.

Preparation

Large sheets of paper (A3 or larger) are needed, along with a supply of markers in various colours.

Procedure

The futures wheel is the simplest, yet in some ways the most versatile, of all the futures tools and techniques. Figure 18 shows how it works. Initially the teacher or students choose a particular development to focus on and, in the figure shown, this is the increasing use of microwave ovens.

'Microwave ovens' is thus placed at the centre of a sheet of paper (see Figure 18) and having decided on the focus one asks: 'What are the *immediate* consequences?' These are roughly arranged in a ring around the primary assumption. Thus 'less heat in the kitchen' leads both to 'less load on air conditioner' and 'new heating ducts'. Once students are satisfied with the immediate consequences they move on to

Figure 18 Futures wheel

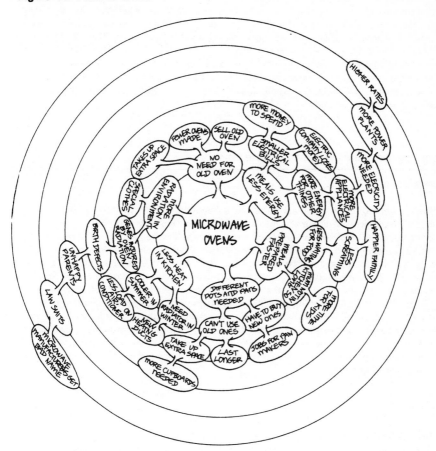

secondary consequences, that is those flowing from the ring which has just been made. In this way a futures wheel is built up which represents a series of judgements about the likelihood and probability of a chain of events consequent upon the first. As the pattern emerges so different relationships can be established between different areas.

Futures wheels can be drawn to explore the possible implications of any issue that the class may be studying, for example expansion of the nuclear power programme, initiating a guaranteed minimum income, or the impact of AIDS.

Note

Futures wheels can be used with any age group from primary upwards. They can be built up by a teacher with children as young as six. He or she simply elicits verbal responses and writes these up on a display board. One of the most valuable aspects

225

of the futures wheel in a peace education context is the way in which it gives students the opportunity to negotiate with each other about whether or not *B* follows *A*. This provides a chance to develop negotiation and conflict-resolution skills. It also allows students to render implicit knowledge and values into an explicit – and therefore accessible – pattern. Hence a good futures wheel is likely to reveal something that one already knew but had not brought to full consciousness. Another useful feature is that the wheel is never simply right or wrong. It represents a series of judgements, not facts. If a wheel doesn't seem quite right it can be restarted using different assumptions.

Dealing with fears about the future

Background

Surveys carried out in many countries show beyond doubt that students are often fearful and depressed about the future that they feel lies ahead for them. Unemployment, nuclear war, terrorism, and pollution are frequently mentioned. Yet the key question is this: 'Are such fears *necessarily* depressing?' This exercise suggests that they need not be for the important reason that negative images of the future can also be understood simply as early warning signals. It makes no more sense to be depressed by them than it does to fear the red lights at a traffic intersection. The crucial thing (and this is what the exercise focuses upon) is how should we respond? This activity therefore suggests that the crucial factor is not the focus of concern, however fearful, but the quality of responses brought to bear upon it. If students can be shown how to take their energy away from despairing about various problems and how to invest it in possible solutions, the whole climate changes for the better.

Purpose

To explore ways of dealing with students' fears about the future. To consider the implications of optimistic and pessimistic options. To learn how to distinguish between 'high' and 'low' quality responses.

Preparation

Encourage pupils to express their fears about a particular issue as fully as they can. Be prepared to admit that the basis of the fear may be entirely rational. If appropriate raise the possibility that, nevertheless, fear alone will not make a difference to the problem. The key is in *using* what is feared to explore possible solutions. Of the many ways to structure and explore responses, two are given in Figures 19 and 20.

Procedure

Copy or redraw Figures 19 and 20 for students. Ask them to think about whether they tend to be optimists or pessimists in life. How would they define each of these? What are the characteristics of each? Lead them to consider that optimism is not

Figure 19 Optimism or pessimism?

Issues to respond to	Optimism		Pessimism	
	Inhibiting response	Empowering response	Inhibiting response	Empowering response
School exams	Over-confidence	Work even harder to get distinction	Resignation to the inevitable	Make up lost ground
Nuclear deterrence	No interest in the issues	Finding out about arguments for and against	Live for today philosophy	Joining Youth CND
etc.				

necessarily useful (if it leads to false confidence for example) and that pessimism is not necessarily negative (if it stimulates active responses). Work through some of the examples chosen, completing Figure 19. Figure 20 offers an alternative approach. Having identified various negative images of the future, students take each in turn and complete the matrix. If they *accept* the negative image of the future they can still choose between low- and high quality responses. What would these be? Again if they *reject* a particular negative image low- and high-quality responses are still possible.

Figure 20 Dealing with negative images

	Low-quality responses	High-quality responses
Acceptance of negative images	Resignation, powerlessness, and continuation of depressive cycles	Negative futures a real posssibility so take avoiding action
Rejection of negative images	Either, don't believe it, all is OK, *or* dive into naïve activism	Empowerment and effective action to realize aspects of liveable futures in the extended present

REFERENCES

Berman, M. (1981) *The Re-enchantment of the World*, Ithaca, NY and London: Cornell University Press.

Dossey, L. (1982) *Space, Time and Medicine*, Colorado: Shambhala.

Gough, N. (1985) *Project IF and other Stories*, Melbourne: Victoria College.

Macy, J.R. (1983) *Despair and Personal Power in the Nuclear Age*, Washington DC: New Society Publishers.

Postman, N. (1985) *Amusing Ourselves to Death*, London: Heinemann.

Schon, D. (1971) *Beyond the Stable State*, London: Temple Smith.

Schumacher, E.F. (1977) *A Guide for the Perplexed*, London: Cape.

Slaughter, R. (1985) 'Metafiction, transcendence and the extended present: Three keys to post-galactic SF', in *Foundation 35*, London: SF Foundation.

—— (1987a) 'Future vision in the nuclear age', *Futures* 19,1: 54–72.

—— (1987b) *Futures Tools and Techniques*, Lancaster: University of Lancaster.

—— (1987c) 'The Machine at the Heart of the World: Technology, Magic and Futures in Children's Media', Lancaster: University of Lancaster.

Wilber, K. (1979) *No Boundary: Eastern and Western Approaches to Person Growth*, Colorado: Shambhala.

PART 3

Connections

14

Changing the curriculum

Robin Richardson

This chapter offers an overview on curriculum change and highlights some of the dilemmas inherent in that process. In particular it draws on experiences from multicultural education and asks: can LEA strategies for change be both humanistic and anti-racist? The issues raised by such a question, for essentially they are about challenging and opposing structural violence in the education system, and are fundamental to the concerns of peace education.

I wish, says a child in a poem by James Berry (1976), reminding us where every article or paper on education ought to start, and from where it ought never to wander far or for long, I wish . . .

> my teacher's eyes wouldn't/ go past me today. Wish he'd know/ it's okay to hug me when I kick/ a goal. Wish I myself wouldn't/ hold back when an answer comes.

When teachers attend to learners, poised and eager to give them praise and affirmation, learners in their turn have the courage and self-assurance to explore, to respond, to venture – 'Wish I myself wouldn't hold back when an answer comes.' Every book about education, every lecture or conference, every in-service course, every education committee meeting, every advisory service meeting, is running the risk of being arid, irrelevant, and downright harmful if it does not start from, and continually hark back to and hearken to, the basic classroom reality of teacher-attending-to-learner, person-attending-to-person. This creature we name education depends on, and is rooted in, that reality. Much of the successful work in peace education and world studies comes, of course, from paying attention to just that reality.

I wish, continues Berry's child,

> I wish I could be educated/ to the best of tune up, and earn/ good money and not sink to lick/ boots. I wish I could go on every/ crisscross way of the globe/ and no persons or powers or/ hotel keepers would make it a waste.

Education, the imagery is recalling, is to do with having a rigorous analytical ('finely tuned') mind, and also a venturing mind – 'wish I could go on every crisscross way of the globe'. And it is to do with gaining economic autonomy, and with developing assertiveness and personal power, the capacity to defend and promote one's rights in all sorts of relationships and role structures, the capacity to speak, to give, to control, to resist, to be productive, not to be wasteful or wasted. Further, it involves being able to say yes more than no, being vibrant, having a song, being recognized and affirmed for your song, your celebration, your affirmations: I wish, continues the poem,

> life wouldn't spend me out/ opposing. Wish same way creation/ would have me stand it would have/ me stretch, and hold high, my voice/ Paul Robeson's, my inside eye/ a sun. Nobody wants to say/ hello to nasty answers.

There is a full programme, sketched here in Berry's brief economic imagery, not just for peace education but for curriculum development and reform more broadly: an interplay of (1) the fine-tuned, scientific, and venturing mind; (2) assertiveness, self-confidence, personal strength, and power; (3) celebration, the arts, and creativity; (4) participation in social and political affairs; and (5) underlying and undergirding the first four, the teacher providing personal attention, recognition, praise, affirmation for the learner, the learner's unique dignity and destiny.

James Berry is not merely, however, evoking and commending a curriculum. For the child in the poem is black, and Berry's implicit cry and contention is that black children in British schools are simply not receiving the curriculum to which they are, like all other children, morally and legally entitled. The poem is about the need for change, major and urgent change. Similarly this chapter is about change – change towards ensuring that that five-part curriculum is received by black children as well as by white. Berry's imagery envisages that classrooms can be and should be both humanistic and anti-racist. But how readily can LEAs in general, and LEA advisory services in particular, be both these things at once? This is the specific underlying question of this chapter and one that highlights some of the tensions inherent in peace education.

If there is a single point which has been learnt about curriculum change during the last twenty-five years or so, it is that successful change depends not only on clear aims but also, and even more importantly, on clear strategies, therefore on sound political skills and dexterity, and a clear understanding of power, of organizational culture, of how adults learn. This is the humanistic emphasis, made in opposition to technocratic and bureaucratic assumptions held by most politicians and many education officers, of much recent literature on curriculum reform and school improvement. It is not true, in the field of curriculum development, that where there's a will there's a way: on the contrary, as Michael Fullan has documented at length in his authoritative study *The Meaning of Educational Change* (1982), strong wills and clear goals more often obstruct and prevent the successful implementation of policy than they facilitate it.

Too much decision-making, management theorists in industry have observed, consists of these three phases: one, get ready; two, fire; three, take aim. If you shoot from the hip, to develop the point with mixed metaphors, you'll shoot yourself in the foot; if you don't aim for clear goals, in another mixed metaphor, you'll score only own goals. Not that, however, taking aim is only or even primarily a matter of having clear goals and high-profile policies: it is a matter also of having clear strategies, of thinking fully and deeply about the whole change process, not about policy only. Michael Fullan quotes wryly the outgoing deputy minister of education in Canada, who is said to have declared to his successor as he left, 'Well, the hard work is done. We have the policy passed; now all you have to do is implement it'. Fullan's whole book is an analysis of the lunacy in that remark, and of international experience over the last twenty-five years or so in developing alternative models and assumptions about change. His book is particularly relevant and challenging for the field of peace education as well as anti-racist and multicultural education – that is for all those who care about the situation sketched in James Berry's poem.

This chapter has a traditional three-part structure: thesis, antithesis, synthesis. First, there is a summary of the humanistic view, as distinct from the technocratic or bureaucratic view, of curriculum reform and school improvement. Second, there is a brief critique and repudiation of the humanistic view, from an anti-racist perspective. In the case of the struggle to create and sustain racial equality and justice in the curriculum, this second part of the chapter argues, the lessons of the international curriculum reform movement are not sufficient. Third, the chapter therefore makes some modest suggestions towards a synthesis.

SOME LESSONS OF THE INTERNATIONAL CURRICULUM REFORM MOVEMENT: 1960–85

The following points have been distilled from the work of academic researchers such as Fullan (1982), Hopkins and Wideen (1984), Dalin and Rust (1983), Everard and Morris (1985), and Galton and Moon (1983). They are presented here in reasonably everyday language because they are also obvious to common sense! However, it is difficult to over-emphasize the view that in much educational activity, particularly in the field of multicultural and anti-racist education, these obvious principles have been honoured more in the breach than in the observance. It is not that they have been tried and found wanting: as with certain other fine aspirations, they have not been tried at all. Also they are often not even advocated, let alone implemented.

Ownership by classroom teachers

New curricular initiatives must be owned by teachers themselves, and are destined to fail if they are merely 'cascaded', handed or ordered downwards from above, or outwards from a centre or project. This means, amongst other things:

1 Teachers must see the need for the change which is proposed.

2 Teachers should take part in actively arguing, pressurizing, and lobbying for change, both as individuals and through their unions and professional associations.

3 Teachers should have opportunities, in atmospheres of security and trust, to talk reflectively and tentatively (viz 'to think aloud') with each other about the change. This involves being able to air their doubts, questions, uncertainties, and resistance without fear of being immediately labelled and rebuked.

4 Teachers must be respected and trusted, as competent, creative, self-managing professionals.

5 Teachers need to be convinced that the proposed change will bring satisfaction and benefit to themselves, both personal and professional and both material and non-material and that these will more than compensate for whatever costs, pains, and discomforts which may be involved.

6 Teachers need to be convinced, in their hearts as well as in their minds, that the proposed change is to the advantage of their pupils.

Continual negotiation and transformation

It has been mischievously suggested that the movement towards teacher ownership of curriculum change has three main phases. In the first phase, the mood is 'This won't work, it can't work, anyway there's no need for it'; in the second, it is 'It might work, and there may be a need, but it's not worth all the time and trouble'; third and finally, people say 'I always did think this was a fantastically good idea'. This process towards ownership is also a process of negotiation of meaning, and therefore a process of change from the original idea or policy.

There must be a positive readiness amongst policy-makers, it follows, for their policies to be reinterpreted, reordered, and reorganized by practitioners, very possibly beyond their own easy recognition. Policy-makers cannot demand, and should not try to demand, perfect fidelity and compliance. Indeed they should not even expect or aim to communicate perfectly, that is to their own satisfaction. They must let practitioners be, not bound them and bind them with tablets of stone.

One theoretical consequence of these emphases is that the customary distinction between policy-formulation and policy-implementation, and between policy-maker and practitioner, are misleading and unhelpful. Ideally they should be dropped from our minds, and from our mouths, pens, and word-processors.

The role of headteachers

Headteachers have many roles – according to one interesting and full analysis, those of figurehead, leader, liaison person, monitor, disseminator, spokesperson, entrepreneur, disturbance handler, resource allocator, negotiator, goal-setter, evaluator, curriculum co-ordinator, teacher, and exemplar of professional values (Coulson 1985). Through this complex mixture of roles Heads can and do exercise very significant influences on any proposed curriculum change. There are three main points worth highlighting in the present context:

1 Heads have the capacity to block or handicap virtually any initiative by withholding or withdrawing essential resources from it. These resources include not only money, and the things which money can buy, but also less material and less tangible factors such as recognition, legitimacy, status, and job-satisfaction.

2 Heads have the capacity to increase the likelihood of success by in fact providing essential resources, and by ironing out various smallish practical difficulties.

3 Heads have great influence on a school's culture and climate, its formal and informal agendas, its openness to new ideas and capacity to learn from others, its capacity to withstand autonomously unwelcome pressure from outside, its readiness to be purposefully self-critical.

It follows from such observations that Heads need a distinctive kind of support for their professional development, not conventional courses. Such support will include on-the-job learning and action-learning, joint reflection with peers rather than with (for example) advisers or inspectors, and consultancy for their teams of senior colleagues as well as for themselves.

Action-learning and action research

A major impetus for change at classroom level, and a major factor underlying the maintenance and continuation of change, arises when teachers replicate

235

for themselves, in their own immediate reality, the research findings which underlie formal policy; and when they engage in action-research, purposefully and reflectively observing their own practice and solving their own immediate practical problems. Such research is particularly influential when it is done collaboratively, or when at least the results are shared with immediate colleagues. Valuable accounts of action research in the gender equality field for example, are contained in *Seeing is Believing* and *It Ain't Necessarily So* (Brent Education Department 1984; 1985).

The sequence in such research is not theory and rationale first followed only later by practical applications; but a continual dialectic of thought and action, with theory typically drawn and crystallized from successful practice not its necessary pre-condition. 'Teaching materials' (textbooks, for example) are misnamed and misconceptualized: we should think rather of developing resources for classroom-action-research.

Individuals and whole schools

Each individual teacher needs new perspectives and skills, developed through action-and-reflection in his or her own classroom. This individual learning needs to be supported, not undermined, by the immediate context – the culture, conversation, and conventions in the staffroom; the everyday taken-for-granted, second-nature procedures of the school; the overall structure of decision-making. The move towards greater participation, democracy, and openness in the individual classroom, for example, has to be strengthened and sustained by analogous changes in school organization and culture.

External support

The individual school, it follows, is the principal arena in which change takes place, or fails to take place. The individual school – not groups of schools and not individual teachers within a school – should be the focus of concern. External support agencies, however, are vital, as sources of assistance and stimulus. To assert this is to make an observation about the nature of institutional and personal change: it is not to imply that schools are inherently deficient.

There is a need both for many different kinds of support and for many different kinds of support agency: no single agency can provide everything which is required. The different kinds of support required by schools are in relation to, amongst other things:

1 the analysis and prioritizing of needs;
2 the development of materials;

236

3 the design and implementation of research, including in particular classroom-action-research;

4 knowledge of developments, trends, and projects – and successes and failures – elsewhere;

5 review, goal-setting, and the formation of objectives;

6 networking, liaison, and contact with others – for mutual moral support as well as for the exchange of information and experience, and a sense of perspective and distance;

7 demonstration-teaching and coaching;

8 in-service;

9 team-building or, as the phrase is, 'capacity-building' – the development of a school's ability to review itself critically, and to engage in self-sustaining change;

10 evaluation;

11 mediation and consultancy in relationships.

External support, as the term is being used here, needs to be distinguished from external, or peripatetic, resources. Many so-called support services in Britain are more accurately described as additional staffing resources – they provide extra pairs of hands, and therefore perhaps valuable organizational slack and space, but do not contribute support in the limited (yet variegated) sense in which it is used in the literature and debate on curriculum reform and school improvement.

Success, failure, and dispute

As those involved in peace education will be well aware, change involves conflict – therefore losses and pain as well as benefits and gains, divided loyalties as well as closer friendships; and disappointments and criticisms, failures and mistakes, ambiguous alliances. The question is not how to avoid these, but how to prevent them being paralysing and demoralizing, and how to transform them from setbacks into resources for learning.

One implication of this point is that it is crucial to identify and reward good practice and success, and to document systematically, and to take a justifiable pride in, progress. Resting on laurels is to be avoided, yes of course, but so also is the despair which underlies the rejection of all laurels, the refusal to accept that praise and pride have their rightful (if also modest) place in the change process. A valuable maxim in this regard is 'Think Big, Act Small': balance the disappointment, pains, and frustration which comes from having high ideals and wide-ranging aspirations with the reinforcement and renewed morale which comes from small-scale, one-step-at-a-time successes.

Change takes time

A new curriculum initiative at school-level takes at least two or three years, and often much longer than this, before its success – or its failure – is at all clear. At LEA-level it takes more like eight to ten years before changes in policy in the education committee begin to involve real changes in what teachers and learners actually do in classrooms. We must therefore resist the temptation to look for, or to deliver, tangible and visible results too soon. Certainly impetus and momentum, and pressure and urgency, are important – crucially important. But also it is important to resist, and to help others to resist, that clamouring voice, inside as well as outside us, which demands, 'I don't want it good, I want it Tuesday.'

THREE SUMMARIES

The first part of this chapter draws to an end with three separate overall summaries of its points and principles. First, there is the account of the ideal LEA advisory service offered in the recent book *Diplomats and Detectives* (Winkley 1985). In so far as the principles outlined here are being applied, an advisory service will have the following main characteristics and emphases:

1 teacher involvement in events;
2 the principle of growth through the identification of good practice;
3 wide use of teachers in INSET;
4 a high valuing of mutual respect and relationships;
5 trust – the foundation of teacher autonomy;
6 emphasis on self-assessment;
7 building on the initiative and ideas of the best practice of all teachers in schools and higher education;
8 a non-hierarchical and open debating system in which teachers are respected as practitioners in the service, with a great deal to offer;
9 encouraging teachers to stand on their own feet, make their own decisions, chair their own meetings, direct their own lives.

A second way of summarizing many of the point and principles is through Figure 21. This focuses on LEA policy-making as a whole and makes five main emphases:

1 Policy-making is a process of negotiation and renegotiation between largely autonomous groupings, not a communication from 'policy-makers', viz politicians and education officers to 'practitioners', viz teachers. A formal policy statement is an event in this process, not a conclusion.

Figure 21 The possible influences of an LEA policy

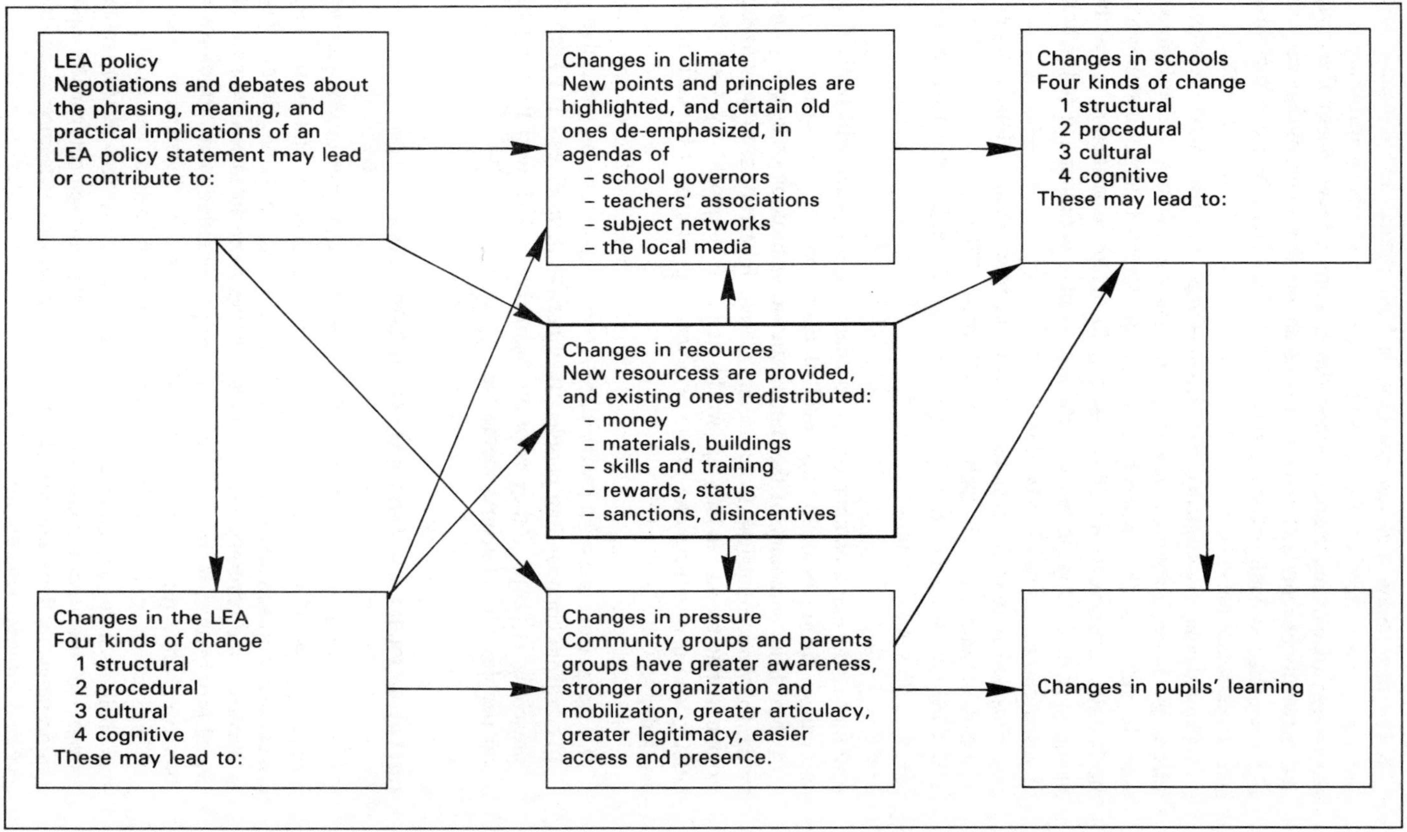

LEA policy
Negotiations and debates about the phrasing, meaning, and practical implications of an LEA policy statement may lead or contribute to:

Changes in climate
New points and principles are highlighted, and certain old ones de-emphasized, in agendas of
  – school governors
  – teachers' associations
  – subject networks
  – the local media

Changes in resources
New resourcess are provided, and existing ones redistributed:
  – money
  – materials, buildings
  – skills and training
  – rewards, status
  – sanctions, disincentives

Changes in pressure
Community groups and parents groups have greater awareness, stronger organization and mobilization, greater articulacy, greater legitimacy, easier access and presence.

Changes in schools
Four kinds of change
  1 structural
  2 procedural
  3 cultural
  4 cognitive
These may lead to:

Changes in the LEA
Four kinds of change
  1 structural
  2 procedural
  3 cultural
  4 cognitive
These may lead to:

Changes in pupils' learning

2 The negotiation and renegotiation is both formal and informal, and is both about meanings of words and concepts and about resources – the distribution of existing resources and the creation of new ones. The distinction between concepts and resources is of course important, but is vulgarized and trivialized if understood merely as the distinction between formulation and implementation.

3 The eventual consequence of policy-making, it is reasonable to hope and intend, is change in pupils' learning. But the causal links and relationships towards this end are indirect, through all sorts of loose couplings, not mechanical. Observers of policy-making, for example academic researchers, should look in the first instance at the effects of negotiation and redistribution of resources to which it may lead.

4 Change has four dimensions – structural, procedural, cultural, individual – and these interact with each other (Haynes 1980).

5 Parents and community groups have an essential role to play in the overall policy-making process.

Any further developments nationally in education for peace will really depend on changes taking place at this level of operation.

A third brief summary of the humanistic orientation on change is provided by the following quotation from ancient China. It refers not to organizational structures but to an underlying world-view. It is quoted by Carl Rogers (1980), who is of course one of the principal high priests of humanistic social psychology:

> If I keep from meddling with people,/ they take care of themselves./ If I keep from commanding people,/ they behave themselves./ If I keep from preaching at people,/ they improve themselves./ If I keep from imposing on people,/ they become themselves.

CRITIQUE FROM AN ANTI-RACIST PERSPECTIVE

The view of change outlined in the first part of this chapter may appeal to the common sense of white academics and peace educators. But is it likely to affect positively and substantially the situation evoked in James Berry's poem? Is it not on the contrary just a recipe, all the more insidious because of its liberal-progressive, humanistic rhetoric, for perpetuating white structures and, therefore, white racism and black under-achievement (Sivanandan 1985)?

There are at least six main sets of questions to be asked, and of objections and challenges to be made and satisfied, before the lessons (or so-called lessons) of the international curriculum reform movement can be applied appropriately to the concerns of peace education and therefore to anti-racist and multicultural education.

Impetus for change

Is it realistic to envisage that the impetus for change can come from the oppressor rather than from the oppressed – that is from those who benefit from an unfair status quo rather than from those who are disadvantaged by it? Is it not more realistic to argue, adapting slightly a political text (Hampton 1984) as follows:

> Intelligence enough to conceive, courage enough to will, power enough to compel: if our ideas of a new curriculum are anything more than a dream, these three qualities must animate the due effective majority of black people, and then, I say, the thing will be done.

White people have a role in helping (or, often, in not hindering) the change process from this perspective, but it is not the same role as from the perspective sketched earlier.

Trust and negotiation

Is it reasonable to trust white teachers and headteachers, and to permit them to negotiate and renegotiate? They are responsible for perpetuating and managing the very system which has been damaging black children. It is surely very naïve to suppose that they will change their ways simply on the basis of appeals to their rationality and good will, and to leave them to renegotiate, and therefore almost certainly transform anti-racist policies back into racist practices.

Urgency

It is completely out of the question to adopt a change strategy which complacently envisages a minimum period of eight to ten years before success or failure will become clear. By then a complete generation of children will have been lost.

Motivation

Is it in fact the case that changes depend largely on rationality – the careful sifting and weighing of objective evidence – and therefore on in-service training? Surely change happens primarily when human beings are seeking certain material rewards and advantages, and when they are seeking to avoid various unpleasant penalties and punishments. What is required is a framework of

241

law and accountability, primarily, not training. A warning given recently to the police applies also to teachers: 'My business is not to train the police officer out of his 'racism', but to have him punished for it – if, that is, he is meant to be accountable to the community which he serves' (Sivanandan 1985).

Staffing

Can we really primarily depend, as seems to be envisaged by the curriculum reform movement, on changing the perception and practice of people already in post? Surely our energy should be directed primarily at removing certain white teachers and headteachers from their posts, and into getting far more black teachers, and anti-racist white teachers, into senior positions.

Vested interests

The humanistic ideology and rhetoric of democracy, participation, gradualism, consensus, consultation, respect for and trust in practitioners, and so on, is arguably nothing more than a disguise for the vested interests of certain academics and LEA advisers – people whose salaries and psychological comfort depend on their saying nice things about teachers, and on not being involved in conflicts and controversies, and in the pain of taking sides. An influential book of the 1960s on humanistic social psychology had as its title 'The Faith of the Counsellors'. In the 1980s we arguably need a book on 'The Vested Interests of the Counsellors' (Selby 1983).

NOTES TOWARDS A POSSIBLE SYNTHESIS

The critical points outlined above were put very briefly. Nevertheless they are all extremely important, and the urgency and desperation behind them must be attended to entirely seriously, not dismissed with sops or with patronizing appeals for patience. The need is for the apparent and real tensions and contradictions between the two perspectives – 'humanistic' and 'anti-racist' – to be teased out, both in theory and in practice. The aspiration must be to achieve a synthesis – not a compromise or middle way ('they're both right if not taken to extremes').

But first, it is appropriate to ask whether such a synthesis is possible. Is the aspiration to achieve synthesis just another liberal naïvety? James Berry himself clearly envisaged, in his imagery, that individual classrooms can be simultaneously humanistic and anti-racist. His five-fold curriculum was humanistic in its person-centred emphasis on praise and affirmation, on the arts and creativity, on personal assertiveness and power, on critical venturing, and so on. At the same time the poem had of course absolutely no doubt that person-centred teaching can be and should be anti-racist. If indeed it is not only desirable but also realistic to aim for this synthesis at classroom-level it is surely not unreasonable to aim for it at LEA-level also. And indeed there would surely be a serious contradiction and disharmony if power-coercive, impersonal, untrusting, controlling, inspectorial methods were used by and LEA Advisory Service to promote person-centred and humanistic education.

Nevertheless we are right to be cautious about the possibility of synthesis. At present the onus is on proponents of humanistic strategies to demonstrate that they can be, and wish to be, anti-racist. It is deeply alarming, and prima facie very significant, that most of the main literature on curriculum development and reform, and on school improvement and organizational development, had made no reference at all, or at best no more than passing ritualistic reference, to racism and racial injustice in schools.

What is needed in practice is a number of projects which are explicitly and thoughtfully both anti-racist and – as the term has been used here – humanistic. Whether synthesis is possible is a matter for energetic action-research, in one specific arena after another, and in thousands of separate arenas at the same time; and there is much that peace educators can do here.

It may be, yes, too late. That possibility has to be faced: there may be ahead of us only a succession of fires and uprisings; projects bound to fail; the inaction of bland policy statements and charitable aid; repression; pointless martyrdoms; burnout; paralysis guilt, despair. Time will tell. In the meanwhile there is James Berry's child in the classroom – there, now, today. Even as we wait for the verdict of history we can attend to persons immediately, urgently: 'I wish the teacher's eyes wouldn't go past me today'.

Note

In its original form this chapter first appeared as an article entitled 'LEA strategies of curriculum change: can they be both humanistic and anti-racist?', *Inspection and Advice* 22,1, 1986.

REFERENCES

Berry, J. (ed.) (1976) in *Blue Foot Traveller*, London: Harrap.
Brent Education Department (1984) *Seeing Is Believing*, Wembley: Brent Education Department.
——— (1985) *It Ain't Necessarily So*, Wembley: Brent Education Department.
Coulson, A. (1985) 'Recruitment and management development for primary headship', *School Organisation*, 5, 2.

Dalin, P. and Rust, V. (1983) *Can Schools Learn?* Walton-on-Thames: NFER/Nelson.

Everard, K.B. and Morris, G. (1985) *Effective School Management*, London: Harper & Row.

Fullan, M. (1982) *The Meaning of Educational Change*, Teachers College Press, and Ontario Institute for Studies in Education.

Galton, M. and Moon, B. (1983) *Changing Schools Changing Curriculum*, London: Harper & Row.

Hampton, C. (ed.) (1984) *A Radical Reader*, adapted from W. Morris, 'On Communism 1893' quoted herein, Harmondsworth: Penguin.

Haynes, R.J. (1980) *Organisation Theory and Local Government*, London: Allen & Unwin.

Hopkins, D. and Wideen, W. (1984) *Alternative Perspectives on School Improvement*, Brighton: Falmer Press.

Rogers, C. (1980) *A Way of Being*, Boston, Mass: Houghton Mifflin.

Selby, P. (1983) *Liberating God: Private Care and Public Struggle*, London: SPCK.

Sivanandan, A. (1985) 'Racism awareness training and the degradation of black struggle', *Race and Class* 26, 4.

Winkley, D. (1985) *Diplomats and Detectives: LEA Advisers at work*, London: Robert Royce.

15

Changing paradigms

David Hicks

A REVIEW OF THE ISSUES

The main substance of this book has been to suggest that an education appropriate for the twenty-first century needs to pay very careful attention both to relevant content and process in the curriculum. Thus one essential element of curriculum content must be learning about contemporary social, political, and economic issues in the world today and, in particular, recognizing the key importance of studying both peace and conflict on scales from the local to the global. The case studies in Part 2 have illustrated admirably both the range of concerns and given some guidance on how these may be approached in the classroom with students.

There is no suggestion here that we should be advocating a new subject called peace studies for inclusion on the timetable, although in some cases this may be appropriate as with the new A-Level in Sheffield (Davies and Munske 1988). Rather, it is being suggested, and this has been the main thrust from all those interested in peace education, that we should be talking about an *approach* to education as much as about content. This approach is both reconstructionist, in arguing that education has a role to play in the transformation of society, and person-centred, in arguing that the development of a centred and assertive self-reliance in the individual is a prerequisite for this.

With the government's current plans for a national curriculum and the present turmoil in education there is great danger that these perspectives may be ignored or even lost. However they are of a long and honourable tradition and have a rightful, indeed an essential place, in the curriculum of the 1990s and beyond. How, and at what point, these matters are explored in school, and in which part of the curriculum, needs to be a matter for discussion by teachers in all the staff-rooms in all our schools. If they are *not* discussed, we do our students a grave disservice, for we send them ill prepared into the world, a world where they will desperately need the skills of conflict resolution and, more than that, a willingness to struggle for justice, both in the context of their own lives and on behalf of the many other groups who find themselves oppressed in the world today.

The table of objectives for education for peace set out in Chapter 1 (p. 14) provides one succinct checklist of the issues. The questions that they raise about knowledge, attitude, and skill acquisition need to be an integral part of all discussion about curriculum objectives. Every teacher, and every school, needs to be quite clear about where and how they are being achieved. If they are not being achieved, we are signally failing to equip our students for life in a fast-changing democratic society. The questions set out in Table 9 also offer another way in to discussion of these crucial concerns. These, together with the objectives, provide one immediate approach for beginning this process of curriculum clarification.

But what impact, if any, has education for peace had on schools and LEAs? There have been many Teachers for Peace Groups active around the country, particularly during the first half of the 1980s, guidelines from LEAs have been published, and in some cases appointments made of both advisers and advisory teachers. While right-wing critics have often deliberately given the impression that such subversive initiatives are spreading rapidly like an undesirable epidemic, a closer and more considered look at the scene suggests a quite different interpretation.

Thus in a recent, quite detailed study by Green (1987), a careful distinction is drawn between the rhetoric, both of protagonists and critics, and the actual extent of successful implementation of peace education programmes and approaches. What becomes quite clear here, as anyone involved in the field knows, is that while there have been a variety of school and LEA initiatives on a small scale, some of which have borne fruit, nowhere have there been the large-scale curriculum changes claimed by some, either in content or methodology. This but serves to remind us that in many ways the structures of education are inimicable to many of the basic assumptions of peace education, that is schools are often hierarchical, inequitable, and structurally violent places, serving generally to perpetuate existing societal patterns.

However, schools are one vital arena for debate and much good work *is* being done which, taken together with developments in world studies, development education, political education, anti-racist and anti-sexist education and allied fields, is of considerable significance. One has only to read accounts such as that by Leimdorfer (1987) to see how far we have come over the last fifteen years. Much ground has been gained and now needs to be held against the incursions of those who see 'relevance' as undesirable in the curriculum. At least, that is, the sort of relevance that is likely to make students more aware of the social, political, and economic contradictions fostered by their masters.

Another way of conceptualizing the concerns of this book is to talk of the three P's: the personal, the political, and the planetary, as essential elements in any definition of good education.

246

Table 9 Education for peace: ten questions to ask

---

1 Local global
Are issues of peace and conflict studied at a variety of scales ranging from both the personal and immediate to the global and long term? Are the rights of the planet considered as well as those of individuals?

2 Conflict analysis
When studying a particular issue, is the exact nature of the conflict analysed into its constituent parts? Is it clear what each party has to gain and what power each has?

3 Conflict resolution
When studying a particular conflict, are a range of possible solutions explored and note taken of who would benefit in each case?

4 Violence
In considering the problems of violence, are examples explored of both direct personal violence and indirect structural violence?

5 Aggression
Is it made clear that there is much debate over the nature of aggression? That it may be culturally learnt and not biologically determined; that some societies are non-aggressive?

6 Non-Violence
In looking at possible solutions to conflict and approaches to life generally are the benefits of less violent and non-violent approaches stressed?

7 Co-operative skills
Are pupils encouraged, and given the opportunity, to acquire and develop co-operative skills via a range of small group activities and situations?

8 Welfare and justice
It is made clear to pupils that any definition of peace must also embody a commitment to human welfare and social justice?

9 Preferred worlds
Are pupils encouraged to visualize and plan personal, local, and global futures which embody their preferred worlds? Are they encouraged to explore the *routes* to such worlds?

10 Medium and message
'There is no way to peace, peace is the way'. If the medium really is the message is this reflected in appropriate teaching/learning methods as well as in the classroom climate and school ethos?

THE PERSONAL

Education for peace is initially about individual actors on the world stage. That is to say it is about people, individually and in groups, and the way in which they interact. It is about what people believe and do, about what they value and about their hopes and dreams. It is, of course, about individual pupils, teachers, and schools, about how they too interact and how they relate to each other. It is about peace, conflict, and violence in our daily lives and immediate experience.

One focus in school thus needs to be very specifically on personal growth and development but, unlike many programmes in personal and social education, set in the broader contexts of both political and planetary awareness. The kinds of skills and attitudes that are necessary here have already been described in Chapter 1 – skills of critical thinking, co-operation, empathy, assertiveness, conflict resolution, and political literacy; attitudes of self-respect, respect for others, ecological concern, open-mindedness, vision, and a commitment to justice.

Since peace education must essentially be holistic in its approach this means that we must pay as much attention to the development of children's feelings, for example, as to their cognitive skills. In particular this requires that both teachers and students learn how to express their feelings rather than denying them. John Heron (1982) highlights the dilemma when he writes:

> culture, through its educational system, offers only one guiding norm about feelings: control. This norm is largely tacit, implied, entailed, by the formal system – in the sense that it is assumed that everyone will be doing it, exercising control, without any clarification being given as to what this means in theory and practice. The result is that throughout [our] culture there is simply no grasp of the distinction between valid, healthy, appropriate control of feelings, and invalid, unhealthy, inappropriate and repressive control of feelings. Thus distress feelings, past and present, become unawarely repressed, denied, then distorted and displaced into rigid and maladaptive behaviours.

This whole area is a crucial one to explore and there is much of practical benefit to teachers in the literature of counselling and therapy, as for example in Murgatroyd (1985), Rowan (1983), Button (1985), Williams (1986), or in works such as Dorothy Rowe's *Beyond Fear* (1987) and Alice Miller's *For Your Own Good* (1987).

It is also important to recall that one outcome of educating for peace should be a change in student's attitudes, so that they learn to prize values which may contribute to peace, whether their own or on a global scale. Bill Eckhardt (1980), for example, has established a range of indicators which show that there are particular attitudes and personality traits which are statistically related to war and peace. Thus one pole of the attitude spectrum, which he calls Compassion, focuses on peacemindedness and worldmindedness, and is defined as a readiness to use persuasion and reason to guide human behavior and resolve social conflicts. The other pole, which he calls Compulsion, is defined as a readiness to use force and punishment to control human behaviour and resolve social conflicts (Eckhardt 1984).

THE POLITICAL

Education for peace must also be centrally concerned about politics in the sense of exploring who gets what, when, where, and how. Since politics is about differing perceptions as to the allocation of resources within society, whether locally, nationally, or globally, it is something that affects everyone. Students thus need to understand about the use and abuse of power and about how decisions are made that affect the future livelihood of themselves and others.

Crick and Porter have written about the need for political literacy (1978), which they define as:

The knowledge, attitudes and skills needed to make students informed about politics; able to participate in public life and groups of all kinds . . . and to recognise and tolerate diversities of political and social values. A politically literate person should know what the main political disputes are about, what beliefs the main contestants have of them, how they are likely to affect them, how they relate to institutions, and they will have a predisposition to try to be politically effective while respecting the sincerity of others.

This is an essential ingredient in peace education, as several of the case studies have indicated, and indeed an essential ingredient of good education in a democratic society whatever some critics may say to the contrary.

Naturally many social, political, and economic issues may be controversial in that there is no broad agreement about their resolution. This is not sufficient reason for their exclusion from the curriculum however, as HMI have indicated (Slater 1986):

We live in an open and pluralist society one of whose characteristics is public debate about issues over which we disagree . . . the testing of fundamental values as well as their preservation lies at the heart of the educational process. Controversial issues cannot be avoided in schools. Many pupils will ask questions about them unprompted, or will have experienced them directly . . . Thus the question is not whether controversial issues should be part of a school curriculum but when, how and with what resources they should be tackled.

The object of discussing controversial issues cannot be to give young people a complete understanding or knowledge of them. None of us has this. If truth cannot be established at least untruth can be avoided. If we cannot know everything at least we can be less ignorant.

Controversial issues can appear in the curriculum of children from the age of five. They are neither subject nor phase specific.

Comment has already been made in Part 1 of this book about the need to teach sensitively about controversial issues and this must be reiterated here. To claim that the issues are too difficult, that they cannot be taught about without bias, that parents and others may complain, is to avoid the professional responsibility that all teachers have in democratic societies. To avoid the study of urgent contemporary issues which our students are, and will have to, deal with directly or indirectly is to commit the gravest irresponsibility to future citizens. There are many ways in which this may be effectively done in the classroom (Harwood 1985).

THE PLANETARY

What motivates many teachers to explore various contemporary issues, whether they specifically talk about education for peace or not, is the state of our planet in this the late twentieth century. Any attempt to take a planetary perspective on matters (let alone a galactic one) has to note the alarming scale on which damage is being done both to people and the biosphere. The scale of the damage is one that we simply cannot afford, as indicated by the following trends (Sivard 1986; Myers 1986; Ehrlich and Ehrlich 1987):

1 The budget of the US Airforce alone is larger than the total educational budget for 1.2 billion children in Africa, Latin America, and Asia, excluding Japan.

2 Each year 40 million people die from hunger and hunger-related diseases, the equivalent of more than 300 jumbo jet crashes a day with no survivors.

3 One in five people in developing countries are undernourished; one in five people in the major industrialized countries are overweight or obese.

4 Every year some 50 million acres of tropical rainforest, which play a key part in the global water-cycle, are lost forever; this equals an area about the size of mainland Britain.

5 After Chernobyl and Three Mile Island public enthusiasm for nuclear power is waning. One Gallup Poll found that 66 per cent of the UK

population said that they didn't want further expansion of nuclear power and 79 per cent said they would prefer alternative energy sources and conservation.

6 Precious topsoil is being lost to world farming at the rate of 25 billion tonnes per annum, that is about 7 per cent of the world's topsoil every decade. Over the last decade in the USA 500 tonnes of soil have gone for every tonne of corn produce.

For every so-called technological 'advance' there is a concomitant human and ecological effect and we would do well to recognize that these 'side' effects often cause long-lasting damage.

We thus see, for example, problems to do with the arms race, world development, health, unemployment, cities, the environment, economic growth and global resources. The key to understanding them, however, is to realize that there is no urban, environmental, or any other, crisis *per se*. Rather we are witnessing a multifaceted global crisis which manifests itself in many ways. All of these are *systemic* problems, that is they are inextricably interrelated and interdependent (Porritt 1984; Johnston and Taylor 1986; Spretnak and Capra 1985). They cannot be understood, let alone resolved, while they are seen as separate and isolated, rather than part of an essentially organic whole. The Chinese ideogram for crisis thus encompasses both danger *and* opportunity and this indeed sums up the global human condition most succinctly. The structure of the global web itself does not need changing but, if we are to survive, then our ideas, our values, our social, political, and economic institutions need to undergo a profound transformation.

Amongst the pertinent developments in education we must note the work of the Centre for Global Education at York University, the *World Studies 8–13 Project* at St Martin's College in Lancaster, the Council for Education in World Citizenship, the education departments of Oxfam and Christian Aid, the Development Education Centres in places such as Manchester, Leeds, Birmingham, and London as well as valuable publications like *Green Teacher*, *Contemporary Issues in Geographical Education*, *Libertarian Education*, and the *World Studies Journal*.

TASKS FOR THE 1990s

How, therefore, might we view some of the possible future developments in these fields? What, for example, are some of the tasks for the 1990s? Richardson's description (1986) of probable future developments in the world studies field is particularly relevant here and has been adapted for this chapter to give the following pointers:

1 *World studies* – there will be an increasing interest in world studies

programmes, and projects such as *World Studies 8–13*, as providing a practical and clear embodiment of education for peace principles in action.

2 *Anti-racism* – there will be increasing recognition that peace education
must be anti-racist in its stance, but also a realization that anti-racism can
learn from the insights of peace education.

3 *Gender* – peace education practitioners will play their part in developing
anti-sexist curricula and equal opportunities for girls and women, and in
challenging male socialization into patterns of violence.

4 *Human rights* – there will be increasing emphasis on teaching and learning about justice, rights, and responsibilities, in both local, national, and
international contexts.

5 *Media* – increasing attention will be paid to the role of the media in
influencing children's attitudes towards violence as well as affecting the
formation of their views of the world.

6 *World development* – there will be a continued emphasis on teaching
about North–South issues and increasing links with those involved in
development education and with Development Education Centres.

7 *Controversy* – more consideration will be given to clarifying the
characteristics of indoctrination and to the specific professional and ethical
responsibilities of teachers when teaching about controversial issues.

8 *International links* – there will be increasing links with peace and global
education initiatives, especially with Europe, the USA, Australia, and
Canada.

9 *National curriculum* – careful attention will be given to the ways in
which specific subject areas can contribute to an understanding of issues to
do with peace and conflict as well as to the ways in which they can benefit
from peace education methodology.

10 *Process* – the process of person-centred education and active learning
will be continually reaffirmed, and particular attention will be given in this
respect to classroom management and school organization.

A TURNING-POINT

The critical question is whether the interest shown in peace education, world
studies, anti-racist and anti-sexist education, development education, political
education and allied fields during the last two decades is merely a passing
fancy, or a part of broader socio-cultural changes that are afoot in the late
twentieth century? It is no accident that the cluster of concerns epitomized
by the above list all focus, in their varying ways, on trying to make both the
content and process of the curriculum more relevant to the needs of the
twenty-first century.

Many writers, among them Fritjof Capra (1983), Marilyn Ferguson
(1982), and Theodore Roszak (1981), have argued that we are in the process

of witnessing some sort of global transformation. In essence this is seen as moving away from a mechanistic to a holistic world view. If this is true it has the most profound implications for us all. Capra (1983), in *The Turning Point*, argues that the mechanistic world view of Cartesian-Newtonian science, from which immeasurable gains have been made, is no longer appropriate, that we now need a more integrated ecological perspective which the old reductionist world view cannot offer. Thus developments in the 'new physics', and indeed a whole range of other fields from economics to health care, reveal an emerging world view which is characterized by words like organic, holistic, and ecological. It is also a systems view, in which the universe is no longer seen as a multitude of separate objects but as one indivisible, dynamic whole, whose parts are all inextricably interrelated.

David Bohm, the physicist, thus writes (1983) about the problem of 'fragmentation and wholeness' which epitomizes the dilemma here:

fragmentation is now very widespread, not only throughout society, but also in each individual: and this is leading to a kind of general confusion of the mind, which creates an endless series of problems and interferes with our clarity of perception . . . Thus science, technology, and human work in general, are divided up into specialities, each considered to be separate in essence from the others . . . [and] society as a whole has developed in such a way that it is broken up into separate nations and different religious, political, economic, racial groups . . . [the] natural environment has correspondingly been seen as an aggregate of separately existent parts, to be exploited . . . Similarly, each individual human being has been fragmented into a large number of separate and conflicting compartments, according to different desires, aims, ambitions, loyalties, psychological, characteristics . . . The attempt to live according to the notion that the fragments are really separate is, in essence, what has led to the growing series of extremely urgent crises that is confronting us today . . . the ability of man to separate himself from his environment and to divide and apportion things ultimately led to a wide range of negative and destructive results, because man lost awareness of what he was doing and thus extended the process of division beyond the limits within which it works properly . . . and begins to see and experience himself and his world as actually constituted of separately existent fragments . . . Man thus obtains and apparent proof of the correctness of his fragmentary self-world view though, of course, he overlooks the fact that it is himself, acting according to his mode of thought, who has brought about the fragmentation that now seems to have an autonomous existence, independent of his will and desire.

It may be no accident here that Bohm talks about 'man' for the old world view based on domination, control, and fragmentation is a specifically male

Table 10 Changing paradigms

Old paradigm	New paradigm
scientific method	ecological awareness
mechanistic	systemic
matter	mind
rational	intuitive
linear	non-linear
pessimistic	optimistic
analytic	holistic
patriarchal	feminist

construct. The world that we have today, it is most important to note, is the outcome of at least 3,000 years of patriarchy in which men – by force, direct pressure, through ritual, tradition, law, language, education, and division of labour – have determined what part women shall play, or not play, and in which female has always traditionally been subsumed under the male.

Table 10 is an attempt to highlight and summarize some of the conceptual shifts between these changing, old and new, paradigms.

This is not in any way to suggest that the key perspectives of the old paradigm are of no value today. Clearly they are and will continue to be so in many ways. The crucial insight, as Bohm points out, is that sole concentration on old paradigm approaches, while offering great gains, has also lead to our present global predicament. The key perspectives of the new emerging paradigm are therefore both timely and essential to our survival. Much of the conflict and anomie that we see around us in the late twentieth century are the result of these paradigms clashing in a wide variety of fields, from the peace movement to education, from health-care to politics.

James Robertson, in his study of alternative futures (1983), has made it quite clear that nothing less than what he calls 'The Sane, Humane, Ecological (SHE) Future' will do. This view, he writes, holds that:

> instead of accelerating, we should change direction . . . the key to the future is not continuing expansion but balance – balance within ourselves, balance between ourselves and other people, balance between people and nature. This is not a recipe for no growth. But the crucial new frontiers for growth now are social and psychological, not technical and economic. The only realistic course is to give top priority to learning to live supportively with one another on our small and crowded planet. This will involve decentralisation, not further centralisation. That is the only way of organising that will work . . . This view appeals to optimistic, participative, reflective people, who reject [other] views as unrealistic or

unacceptable and believe that a better future is feasible. It is only fair to say that it also appeals to quite a large number of cranks.

AND FINALLY

So what are we to make of claims that world views are changing, that we need radically different images of the future, that education is in danger of losing its sense of direction? Is this a *'fin de siècle'* malaise or something more? Clearly at present it appears to be primarily in the industrialized world that such views are changing and it remains to be seen whether this debate has much to offer the less affluent areas of the globe. It is worth noting that many elements of the new paradigm are in broad accordance with the world view of many indigenous peoples: a stress on interconnectedness, on the sacredness of the earth and respect for the needs of future generations. A book on peace education, as all the contributors have indicated, requires by definition images of the future which are more just, sustainable, and peaceful. While the range of preferred futures may vary quite widely, there are some broadly agreed indicators (Hicks 1988), and the task is to examine just how we can get there from here. Frankel, in his study of *The Post-Industrial Utopians* (1987), argues that we need to pay much more attention to this crucial problem and look very critically at many of the proposed strategies for change.

If we wish things to change for the better then we have to work both on ourselves and on society. Joanna Macy, in her work on despair and empowerment (1983), has shown quite clearly the sort of work that needs to be done. Maslow (1976) too has reminded us that the personal and the political are inextricably intertwined:

> The empirical fact is that self-actualising people, our best experiences, are also our most compassionate, our great improvers and reformers of society, our most *effective* fighters against injustice, inequality, slavery, cruelty, exploitation (and also our best fighters *for* excellence, effectiveness, competence). And it also becomes clearer and clearer that the best 'helpers' are the most fully human persons. What I may call the bodhisattvic path is an *integration* of self-improvement and social zeal, i.e., the best way to become a better 'helper' is to become a better person. But one necessary aspect of becoming a better person is *via* helping other people. So one must and can do both simultaneously.

The signs of change are all around us, particularly in the rise of green politics (Spretnak and Capra 1985; Bahro 1986; Hutton 1987) and in redefinitions of sexuality and spirituality (Spretnak 1982; Starhawk 1982). The

Taylor Nelson Monitor Surveys also indicate that these shifts are now visible in their studies of long-term social change in the UK. Thus it has been possible to aggregate the seven social value groups that they have identified into three major groupings labelled Inner Directed, Outer Directed, and Sustenance Driven. Of these three social value groups it is the Inner Directed that is on the increase (MacNulty 1985).

Perhaps the last word should really lie with Paul Goodman (1957) who, in exploring the need for young people both to love and to be critical of their immediate environment, wrote:

'Fundamentally, our kids must learn two things: skills and sabotage. Let me explain.'

'We have here a great city and a vast culture. It must be maintained as a whole: it can and must be improved piecemeal. At the same time, it is a vast corporate organisation: its enterprise is bureaucratised, its arts are institutionalised, its mores are far from spontaneity. Therefore, in order to prevent being swallowed up by it or stamped by it, a kid must learn to circumvent it and sabotage it at any needful point as occasion arises.'

'Wait up! Wait up!' said Horace. 'Ain't this a contradiction? You say we got to learn to be easy at home here, then you say we got to sabotage at every point. On the one hand, you gotta love an' serve 'em: on the other hand, you gotta kick 'em in the shins. Does it make sense to you?'

'There's nothing in what you say, young man. In the Empire City, these two attitudes come to the same thing: if you persist in honest service, you will soon be engaging in sabotage. Do you follow that?'

'Yes, I think we follow that', said Eliphaz quietly. 'But I doubt that other people do.'

REFERENCES

Bahro, R. (1986) *Building the Green Movement*, London: GMP Publishers.

Bohm, D. (1983) *Wholeness and the Implicate Order*, London: Ark Paperbacks, Routledge & Kegan Paul.

Button, J. (1985) *Making Love Work: A Radical Approach*, Wellingborough: Turnstone Press.

Capra, F. (1983) *The Turning Point: Science, Society and the Rising Culture*, London: Fontana.

Crick, B. and Porter, A. (1978) *Political Education and Political Literacy*, London: Longman.

Davies, R. and Munske, B. (1988) *An A-Level Peace Studies Reader*, London: Pergamon.

Eckhardt, W. (1980) *A Manual on the Development of the Concept of Compassion*, 1962–1980, 3rd edn, St Louis, Missouri: Peace Research Laboratory.

—— (1984) 'Peace studies and attitude change', *Peace and Change* 10, 2.

Ehrlich, A. and Ehrlich, P. (1987) *Earth*, London: Thames Methuen.

Ferguson, M. (1982) *The Aquarian Conspiracy: Personal and Social Transformation in the 1980s*, London: Granada.

Frankel, B. (1987) *The Post-Industrial Utopians*, Oxford: Polity Press–Blackwell.

Goodman, P. (1957) *The Empire City*, New York: Bobbs-Merill Inc.

Green, K. (1987) *Education for Peace in the United Kingdom*, M Phil. thesis, Bradford University, School of Peace Studies.

Harwood, D. (1985) 'We want political not Political education for 5–13 year olds', *Education 3–13* Summer.

Heron, J. (1982) *Education of the Affect*, University of Surrey, Human Potential Research Project.

Hicks, D. (1988) 'Teaching geography for a better world', in J. Fien and R. Gerber, (eds) *Teaching Geography for a Better World*, Edinburgh: Oliver & Boyd.

Hutton, D. (ed.) (1987) *Green Politics in Australia*, Sydney: Angus & Robertson.

Johnston, R.J. and Taylor, P.J. (1986) *A World in Crisis? Geographical Perspectives*, Oxford: Blackwell.

Leimdorfer, T. (1987) *Aspects of International Understanding and Global Perspectives in Curriculum*, M.Ed. Dissertation, University of Bristol.

Macnulty, W.K. (1985) 'UK social change through a wide-angle lens', *Futures* August: 331–47.

Macy, J. (1983) *Despair and Personal Power in the Nuclear Age*, Philadelphia, Pa: New Society Publishers.

Maslow, A. (1976) *Religions, Values and Peak Experiences*, Harmondsworth: Penguin.

Miller, A. (1987) *For Your Own Good*, London: Women's Press.

Murgatroyd, S. (1985) *Counselling and Helping*, London: Methuen.

Myers, N. (1986) *The Gaia Atlas of Planet Management*, London: Pan.

Porritt, J. (1984) *Seeing Green: The Politics of Ecology Explained*, Oxford: Blackwell.

Richardson, R. (1986) *The World Studies Story: Projects, People, Places*, a paper drafted to support some Berkshire in-service courses.

Robertson, J. (1983) *The Sane Alternative: A Choice of Futures*, The Old Bakehouse, Cholsey, nr Wallingford, Oxon OX10 9NU.

Roszak, T. (1981) *Person/Planet: The Creative Disintegration of Industrial Society*, London: Granada.

Rowan, J. (1983) *The Reality Game: A Guide to Humanistic Counselling and Therapy*, London: Routledge & Kegan Paul.

Rowe, D. (1987) *Beyond Fear*, London: Fontana.

Sivard, R.L. (1986) *World Military and Social Expenditures 1986*, Washington, DC: World Priorities.

Slater, J. (1986) *The Teaching of Controversial Issues in Schools: An HMI View*, paper presented at Schools Curriculum Development Committee seminar, April.

Spretnak, C. (ed.) (1982) *The Politics of Women's Spirituality*, New York: Ancho-Doubleday.

Spretnak, C. and Capra, F. (1985) *Green Politics: The Global Promise*, London: Paladin–Collins.

Starhawk (1982) *Dreaming the Dark: Magic, Sex and Politics*, Boston, Mass: Beacon.

Williams, S.K. (1986) *The Practice of Personal Transformation*, Wellingborough: Aquarian Press.

Index